Praise for

John Noble Wilford's

The Mysterious History of Columbus

"An excellent introduction to Columbus and the current scholarship on the man and his accomplishments. The balanced and lucid writing make it a joy to read."

—*Dallas Morning News*

"Wilford approaches this subject with a sensitivity for its explosive nature, and offers an even-handed...reading of the events.... [His] careful approach to Columbus greatly helps his readers sidestep many of the impediments which legend and lore have placed there."

—*Cleveland Plain Dealer*

"This judicious biography...makes the best starting point for a lay reader."

—*Chicago Sun Times*

"Wilford achieves true eloquence in distinguishing Columbus's achievements."

—*Boston Globe*

"Wilford deftly tells the story by showing readers the many faces of Columbus throughout the years...a highly readable book."

—*Los Angeles Daily News*

John Noble Wilford

The Mysterious History of Columbus

John Noble Wilford is a science correspondent for *The New York Times*. He won the 1983 American Association for the Advancement of Sciences/Westinghouse science-writing award and two Pulitzer Prizes—one in 1984 for his reporting of space and science and the other in 1987 as a member of the *Times* team reporting on the aftermath of the Challenger accident. He was a Visiting Journalist at Duke University in 1984, the McGraw Lecturer at Princeton University in 1985, and Professor of Science Journalism at the University of Tennessee in 1989–90. He has worked for *The Wall Street Journal, Time* magazine, and, since 1965, the *Times*. He is the author of *We Reach the Moon* (1969), *The Mapmakers* (1981), *The Riddle of the Dinosaur* (1985), and *Mars Beckons* (1990), co-author of *Spaceliner* (1981) and *The New York Times Guide to the Return of Halley's Comet* (1985), and editor of *Scientists at Work* (1979).

ALSO BY JOHN NOBLE WILFORD

We Reach the Moon (1969)

Scientists at Work (1979)
(editor)

The Mapmakers (1981)

Spaceliner (1981)
(with William Stockton)

The Riddle of the Dinosaur (1985)

The New York Times Guide to the Return of Halley's Comet (1985)
(with Richard Flaste, Holcomb Noble, and Walter Sullivan)

Mars Beckons (1990)

The Mysterious History of Columbus

The Mysterious History of Columbus

An Exploration of the Man, the Myth, the Legacy

John Noble Wilford

Vintage Books • A Division of Random House, Inc. • New York

First Vintage Books Edition, October 1992

 Published in the United States by Vintage Books, a division of Random House, Inc., New York, and simultaneously in Canada by Random House of Canada Limited, Toronto. Originally published in hardcover by Alfred A. Knopf, Inc., New York, in 1991.

Owing to limitations of space, acknowledgments for permission to reprint previously published material may be found following the Index.

Library of Congress Cataloging-in-Publication Data
Wilford, John Noble.
The mysterious history of Columbus: an exploration of the man, the myth, the legacy / John Noble Wilford, — 1st Vintage Books ed.
p. cm.
Originally published: New York: Knopf: Distributed by Random House, 1991.
Includes bibliographical references and index.
ISBN 0-679-73832-0 (pbk)
1. Columbus, Christopher. 2. Explorers — America — Biography. 3. Explorers — Spain — Biography. 4. America — Discovery and exploration — Spanish. I. Title.
E111.W65 1992
970.01′5 — dc20 92-50088
CIP

Manufactured in the United States of America
10 9 8 7 6 5 4 3 2 1

For Nona

Contents

PART THREE

Preface

Few stories in history are more familiar than the one of Christopher Columbus sailing west for the other side of the Old World and finding a world then unknown to Europe: the New World. Our minds may misplace this or that date of personal and national history, but indelibly imprinted in our memory is the verse from childhood: "In Fourteen Hundred and Ninety-Two / Columbus sailed the ocean blue." The names of his ships, the *Niña,* the *Pinta,* and the *Santa María,* roll fluently from our lips. We know—at least in outline—the rest of the story. Of how Columbus, a seaman of humble and obscure origins, pursued a dream that became his obsession. Of how Columbus found not the riches of Cathay or the resplendent court of the Great Khan, as evoked in the alluring tales of Marco Polo, but a sprinkling of small islands inhabited by gentle people living in nature and innocent of any European idea of wealth and civilization. Of how he called these people Indians, thinking that surely the mainland of the Indies lay just over the horizon. And of how he died believing he had reached the Indies, having closed his mind to the realization, growing among those who followed in his wake, that his vision and determination had carried Europeans to a discovery far greater than anything dreamed of by the man who had found the way.

The familiarity of the story is deceptive, leaving the impression that it is firmly grounded in fact and that historians agree on those facts and their interpretation. Nothing could be further from the truth. The history of Columbus is frustratingly incomplete.

The origins and early life of Columbus are not known in so many important details. When and how in the mists of his rootless life did he conceive of his audacious plan? We cannot even be sure what he had in mind. Was he really seeking the Indies? We can admire his perseverance in the pursuit of his ambition and his courage and skill as a mariner. But how are we to navigate the poorly charted waters of ambiguity and conflicting documentation everywhere Columbus went and in everything he did? We are not certain how he was finally able to win royal backing for the enterprise. We know so little about his ships and the men who sailed them. We cannot pinpoint exactly where he made first landfall. He was an inept governor of Spanish settlements in the Caribbean and had a bloodied hand in the brutalization of the native people and the start of a slave trade. How could such a man be honored and even idealized in popular lore? Should he be condemned instead? In rehearsing his life and accomplishments, we can glimpse in Columbus the best and worst of humanity.

All the more reason for us to see him as a tragic figure and wish to strip away the myths and misconceptions and look for the real man.

Leopold von Ranke admonished his fellow scholars to write history "*wie es eigentlich gewesen*"—how it really was. But this ideal, as Bernard Lewis of Princeton University says, "is neither as simple nor as easy as it sounds." Lewis was speaking of the profession of history in general, but the Columbus story presents a textbook example of the problems. History has given us many Columbuses and left us an incomplete record from which to reconstruct the Columbus who really was.

Part of the problem is the understandable consequence of the passage of time. Although the record of Columbus by contemporaries is more substantial than that for any other fifteenth-century explorer, surviving accounts are often difficult to assess from this temporal distance. Whose version is to be trusted? Too many important documents either are missing or exist only in extracts. These lacunae are an invitation to confusion: Hagiographers can fill the gaps in ways that magnify their hero. Detractors can make a case diminishing the man. Who is closer to the truth? Serious historians can honestly arrive at widely differing interpretations of motives and actions, and so they have.

Much of the confusion is traceable to Columbus himself. His own words are not always revealing or trustworthy. He was secretive. He had almost nothing to say on his early life or the genesis of his plan for the voyage of discovery. He could be vague, contradictory, and self-serving in what he did write. Then, late in his life, his mind seemed to slip its mooring and drift into mysticism. Had this been the essential Columbus all along?

The elevation of Columbus to heroic stature has further distorted history. Over the five centuries since the epochal voyage, the story of

Columbus has assumed the character of legend. We want—or used to want—our heroes to be larger than life. But legends have a way of transmuting the person and the achievement they celebrate. The result can sometimes be ridiculous. Not that anyone still seriously believes the tale that Columbus set out to prove the world round at a time when most people thought it flat (a mistaken view perpetuated every time Ella Fitzgerald enchants us singing, "They all laughed at Christopher Columbus when he said the world was round"); that notion has been tossed out of popular history along with little George Washington's cherry tree. Iconographers do their subject a disservice, creating and venerating a caricature that is a plastic saint inviting iconoclasts to step forward with their own images, which likewise ignore the complexity of human reality. Even though a more measured approach to Columbus is now largely the rule, many aspects of his story remain riddled with fanciful conjecture told as truth—a legacy of his devoted son's biography and the hero-worship that soared to a zenith in the nineteenth century.

The incomplete state of Columbus scholarship was brought home to me a few years ago when I was reporting a story on nautical archeology for *The New York Times.* I learned to my surprise that no one really knows the dimensions and rigging of Columbus's ships, or much about the shipbuilding technology that made the voyages of discovery possible. If we have such scant knowledge of the ships, what else do we *not* know about Columbus? How certain are we of the particulars of this pivotal event in history? I soon learned how long is this list of uncertainties.

It was this revelation, of our ignorance on so many matters involving Columbus, that sent me off on an exploration into the mysteries and controversies surrounding the man who opened the modern age.

The purpose of this book is not to present a full-scale biography of Columbus. It is to tell the story of the story of Columbus—that is, to describe what we do know about him and his achievements and how this knowledge has come down to us, and also to review and assess the numerous questions that persist and cause such heated dispute among historians. The many Columbus riddles will each be addressed, with possible solutions weighed on the basis of new discoveries and interpretations. Special attention will be given to recent archival and archeological findings and to changing interpretations, particularly those dealing with topics that earlier historians tended to ignore, such as the consequences of the encounter between Europeans and indigenous Americans, the story behind the naming of America, the mind of Columbus, and the way his reputation has changed through the centuries. It is hoped that the result will be a useful guide to readers who are sure to be overwhelmed during the Columbian Quincentennial with a puzzling mix of interpretation, hypothesis, and both popular and scholarly rehearsals of every imaginable aspect of the man and his discoveries.

But the story of Columbus is incomplete not only because of missing or conflicting documentation. It is incomplete also because that is the nature of history. All works of history, it has been said, are interim reports.

History does not exist in itself. What people did in the past cannot be preserved in amber, a moment captured and immutable through time. Their lives and actions may well be unchangeable. What they did cannot be undone, and why and how they did it can only be seen in the context of their times. Telling history this way, insofar as it is possible, is as close as one can come to Ranke's ideal. That is one side of history—the story of events past. There is another side.

Each generation looks back on the past and, drawing on its own experiences, presumes to find patterns that illuminate both the past and the present. This is natural and proper. The temptation, though, is to rewrite history as we would wish it had been, which has happened all too often regarding Columbus and produced myth and propaganda in the guise of history. But a succeeding generation can properly ask questions of the past that those in the past never asked of themselves. Columbus could not know that he had ushered in what we call the Age of Discovery, with all of its implications, any more than we can know what two world wars, nuclear power, the collapse of colonial empires, the end of the Cold War, and the beginning of space travel will mean to people centuries from now. Perceptions change, and so does our understanding of the past. Accordingly, the image of Columbus has changed through the years, sometimes as a result of new information but most often because of changes in the lenses through which we view him.

Consider just one example. Samuel Eliot Morison's *Admiral of the Ocean Sea: A Life of Christopher Columbus* is generally regarded as the best and most popular book on the subject. Morison, an eminent historian at Harvard University, wrote the book in 1942. In the foreword to a new edition in 1983, David Beers Quinn, another distinguished historian of exploration, praised the book's dramatic sweep and literary style, but noted that "there are other perceptions of the Discoverer that must now be taken into account." Quinn feels that Morison ignored or dismissed Columbus's failings. Columbus, Quinn writes, "cannot be detached from the imperialist exploitation of his discoveries and he must be made to take some share of responsibility for the brutal exploitation of the islands and mainlands he found." Times and sensitivities change in less than half a century, and so can the telling of history.

No doubt Morison, if he were alive, would defend his excellent book and his heroic Columbus with customary force and eloquence. But he, too, was aware of the protean nature of written history. In his 1950 presidential address to the American Historical Association, Morison declared that the historian "is writing of the past, but not for the past; he is writing for the public of today and tomorrow." Though endorsing Ranke's view that the historian must apply himself to ascertaining what really happened, he quoted with approval Benedetto Croce, the Italian historian, to the effect that all history to some extent is "contemporary history because, however remote in time events there recounted may seem to be, the history in reality refers to present needs and present situations wherein those events vibrate."

The following, then, is the story of Columbus, in fact and legend, and an exploration of it as a striking example of how history is forever being revised and rewritten. History is not only what happened long ago but it is also the perception by succeeding generations of those events and those people.

Part One

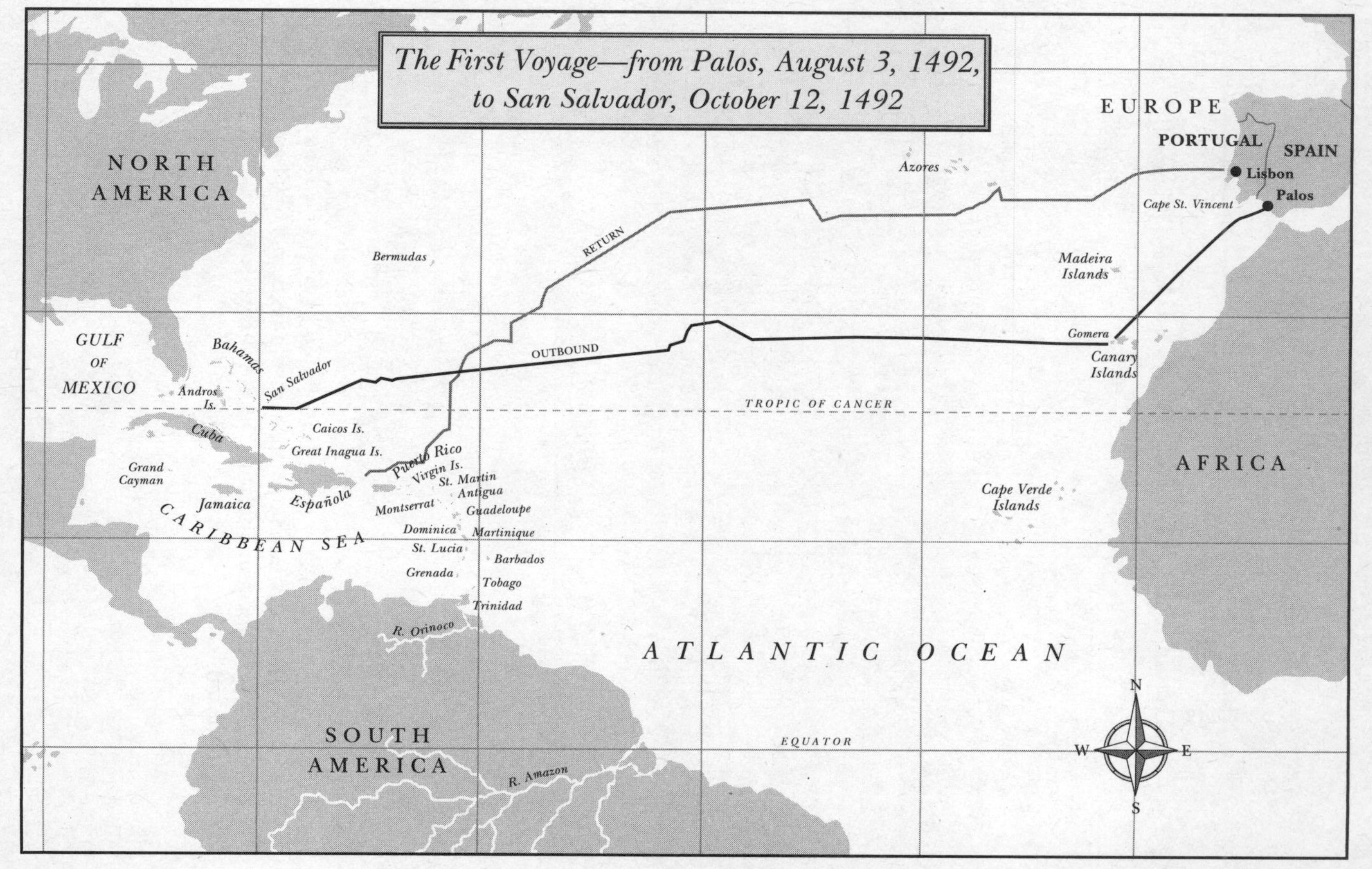
The First Voyage—from Palos, August 3, 1492, to San Salvador, October 12, 1492
NORTH AMERICA
EUROPE
PORTUGAL
SPAIN
Lisbon
Palos
Cape St. Vincent
Azores
Madeira Islands
Gomera
Canary Islands
AFRICA
Cape Verde Islands
Bermudas
RETURN
OUTBOUND
TROPIC OF CANCER
GULF OF MEXICO
Bahamas
San Salvador
Andros Is.
Cuba
Caicos Is.
Great Inagua Is.
Grand Cayman
Jamaica
Española
Puerto Rico
Virgin Is.
St. Martin
Antigua
Montserrat
Guadeloupe
Dominica
Martinique
St. Lucia
Barbados
Grenada
Tobago
Trinidad
CARIBBEAN SEA
R. Orinoco
ATLANTIC OCEAN
SOUTH AMERICA
R. Amazon
EQUATOR
N
W
E
S

1

An Exclamation of Discovery

Homeward bound, his mind alive with glittering images of verdant islands he had seen that surely must be stepping-stones to the fabled Cipangu, his heart racing ahead to the glory that should be his, Christopher Columbus composed a letter to the court of Ferdinand and Isabella. He had made good his boast to one and all. He may have harbored some disappointment in not reaching the Asian mainland or in seeing so little evidence of the gold and spices he had expected to find in abundance. But look what he had accomplished. Columbus felt sure he had fulfilled his extravagant promise to his patrons, the king and queen of Spain. He had sailed across the Ocean Sea and found lands and people unknown to Europeans. Since these islands were very near to the latitude and distance where Cipangu (Japan) ought to be, by his calculations, and so were not far off the mainland, he believed in his mind and heart that he had established a western sea route to the riches of the Indies. Columbus could hardly wait to spread the word.

"Sir: Because I know you will take pleasure in the great victory that Our Lord has given me in my voyage," Columbus began the message, writing in Spanish on vellum, "I write this letter to inform you of how in twenty days* I reached the Indies with the fleet supplied to me by the most illustrious King and Queen, our Sovereigns, and how there I discovered a great many islands inhabited by people without number: and of them all I have taken possession on behalf of Their Highnesses by proclamation and with the royal flag extended, and I was not opposed."

*In a postscript added at the conclusion of the voyage, Columbus corrected himself on the duration of the outward voyage; it took thirty-three days from the Canary Islands to landfall. Scholars suspect that the large discrepancy was the result of a misprint, *veinte,* twenty, appearing in printed versions instead of *treinta,* thirty. The original manuscript of the letter is lost.

The letter is our first glimpse into the mind of Columbus in triumph. It reveals him to be positive, credulous, and, above all, enthusiastic. Like so many who perform on history's stage, Columbus wanted to have the first word, the first revelation of the discovery to be read and pondered back home in Europe. But, most of all, he was reporting what he wanted the king and queen to know, especially since it justified his claim to the generous emoluments due him pursuant to the deal he had struck with the court.

The letter also was his bid for a place in history. In this regard, Columbus showed his understanding that the achievement would go for naught unless the news got back to others. To explore (the word, in one version of its etymology, comes from the Latin "to cry out") is to search out and exclaim discovery. To discover, as the dictionary defines the word, is to make known something secret, unknown, or previously unnoticed. Simply reaching a new land does not in itself constitute a discovery. How can there be a discovery if the event is never announced and then recorded in history? The question brings to mind that hoary conundrum about whether a tree makes a sound if it falls in the forest and there is no one there to hear the fall.

If others besides the indigenous people themselves preceded Columbus in finding America, and they almost certainly did, their imprint on history was negligible. They may have crossed the Ocean Sea, or Western Sea, as the Atlantic was then called. But they either failed to make their way back or left no account to inform and inspire succeeding generations.

More than a century before Christ, according to one line of speculation, Phoenicians coasting Africa were "blown across" to Brazil. People from Guinea in West Africa may also have made their way to the Brazilian coast. In the sixth century, the legendary Irish monk St. Brendan sailed across the ocean and discovered the "Promised Land of the Saints," which may or may not have been a part of North America. An account of the voyage, a popular piece of tenth-century literature, revealed some knowledge of Iceland and possibly Newfoundland and of icebergs, volcanoes, and the more southerly islands, possibly the Azores. But this was more medieval fantasy than a report of discovery. In descriptions attributed to the Brendan voyagers, the islands visited seemed to be no more than idealized versions of Ireland, and they were surrounded by waters alive with sea monsters breathing fire from their nostrils, Once, we are asked to believe, the monks landed on the back of a whale, taking it to be an island, and did not recognize their mistake until they started a fire and aroused the dozing creature.

At about the same time, Chinese legend has it that Hoei-Sin sailed east and raised a continent that he called Fusang. Fusang was also his name for the maguey cactus, which to him resembled a Chinese plant of that name. Had he reached Mexico? Some accounts suggest that Polynesian navigators made it to the western coast of America in pre-Columbian times. Even more plausibly, Portuguese literature hints of the occasional mariners who cast their eyes west of the farthest Azores. In 1452, Diego de Teive, a merchant from Madeira, might have gone all the way to America if his ship had not been driven by winds into the Gulf Stream, which carried him instead to Ireland. This adventure and perhaps others must have been behind the alluring stories of western discovery making the rounds before Columbus sailed. Breton or Basque fishermen may also have reached America before Columbus. As recently as the 1480s, it has been argued, fishermen out of the English port of Bristol glimpsed unknown lands across the Western Sea. But a land to fishermen was no more than the frustrating boundary to their fishing grounds, a limitation of no other importance.

More firmly documented is the Norse presence on American soil in the early eleventh century. Slowly and methodically, the Norse had extended their reach across the northern waters. "Only a fool with a new theory would sail off into an ocean without a very specific idea of where he was going," writes Alfred W. Crosby in *Ecological Imperialism: The Biological Expansion of Europe, 900–1900.* "The Norse always had a specific idea."

Following the lead of holy men from Ireland, they established Europe's first large overseas colony on Iceland in the ninth century. To learned Europeans this was assumed to be the northern land that Ptolemy, the classical authority on geographic matters, had called Ultima Thule. But in time the Norse proved Thule not to be the ultimate land, but only one destination in the northern ocean where no more than 500 miles separates landfalls. From Iceland these hardy seafarers, led by Erik the Red, an outlaw from both Norway and Iceland, found their way in the tenth century to the southern shore of a new land. With the instincts of a real-estate developer, Erik disregarded the frigid evidence all around and, hoping to promote colonization, named the place Greenland. In 986, another Norseman, Bjarni Herjolfsson, became lost trying to reach Greenland and came upon the coast of what would prove to be North America. But he showed no interest. Without so much as going ashore, he turned and made it to Greenland. In subsequent decades, the Norse under Erik's son Leif Eriksson went looking for the coast Herjolfsson had glimpsed. They came first to the rocky littoral he called Helluland, probably present-day Baffin Island, and then to a wooded coast of a place he named Markland, probably Labrador. Finally, Leif reached a land to the south where the wild "grape" (red currant?) grew. The Norse called it Vinland the Good, a place now assumed to be Newfoundland. Recent excavations of hearths and middens locate the probable site at L'Anse aux Meadows, on a northern finger of Newfoundland.

A valiant attempt to colonize Vinland was made with the arrival of women to join the men and also the introduction of livestock. But the venture ended in utter failure. Vinland was simply too far away in those days. If the Norse had assumed their swords and axes of metal gave them an advantage over the indigenous people, whom they called Skraelings, they soon realized their mistake. The Skraelings, with only stone weapons, easily routed the would-be settlers, and they were not without justification. Having killed eight of the first Skraelings they met, the Norse could hardly have expected a cordial welcome. According to Norse legend, Thorvald Eriksson, brother of Leif, was mortally wounded by a stone-tipped arrow while he was choosing a site in Vinland for his grave. As he lay dying, Thorvald is supposed to have said: "I seem to have hit on the truth when I said that I would settle there for a while."

Such exploits entered folk history, tales told and retold by a people and eventually recorded as the Icelandic Sagas, but they were not generally known to other Europeans until after the fifteenth century. These previous encounters, assuming the veracity of at least some of the storytellers, might as well not have occurred for the lack of practical effect they had on subsequent history. Eriksson and the others may have reached America, but they failed to discover it.

Columbus was making sure this could never be said of him and his achievement. But first he had to deliver the letter.

Many histories give short shrift to Columbus's return voyage from the newfound lands, dwelling instead on the outward passage. They properly dramatize the daring and terror of sailing west into the unknown, the alarm of wallowing in the matted seaweed of the Sargasso Sea, the dashed hopes of false landfalls, and the incipient mutiny. Yet Columbus and the crews of his three ships were fortunate to have a fair wind all the way out: no storms or heavy seas, and a warm breeze generally to their backs. In the strict nautical sense, it could hardly have been a more uneventful voyage. By contrast, the homeward voyage was too eventful, and everything—the lives of the discoverers and Columbus's place in history—depended on its successful completion.

Columbus very nearly did not make it home. If he had not, his name would be little more familiar to us than that of Fernão Dulmo or João Estreito. In 1487, under a license from the king of Portugal, these mariners presumably set sail to find the legendary Antilla, the island of the Seven Cities said to be settled by Christian bishops "opposite" Portugal. Dulmo and Estreito were never heard from again. If Columbus had fared no better, all that would have been recalled of him, in tales told on Iberian waterfronts, was that he was among some adventurous men who sailed west in 1492, boldly proclaiming the Indies as their destination, and they, too, never returned. Bless their souls, and let that be a warning. In time, someone would have made the round-trip crossing of the Western Sea, but it would never have been known that a man named Columbus had been there first, to a place he believed to be the Indies.

Here, then, with the writing of a letter and the tempest-tossed return voyage, begins the record of the fateful encounter between people who had long shared the same planet but were unknown to each other. Here begins the recorded history of the New World, America, in global affairs. Here, too, is a fitting point to launch an exploration of Columbus the man and of his place in history.

Columbus presumably retired to his cabin on the *Niña* and began the letter soon after heading home, January 16, 1493. The skies were clear and the seas smooth. He was beating to windward, east by north. He may have acted on instinct or on some knowledge about ocean winds; about one thing nearly all historians agree—Columbus was a mariner of surpassing skill and intuition. It was said of this man that he had "a wind-rose in his head." For his return, Columbus knew that he must avoid running against the constant trade wind that had borne him from the Canary Islands to his momentous landfall. So he adopted a different strategy. He would seek out a northern latitude—that of Bermuda, it turns out—where he hoped to catch the westerly winds he inferred to exist from his experience sailing off Portugal. Or perhaps he was simply looking for the most direct route back to Palos, the Andalusian port whence he had embarked August 3, 1492. In any case, he found the wind he needed. "Whether by luck or judgment," John H. Parry writes in *The Discovery of the Sea,* Columbus "sailed nearly the best possible course throughout most of the passage." Indeed, historians of seafaring point out that on this one round-trip voyage Columbus not only found lands new to Europeans but discovered the best possible sailing route from Europe to North America and back again.

The weather favored him, in the beginning. Day after day, Columbus's terse entries in the journal read: The sea is "very smooth, thanks be given to God," or "The sea very smooth, thanks to God, and the breeze very agreeable." Once he headed due east, with the wind astern, he made especially good time, regularly eight miles an hour, sometimes fourteen miles. He took note of floating seaweed, frigate birds, and plentiful schools of tuna. Sailors killed a porpoise and a shark, which were a welcome change in diet from the bread and yams that were about all the sustenance they carried below. On February 6, Columbus reckoned, a following wind took them 222¾ miles. If he had not already written the letter, a run like that, the best of the entire trip for a single day, would inspire soaring confidence in a successful return and move him to write a summing-up of his impressions of the new lands and people.

The letter, whenever it was written, summarized observations Columbus had already entered in the journal he had kept throughout the voyage. From its opening sentence it is clear that he believed, or wanted to believe, that he had been to the Indies. (In his time, India had no exact geographic meaning to Europeans; it was the general area east of Islam. Wilcomb E. Washburn, a historian at the Smithsonian Institution, notes that, in adopting the expression "the Indies," Columbus was using "the vaguest, most inclusive term he could find to suggest Indian without doing violence to the public imagination back home.") Columbus declared, "I reached the Indies," and elsewhere he included the phrase "As soon as I arrived in the Indies." He referred to the inhabitants as Indios, Indians, and so the aboriginal people of America were henceforth Indians. These people, Columbus was pleased to report, had never seen Europeans; he was first.

Columbus the explorer was exclaiming discovery and, thinking of the years it took to win authorization for the expedition, knowing the risks he had faced, and desiring the rewards, was promoting its importance to the hilt.

But Columbus was honest enough to recount the difficulties of trying to get confirmation that he had indeed reached the Indies. Following the coast of Cuba, which he called Juana, he let expectations color his vision. "I thought it must be the mainland, the province of Catayo [Cathay]," he wrote. Europe knew of fabulous Cathay, or China, mainly through the fourteenth-century reminiscences of Marco Polo, and by most evidence this was one of the more enticing lures that drew Columbus across the ocean. He had carried with him a letter from Ferdinand and Isabella to the Great Khan. A converted Jew, Luis de Torres, who knew some Arabic and other eastern languages, was a member of the crew expressly to act as interpreter between Columbus and the oriental potentates he expected to meet. To his disappointment, Columbus presently learned from inhabitants that Juana could not be Cathay, for they told him it was an island. Columbus, nevertheless, continued to affirm his belief in the proximity of the Asian mainland. He wrote of the fort he established on Española that it was convenient "for all kinds of trade with the nearest mainland as well as with the farther one of the Great Khan."

Columbus's descriptions of the Indians were generally admiring. They were "so artless and so free with all they possess." . . . Their "good looks [were] esteemed," and they were not "Negroes, as in Guinea, but with flowing hair." They went "naked, men and women, as their mothers bore them, except that some women cover one place only with the leaf of a plant or with a net of cotton which they make for that."

Their nakedness set the Indians apart from the Asians Marco Polo had described, and this must have been another source of disappointment. Where was all the silk brocade? Columbus noted in the letter that the people gave impressive accounts of their travels by sea to neighboring islands, but that it was the first time they had seen anyone in clothes. Even if this supported his primacy as an explorer, Columbus must have heard these stories with mixed feelings: the islands evidently were not as close to Cipangu or Cathay as he wanted to believe.

Unfortunately, we have no record of the first impressions the people Columbus called Indians had of the Europeans who appeared on their sandy shores. What did they think of these white men with beards? Their sailing ships and their weapons that belched smoke?

Their Christian God and their inordinate interest in gold and a place beyond the horizon they called the Indies? We will never know. They could not put their feelings into writing; they had no writing. And the encounter itself doomed them. Within a generation or two, these people became extinct and so could not pass on by word of mouth stories about the moment white men entered their lives.

The only insights into their thinking to be found in Columbus's letter were descriptions of their timorous and trusting behavior in the presence of the Spaniards, the eagerness with which they bartered for European goods, and their apparent belief that Columbus and his ships had come from the sky. Indians forced to accompany the Spaniards would run into the villages shouting, "Come! Come! See the people from the sky!" The Indians, he further wrote, would come out, "so that not one, big or little, remained behind, and all brought something to eat and drink, which they gave with marvelous love."

So intent was Columbus on presenting an optimistic account that he neglected to report in the letter the expedition's one serious misfortune. On the night before Christmas, off the northern coast of Española, his flagship, the *Santa María,* went aground on a reef and was hopelessly stranded. Abandoning ship, the crew sought refuge in the nearby town of a friendly Taino chief. Timbers from the ship were hauled ashore and used to construct a fortress within the Taino town. Columbus left thirty-nine men there, with instructions to hunt for gold while awaiting his next voyage, and then he sailed away on the *Niña.*

His letter gave a disingenuous version. "In . . . Española . . . I have taken possession of a large town to which I gave the name *La Villa de Navidad,*" Columbus wrote, pointing out what he said was its strategic location for "great trade and profit" in subsequent commerce with Cathay. "In it I have built a fort and defenses, which already, at this moment, will be all complete, and I have left in it enough people for such a purpose, with arms and artillery and provisions for more than a year, and a fusta, and a master of the sea in all arts to build others; and great friendship with the king of that land, to such an extent that he took pride in calling me and treating me as brother." Then, without suspecting the prescience of his assertion, he concluded: "The island is without danger for their persons, if they know how to behave themselves."

The Columbus letter, whether he intended it or not, was misleading in other respects, such as the extravagant assessments of all he had seen. The harbors are "incomparable to others which I know in Christendom, and [there are] numerous rivers, good and large, which is marvelous." Juana is "larger than England and Scotland together." Beautiful Española "in circuit is greater than all Spain."

Columbus was also exuberant in his descriptions of the beauty and promise of these islands. Española was "marvelous." The "trees of a thousand kinds" there were "tall, and they seem to touch the sky," and in November they were "as green and beautiful as they are in Spain in May." The lands abounded in fruit, honey, cotton, aloe, mastic, and spices. In the mountains there was gold. All this wealth, he said, could be shipped to the monarchs on future voyages. "I shall give them as much gold as they want," Columbus wrote to the court, reflecting his consuming interest in wealth, and "slaves, as many as they shall order," reflecting the dark side of contemporary labor economics.

Columbus was neither the first explorer nor the last to exaggerate his discoveries. In the mind of an explorer, it seems, the goal reached should be commensurate with the vision that drove him to endure the hardship and risk preceding discovery. Admiral Robert Peary's claim to have reached the North Pole is a case in point; it is not altogether clear from his own navigation data that he did make it, but his desire was too great to let ambiguity deny him the satisfaction and honor. So it may have been with Columbus. Some of his glowing descriptions, however, were not far-fetched. Those islands, beautiful as they are now, were still more beautiful and luxuriant then. Parry offers another plausible explanation. To sailors long at sea, often despairing of ever seeing land again, any island is Eden. To sailors who have lived weeks on hard biscuits and beans, the sight of fruit and fresh water is a vision of plenitude. Columbus the sailor must have shared these feelings. But the Columbus in pursuit of loftier ambitions had other reasons to put the best face possible on what he had found. There was no place in his vision for small islands inhabited by naked people with none of the wealth and gold-roofed splendor celebrated by Marco Polo. Columbus, who had importuned Ferdinand and Isabella to back his venture, was applying his considerable gifts of persuasion to the task of convincing them that their trust in him had been well placed.

Imagine, then, the desolation of his soul when, on February 12, the two returning caravels ran into the thick of a terrifying storm. Powerful winds lashed the rigging. High waves pounded the worm-eaten hulls. In the night, Columbus counted three lightning strikes to the north-northeast and knew the worst was yet to come. Winds blew harder the next night, and waves rose higher, crossed each other, and crashed over the decks. Sailors, cold and wet and cursing, pumped furiously. They burned flares to maintain contact between the *Niña* and the *Pinta,* but at dawn on the 14th the *Pinta* was nowhere in sight of Columbus on the *Niña.* Columbus and all those on board feared that they would never again see the *Pinta*—or land.

On that day, the tempest at full fury, they fell to their knees and prayed. If the Lord in His tender mercy would only spare them, they vowed to go barefoot and in nothing but their shirts to the first shrine to the Blessed Virgin and offer thanks for their deliverance. Columbus admitted his own grave thoughts. He "ought not to fear the storm," he confessed in his journal, but his "weakness and faint heart" would not allow his mind to be reassured.

Columbus fretted that the world would never hear his "prosperous news." One can guess his thoughts. If the *Pinta* should likewise be lost, the discovery might never be known. No one would know to rescue the crewmen left on Española, and they, too, might perish without a trace. Someone might eventually reach those islands and hear tales of white men who came there long ago in ships. And that would be that. Columbus could scarcely bear the thought that his achievement might go unrecognized in history. In desperation, he decided to write another message of discovery.

As he explained in his journal, Columbus also had in mind the welfare of his two sons. If the king and queen only knew of the service he had performed for them on this voyage and the very important news he was carrying to them, they would be moved to see his sons well cared for. The message he had prepared, he said, included a brief report on parchment of everything concerning what he had found, "greatly beseeching him who might find it to take it to the Sovereigns." He sealed the parchment in a waxed cloth, ordered a wooden barrel brought to him, and placed the message in the barrel. He had the whole package tossed into the stormy sea.

The message in the barrel vanished forever, though it inspired a clumsy hoax four centuries later. In 1891, a London publishing firm claimed to have come into the possession of the paper, said to have been picked up by a fisherman off the coast of Wales. The writing was in English, but the publisher had a ready, if anachronistic, explanation: Columbus had used the universal maritime language to improve chances that the message would be understood. As transparent a fake as this was, Samuel Eliot Morison writes in his biography of Columbus, a "facsimile edition" of the message "found many credulous purchasers, several of whom have tried to unload their unhappy acquisitions on the present writer."

But the crisis passed, and Columbus had no further need of communicating with the world by barrel. After sunset the same day, he glimpsed clearing skies to the west, and the next morning, the 15th, a sailor caught sight of land off the prow. This was not Castile or any other continental shore, but an island in the Azores. While the pilots and sailors argued over where they were, Columbus went to his cabin that day and, his spirits obviously much revived, completed his formal message to the Spanish court.*

The letter's peroration was vintage Columbus. The pious Columbus praised "God, Our Lord, Who gives to all those who walk in His way victory over things which appear impossible." The apostolic Columbus, who believed himself chosen by God to carry the Cross to the Indies, proclaimed that "all Christendom ought to feel joyful and make great celebrations and give solemn thanks to the Holy Trinity with many solemn prayers for the great exaltation which it will have, in the turning of so many peoples to our holy faith." The suppliant Columbus beseeched Their Highnesses to support further expeditions to "find a thousand other things of value." The imperial Columbus called attention to the "material benefits, since not only Spain but all Christians will hence have refreshment and profit." The proud Columbus, triumphant and vindicated, stressed the fulfillment of his geographical prophecy: "For although men have talked or have written of these lands, all was conjecture, without getting a look at it." The bold and resolute Columbus had gone and seen these lands and now was exclaiming the discovery.

In closing, Columbus noted that the letter was written "in the caravel off the Canary Islands, on the fifteenth of February, year 1493." Columbus could be careless in his writing, as historians are always finding to their dismay and puzzlement, and this was one of

*Because the letter is dated February 15, 1493, many historians concluded that it was written then, off the Azores. Morison, however, believes that Columbus wrote the letter before and dated it while off Santa Maria. The fact is that no one knows or is likely to. But Morison's interpretation is more satisfying. If you were Columbus, would it not make sense to write the letter while the experience was fresh and the seas smooth?

those inexplicable mistakes. He should have known better. He had stopped off at the Canaries on the outbound voyage and knew they lay to the south, off Morocco, where the winds blow out of the east. He had been trying to make it home on the westerly winds of a northern course, and in his journal that day, he entered his belief that the land ahead was an island in the Azores. And so it was. Columbus had returned to the known world, although he undoubtedly wished that he had raised the Canaries, which were under Spanish authority, rather than the Azores, which were Portuguese.

Luck seemed to be running out on Columbus. A desperate need for fresh water and wood left him no choice but to put in at Santa Maria, the southernmost island of the Azores, and take his chances with the Portuguese authorities. Their reception was hardly cordial. While half the crew were praying at the altar of a nearby chapel, fulfilling their vows made in the storm, they were set upon by armed men and taken prisoners. Several tense days followed. Columbus met with local officials and found them suspicious of any Spanish ship because of recent raids on Portuguese territory on the African coast. They were in no way reassured by the yarns they were told about returning from the Indies. Columbus showed them his credentials from the king and queen, threatened to sail away and come back with an avenging Spanish fleet, and in anger swore that he would "blow up the entire island." The Portuguese captain finally relented and permitted Columbus to rescue his crew. After six tumultous days, Columbus weighed anchor on February 24 and sailed with the southwesterly wind.

Before long, the hardy little caravel ran into more heavy seas and squalls. She rode out a fierce storm through the night of March 3 into the early hours of March 4. The winds and the seas came at them from two directions and "seemed to lift the caravel in the air," Columbus wrote in his journal. "It pleased Our Lord to sustain [us], and [we] went on this way until the first watch, when Our Lord showed [us] land."

It was Europe. Europe, at last. Columbus had hoped to sight land somewhere near Cape St. Vincent, where it would be a short, direct sail along the southern-Iberian coast to Palos. He saw instead the Rock of Sintra, the mountainous peninsula that is the sailor's landmark for the approach to the Tagus River and Lisbon. Once again, since he was in dire need of repairs after the storm's damage, his only realistic option was to seek shelter in Portuguese waters. At 9:00 a.m. Monday, March 4, he anchored off Restelo in the Tagus estuary near Lisbon. The anchorage was near the site of the Tower of Belém, which would be erected in 1512 to commemorate the great Portuguese navigators whose opening of the Age of Discovery had set the stage for Columbus.

In one of those ironies of history, the winds had driven Columbus to harbor at the capital of Spain's principal seafaring rival and sometime enemy. He found himself in the uncomfortable position of rendering the first official account of his exploits not to Ferdinand and Isabella, his patrons, but to John II, the king of Portugal and one of the ablest rulers of the century, who some years before had rejected his pleas for support.

On Tuesday, compounding the irony, the man mainly responsible for the king's rejection, Bartolomeu Dias,* came aboard the *Niña* to pay his respects. Dias was one of the greatest fifteenth-century navigators, who discovered the Cape of Good Hope in 1488, thus revealing the promising eastern sea route to India. His return from the successful African expedition coincided with Columbus's final appeal to the Portuguese court, and that did it. The court's experts in cosmography had been dubious all along—and correctly so—of some of Columbus's geographical premises concerning the distance to Asia by the supposed western ocean route. The king himself, though intrigued and tempted, had not been sure he should trust this engaging but boastful man. With the knowledge brought back by Dias, John II decided that there was no longer a pressing need to sail west into the unknown, as this man Columbus proposed. Now, more than four years later, Columbus was the one returning in triumph. He let Dias know in no uncertain terms that he expected to be shown all the respect due the admiral of the Ocean Sea. He would not go to Dias's captain with a report of his voyage, as requested; the captain could come to him—which he did, Columbus said, "with great ceremony, and with kettledrums, trumpets, and horns sounding gaily."

One must hand it to Columbus. If he felt uneasy in the rival harbor, in the company of menacing warships, he was not intimidated. He was not some ordinary windswept mariner. The force of character—self-assurance, courage, and stubborn resolution—that it had taken to bring off the Enterprise of the Indies, Columbus now applied to

*Historians are not certain that this man and the discoverer of the Cape of Good Hope are indeed the same Dias. Morison, however, believes they are one and the same.

securing his just reward. The king and queen of Spain had promised to crown his success with, among other emoluments, noble rank and the title of "admiral of the Ocean Sea and viceroy of the Indies." He saw no need to await investiture. He had succeeded and, by San Fernando, to use his favorite oath, the Portuguese would accord him the respect due one of heroic accomplishment and exalted rank.

The people of Lisbon flocked to the *Niña* to hear the story of the voyage and see and touch the Indians Columbus had brought back. "They all marveled, giving thanks to Our Lord," he wrote in his journal. At the end of the week, Columbus accepted a royal invitation and traveled by mule to a monastery outside the city for an audience with John II, taking with him two or three of the captive Indians.

The meeting between king and admiral was the first test of European credulity upon hearing the story Columbus told. John received him with courtesy and put the royal shipyard at his disposal for repairs on the *Niña.* Columbus said that the king "took much pleasure from the voyage having had a good ending and having been made."

For the first time, we need not rely solely on Columbus's version of events. Among those present at the meeting was Rui de Pina, the court chronicler. He wrote that the king, despite his cordiality and expressions of pleasure over Columbus's success, was seething with anger as he listened to Columbus the discoverer and regretted his rejection of Columbus the boastful petitioner.

A story of that meeting, presumably related by Columbus and recorded in later histories, reflects the king's mood. As a test of Columbus's claims and the Indians' intelligence, John commanded that a bowl of dried beans be brought to him and had them scattered on a table. One of the Indians was directed by sign to arrange the beans as a rough map of the islands Columbus claimed to have discovered. The Indian laid out the beans to show Española, Cuba, and the Bahamas, whereupon the king grew sullen and, as if by accident, upset the map and ordered another Indian to reconstruct it. As he did so, adding many more islands, John is reported to have beat his breast and exclaimed: "O man of little understanding! Why did you let such an enterprise fall from your hands?"

Columbus's proud demeanor apparently did not improve John's humor. The king was especially annoyed, De Pina said, "because the said Admiral was somewhat elevated above his condition and in telling his tale always exceeded the bounds of truth and made the tale of gold, silver and riches much greater than it was."

The court of Portugal once again was responding to Columbus with skepticism. It had been correct in the first place in doubting that Cipangu was near enough to the west that Columbus could make it by sailing across the Western Sea. Now, whether it was a case of sour grapes or something in the admiral's manner—probably both—the court in its reaction was reaching what turned out to be a sound assessment. Again, Portugal was absolutely right but shortsighted.

"If Columbus had indeed discovered part of the 'Indies,'" Parry writes, discussing John II's reaction, "it was a part in which Portugal was not immediately interested; if, as was more likely, he had found an extensive but remote group of oceanic islands, Portuguese plans need not be seriously endangered."

At the meeting, as both Columbus and De Pina reported, the king expressed the opinion that the lands discovered might well lie within Portugal's sphere of influence, as established in a treaty with Spain and recognized in a papal bull of 1481. By these agreements, Portugal claimed exclusive rights to the western coast of Africa, its primary interest, and any islands south of the Spanish-held Canaries. Columbus handled this potential diplomatic crisis with aplomb. He told the king that he knew nothing of the treaty but reassured him that the Spanish monarchs had specifically instructed him not to go anywhere near the African coast. "The King graciously answered he was sure that there would be no need for arbitrators to settle this," Columbus wrote in his journal.

Some of John's advisers had ungracious ideas about what to do with this man Columbus. According to De Pina, courtiers urged the king to have Columbus murdered, supposing that this would put an end to Spanish advances in the Portuguese ocean. Perhaps the king, whose nation had so long led in oceanic discovery, recognized the futility of trying to impede the course of exploration by the death of one man. Perhaps he simply wanted to avoid offending Spain. In any event, he vetoed the idea and saw to Columbus's safety until his departure from Lisbon Wednesday morning, March 13, on the final leg of the voyage.

Columbus could relax now. His letter, his formal exclamation of discovery, was on its way to the Spanish court. On the day of his arrival in Lisbon, suspecting that there might be Portuguese with murderous intent, Columbus had immediately dispatched the letter. He addressed it to Luis de Santángel, the court treasurer, who had finally persuaded Isabella to back Columbus and had helped find the money for the enterprise. In history, this is known as the Letter to Santángel.

It is likely that Columbus, taking no chances that a single letter would get through, addressed copies to others in the court; several versions are extant. Friends he had known as a younger man living in Lisbon presumably arranged for the couriers to deliver the letter at once to Barcelona, more than 700 miles overland.

On March 15, 1493, two days after leaving Lisbon, the *Niña* rode a floodtide into the harbor of Palos. By a remarkable coincidence, the *Pinta* arrived a little later on the same tide. She had survived the storm, bypassed the Azores, and reached land first in Galicia, just north of the Portuguese border. Exactly thirty-two weeks after their departure, the *Niña* and the *Pinta* were back home.

Columbus had crossed the uncharted Western Sea. He had come upon lands unknown to Europeans and managed to get back to tell the tale. It was said of Columbus that any land he sighted he could return to with uncanny precision, and this he would do in three subsequent voyages. Never mind that he misunderstood what he had found and was to return to. He knew the way, no doubt about it, and this encouraged others to follow, and it would be up to those others to make the intellectual leap in discovering the reality of what it was he had found. Never mind that so much about his background, motives, and aspirations is the stuff of earnest and sometimes outrageous dispute. About Columbus history has many open questions—with one exception. Undisputedly, this superb seaman was, first and foremost, a discoverer: he spread the word. And, though he could not know it, his voyage would alter forever the course of history.

2

His Shining Hour

The message from Columbus was received and accepted, disseminated and celebrated. He had done his part. The discovery was complete. It could be acted upon, and in the acceptance and action the achievement entered the flow of history.

The news spread swiftly in official and influential circles throughout Iberia, then across to Italy. In the absence of mass communications—the newspaper did not come into being until the seventeenth century—letter-writing was the usual means by which educated people far apart exchanged news and gossip, and their messengers were kept unusually busy in the weeks and months after Columbus's return. His own letter was circulated widely in printed form, one of the earliest examples of broadcasting news by means of the century's most revolutionary invention: printing with movable type.

The first letter known to be written in reaction to the discovery came from the hand of Luis de la Cerda, the duke of Medina Celi. The letter was dated March 19, 1493, four days after the return of the *Niña* and the *Pinta* to Palos, and was sent to Pedro Gonzales de Mendoza, archbishop of Toledo and grand cardinal of Spain, who was, next to the king and queen, the most powerful person in the country. The duke, a prosperous Cádiz shipowner, had somehow received word, probably from a correspondent in Lisbon, that Columbus "has returned after eight months and has found what he searched for and that very completely." But his message was hardly a selfless expression of joy for Spain and Christendom. He wanted a share of the profits.

Proving once more that success has many fathers while failure is an orphan, the duke called attention to what he claimed was his crucial role. He had befriended Columbus when his spirits were sagging, lodging him at the ducal castle, and had dissuaded him from taking his proposal to the king of France. He was the one, the duke reminded the cardinal, who had persuaded Columbus instead to make one more plea to Isabella. Approval followed, and then discovery. In return for this service to Spain, the duke sought not only reward but the right to send his own caravels to the new lands. The letter portended Columbus's eventual loss of control over his discovery.

By the last week of March, the discovery was the talk of Barcelona, where Ferdinand and Isabella were holding court. The city bustled with representatives of foreign kingdoms and principalities, agents or ambassadors paid to report regularly on news and political activities. Envoys followed the court from city to city, there being no permanent seat of the kingdom. This traveling entourage reminded one historian of a "tribal migration." Butchers and armorers, harness-makers and saddlers, surgeons and teachers tramped behind and beside mule-drawn litters (carriages were not sturdy enough to endure the rough roads and rugged terrain) bearing the women and children and the royal couple as well as the jewels and finery to grace their next venue. Soldiers rode and marched in watchful escort, and hunting dogs sniffed and yelped on the fringes. Slowly, the caravan made its way from Valladolid to Seville to Barcelona and points in between.

Especially well represented at the court were Italians, who had many financial and religious interests in common with the Spanish. Before the month was out, a letter from one of these envoys reached an official in Florence reporting that caravels had returned from new lands "not already seen by the King of Portugal." The discoverers had found a large island inhabited by naked people rich in gold and with no knowledge of iron. Obviously, the contents of the Letter to Santángel were familiar to everyone around the court.

The original manuscript of that letter is lost. But an enterprising printer in Barcelona obtained a copy, set the type by hand, and on April 1 produced the first printed edition. Entitled Letter of Christopher Columbus Concerning the Newly Discovered Islands, it was no more than a two-leaf folder of folio size, one copy of which has survived. The publication and others like it became immediate best-sellers, or what passed for best-sellers in the fifteenth century, when the average press run for a book was 200 copies and few books other than *The Imitation of Christ,* by Thomas à Kempis, enjoyed so much as a 1,000-copy printing. Copies of the Barcelona edition made their way to Italy, and within a month an edition in Latin appeared in Rome. Since the introduction of movable type in 1440 by Johannes Gutenberg, a goldsmith in Mainz, printing presses had been set up in the larger cities in most of the countries of Europe. Ten more editions of the Columbus letter were published within the year, at Paris, Antwerp, Basel, and Florence. Within five years, the letter could be read in four languages and in six different countries.

The news, however, did not spread immediately beyond the Alps. *The Nuremberg Chronicle,* a compendium of current events printed on July 12, 1493, made not a single mention of the voyage.

No such ignorance existed in northern Italy, where interest was especially keen. On April 9, a Barcelona merchant named Hannibal Januarius wrote his brother in Milan a letter that no doubt reflected the information and misinformation then currrent. After promising to send a letter "by each courier," Januarius turned immediately to news of the discovery, writing:

> Last August these Lord Sovereigns, on the plea of a certain Colomba, were content that the aforesaid should equip four caravels, because he said he wanted to pass over the Great Sea and sail directly to the west, in order to reach the Orient. . . . And so he did; the said caravels were accordingly equipped and the westward course was taken from outside the Straits, according to the letter which he wrote and which I have seen. In 34 days he arrived at a great island inhabited by naked people of olive complexion without any skill in fighting and very timorous. And, some having landed, they took some by force, so as to have knowledge of them, and to learn their language, in order that they might understand. . . . [Columbus and his men] accomplished their object, and by signs and other means it was learned that they were among islands of India. . . . In that island they say they found pepper, lignum aloes, and a mine of gold in the rivers, i.e., a river, which has sand with many grains of gold. . . . I expect to have a copy of that letter which he has written, and shall send it to you, and when he has come and I learn anything further I shall let you know. And this is regarded as certain in this court; and, as I have said, I have seen the letter which says, furthermore, that he has not observed among those people any law or religion, except that they believe that all things come from Heaven, and that there is a creator of all things; whence cometh hope of their easy conversion to the Holy Catholic Faith. He says further that he was afterwards in a province where men are born with a tail.

Columbus, meanwhile, was biding his time. He spent ten days or so at the monastery of La Rábida, near Palos, resting from the ordeal and sharing his delight with the Franciscans whose aid and encouragement had meant so much in the past. Most of all, he waited for word from Ferdinand and Isabella. Finally, Columbus assembled his own modest but exotic entourage of crew members and six Indians and set out for Seville.

A young man named Bartolomé de las Casas saw Columbus make his entrance to Seville on Palm Sunday, March 31. Columbus, he recalled, wore "the finest clothing he possessed" and was received "with much honor." Besides the Indians, Las Casas said, "he also brought green parrots, which were very beautiful and colorful, and also guaycas, which are jewelled masks made from fishbones, inlaid and decorated with pearls and gold, as well as some belts made in the same way . . . and many samples of the finest native gold work."

In a week, while still in Seville, Columbus received the invitation he had been expecting. The letter from the king and queen was dated March 30, a measure of the speed of fifteenth-century courier service.

"Don Cristóbal Colón," they wrote, "our Admiral of the Ocean Sea and Viceroy and Governor of the islands that have been discovered in the Indies: We have seen your letters and we have much pleasure in knowing what you write to us by them and that God has given so good an issue to your enterprise." These words must have gladdened his heart. All the titles he had been promised were used in addressing him. And the king and queen explicitly accepted his interpretation of what he had discovered. Now they commanded him to come to Barcelona at once for the fanfare to triumph.

Columbus may have had another reason to feel reassured that the monarchs had been faithful to their contract with him. According to a story related by his son Ferdinand Columbus, Martín Alonso Pinzón, captain of the *Pinta* and sometime rival, had himself written to the king and queen as soon as he reached port in the northern-Spanish province of Galicia, about the time Columbus had arrived in Lisbon. Pinzón reported the successful crossing and proposed to go to Barcelona to give a full account to the court. The monarchs supposedly sent Pinzón word "that he must not come save in the company of the Admiral, with whom he had sailed on that voyage of discovery." This snub, Ferdinand wrote, "caused Pinzón such chagrin and annoyance that he went home to Palos a sick man, and a few days after his arrival died of grief."

Although this sad postscript to the discovery has entered history as fact, there is no supporting documentation—only the word of Columbus's son, and there are reasons to suspect his credibility on the subject. Annoyed by claims of Pinzón heirs to a share of the credit for the discovery, Ferdinand passed up few opportunities to disparage the Palos mariner. Antonio Rumeu de Armas, a Spanish scholar writing in 1968, maintains flatly that the sovereigns never rejected a request of Pinzón to come to Barcelona—if any such request was made. Other scholars have suggested that it may have been syphilis, not chagrin, that killed Pinzón. If so, he was the first victim of the scourge that swept Europe shortly after the voyage and so has been identified by some historical epidemiologists as an unwanted import from the newly found lands.

The story of the Pinzón rejection, though no more than a minor moment in the history of Columbus, alerts us to the dangers in the writing of any history, but especially the story of Columbus. Events are embellished, facts are invented or forgotten, and in time a fog of legend obscures all. On these shoals the history of Columbus has often run aground, its passage to the discovery of larger meanings frustrated by interminable disputes.

But Columbus was as blissfully unaware of the troubles that lay ahead for him in history as he was of the efforts by people like the duke of Medina Celi to cash in on his hard-won discovery. Leaving Seville for the journey to Barcelona, Columbus had every reason to feel in control of his destiny. He could see that word of his discovery had reached the common people as well. Las Casas is again history's witness. "As the news began to spread throughout Castile that new lands called the Indies with a large and varied population had been discovered, as well as other things, and that the person who discovered them was coming on such-and-such a road, bringing these people with him," he wrote, "not only did everyone in the towns along his route turn out to see him, but many towns far from his route were emptied."

The journey took him to Córdoba, where he stopped to visit his two sons and his mistress, Beatriz Enríquez de Arana. She was the mother of Ferdinand, the younger, illegitimate son. Diego was his son by a marriage in Portugal to Felipa Perestrello e Moniz, who apparently died sometime in 1485. But Columbus did not tarry. He could not keep the king and queen waiting.

Barcelona in April 1493 was a growing seaport that had yet to reach the bounds of its ambition. The city walls, erected in the middle of the fourteenth century, enclosed extensive gardens and fields for grazing flocks—a bit of contingency planning in the event of a siege. It took two centuries, the historian Fernand Braudel has written, for the city to grow "into this outsize garment."

Columbus arrived there between April 15 and 20. The exact date is unknown, for there is no court record extant describing the events. We must depend largely on the word of his son Ferdinand, a very young boy then, and hence must be wary of exaggerations. But Peter Martyr d'Anghiera, the Italian courtier who was there, testified that Columbus "was honorably received by the king and queen, who caused him to sit in their presence, which is a token of great love and honor among the Spaniards."

On the day of the ceremonial reception, Ferdinand reported, "All the court and all the city came out." The streets near the harbor were crammed with people eager for a glimpse of Columbus and the Indians and parrots they had heard so much about. The admiral made his way slowly and solemnly through a corridor in the crowd and reached the royal stand in King's Square by the cathedral. Near this site today there stands on a tall column a statue of Columbus with the index finger of his right hand pointing in the direction of the lands of his discovery. The king and queen sat, waiting, on chairs draped with velvet under a canopy of gold cloth.

Ferdinand was born in 1452 and ascended to the throne of Aragon in 1479. Though his education was scant, he could hold his own in conversation with learned men, and no less an authority than Machiavelli would judge him to be one of the best European diplomats of his generation. He was a swarthy man of medium stature, balding and bearded, an excellent horseman who had a passion for hunting, especially falconry. Hernando del Pulgar, the queen's confidential secretary and chronicler, said Ferdinand "enjoyed all kinds of games such as ball, chess or royal tables, and he devoted to this pleasure more time than he ought to have done; while he loved the Queen his wife dearly, yet he gave himself to other women." On this day, Ferdinand, wearing a garnet crown, had to prop up his back with a cushion, favoring a painful wound inflicted by a deranged peasant.

Isabella was born in 1451 and became queen of Castile in 1474, reigning with shrewd and pious intelligence. Pulgar said she was "both clever and sensible, which is rarely to be seen together in one

Columbus with Queen Isabella and King Ferdinand

person." She was a handsome woman with dark-blue eyes and auburn hair. "She loved much the King her husband and was jealous about him beyond all measure," Pulgar reported. For the occasion of Columbus's return she wore a white veil that framed her round face, but otherwise her attire has gone unrecorded, though she was known to favor robes of velvet and a full complement of jewels and precious stones, on account of which her confessor sometimes reproached her vanity.

The marriage of Ferdinand and Isabella in 1469, arranged with a forged papal dispensation, led first to civil war but then to the confederation of the two kingdoms and ultimately the unification of Spain as, in the opinion of some scholars, the first modern state. Their victory in driving out the Moors was to earn them the title, conferred by the pope, by which they are known in history—the Catholic Kings.

Columbus had been at the court at Santa Fé, a town hastily erected as the base for the final siege of Granada. When Granada, capital for the Moors and their last stronghold in Christian Iberia, capitulated on January 2, 1492, he saw Ferdinand and Isabella enter the city in their own moment of triumph. "I saw the Royal Standards of Your High-

Isabella I

nesses placed by force of arms on the towers of the Alhambra," Columbus wrote in the preface to his journal of the first voyage, "and I saw the Moorish King come out to the gates of the city and kiss the Royal Hands of Your Highnesses and of the Prince my Lord."

Now Columbus stood before the king and queen, the supplicant returned triumphant. "He looked like a Roman senator: tall and stately, gray-haired, with a modest smile on his dignified face," Las Casas reported. "When he came forward to kiss their hands, they rose from their thrones as if he were a great lord, and would not let him kiss their hands but made him sit beside them."

After the public ceremony, the king and queen led Columbus inside the hall and, in the company of various courtiers, heard him tell of the voyage and the customs of the Indians, who he said were ready to receive the blessings of Christianity. "The king and queen heard this with profound attention and, raising their hands in prayer, sank to their knees in deep gratitude to God," Las Casas wrote. "The singers of the royal chapel sang the *'Te Deum laudamus,'* while the wind instruments gave the response and indeed, it seemed a moment of communion with all the celestial joys. Who could describe the tears shed by the king, queen and noblemen?"

Columbus remained in Barcelona five or six weeks. One royal feast followed another. At one celebration Columbus supposedly called for an egg to illustrate his singular role in history. As the familiar story has been related, some noblemen insisted that if Columbus had not undertaken the enterprise someone else, a Spaniard and not a foreigner, would have made the same discovery. At this, Columbus took an egg and had it placed on the table. "Gentlemen," he was reported to have said, pointing to the egg, "you make it stand here, not with crumbs, salt, etc. (for anyone knows how to do it with meal or sand), but naked and without anything at all, as I will, who was the first to discover the Indies." Each nobleman tried without success to make the egg stand up. When it was Columbus's turn, he crushed one end of the egg and had no trouble making it stand up on the table. An Italian historian, telling the story in 1565, wrote: "Wherefore all remained confused, understanding what he meant: that after the deed is done everybody knows how to do it; that they ought first to have sought for the Indies, and not laugh at him who had sought for them first."

The anecdote has proved irresistible to historians and storytellers, even though it never happened. The story was not only apocryphal, Morison points out, but it "had already done duty in several Italian biographies of other characters." In time, legend colors the reality of great people and deeds, and so it has with Columbus, further complicating the tasks of more judicious historians.

For the moment, Columbus had no need to resort to eggs to win over his audiences. Members of the court hung on his every word about the Indies, and on a number of occasions he was seen riding about the city beside the king. The Indians were duly baptized, but no one seems to have thought to record their feelings about the strange people and customs they, too, were discovering for the first time.

Rumor had reached the court from Lisbon that John II might be readying a fleet to sail for the new lands. Columbus was commanded to hasten preparations for a second expedition. The monarchs, in consultation with Columbus, moved to obtain exclusive title to the territory. For this they looked to the pope, the one supreme authority in such matters recognized by all the sovereigns of Christian Europe.

At the time, Portugal had a presumptive claim to new discoveries in the Atlantic. In the Treaty of Alcáçovas, signed in 1479 to end the war between Castile and Portugal, Isabella had agreed to recognize the Portuguese monopoly on trade and exploration in West Africa and to accept Portugal's title to the Azores, the Madeiras, and the Cape Verdes. In return, Portugal recognized Castilian rule over the Canaries. Two years later, a papal bull gave Portugal full rights to lands south of the Canaries and west of Africa. If Ferdinand and Isabella did not move fast, Portugal might be within its treaty and papal rights to claim the Columbus discoveries.

All the king and queen had to do was ask Pope Alexander VI and it would be granted. The pope was a Spaniard himself, Rodrigo Borgia of the notorious Borgia family, and owed his office to the Spanish monarchs. He was further indebted because Ferdinand and Isabella had nominated one of his bastard sons, Cesare Borgia, to prosperous bishoprics. The first of the accommodating Alexander's four bulls, issued May 3, contained language straight out of the Letter to Santángel. It granted Spain jurisdiction over the "islands and firm land" located in "the western parts of the Ocean Sea, toward the Indies" that Columbus had found. (The pope and the crown were neither accepting nor rejecting Columbus's claim to have reached the Indies.) In the third bull, which followed in a few weeks, Alexander drew a north–south line 100 degrees west of the Azores and the Cape Verdes; any lands east of the line were Portuguese, and anything found west of it, and not previously possessed by a Christian prince, would be Spanish. Columbus presumably suggested where the line of demarcation should be drawn. About 100 leagues west of the Azores, he had noted, there was a perceptible change in the temperature, the sea and wind, and the pattern of stars.

John II could not acquiesce to such a pro-Spanish arrangement, because it threatened Portuguese trade routes to the Indies by way of the South Atlantic and around the tip of Africa. If Columbus had found a western route to the Indies for Spain, John was all the more determined to exploit the eastern route. Although he dared not challenge the pope, he possessed a navy of sufficient power to bring Ferdinand and Isabella to the negotiating table. In a treaty concluded June 7, 1494, at Tordesillas, in northern Spain, the two countries agreed to move the line of demarcation farther west—370 leagues west of the Cape Verde Islands—"for the sake of peace and concord."

If the Middle Ages can be said to have ended with Columbus's achievement, then it is not surprising that the first diplomatic maneuvers in its aftermath should take a decidedly post-medieval turn. In bypassing the pope, John II established a new secular tradition in European diplomacy that would find its ultimate expression at the end of World War II, when Stalin asked derisively how many divisions the pope had.

As a result of the treaty, Brazil, when discovered in 1500, came under the Portuguese empire, and nearly all the rest of South America, as well as the islands of the Caribbean, became Spanish. The Tordesillas settlement cleared the way for surprisingly amicable relations between competing empires in the Americas, at least until the decades after the Reformation, begun in 1517 when Martin Luther posted his ninety-five theses on the door of Wittenberg's Castle Church. Late in the sixteenth century, Protestant rulers of northern Europe and even the king of Catholic France ignored Rome, asking what provision in Adam's will gave the popes the right to divide up the world. The sources and exercise of power were changing and reaching far beyond the continent of Europe.

How much Columbus must have savored the moment. Who would not? Give the man his due. With only grudging support, in defiance of wise experts, he had accomplished a feat of daring and of astounding discovery. The obscure but ambitious mariner had now moved easily among the learned and powerful, relishing the knowledge that he had proved all his detractors wrong and barely containing (for now) the human impulse to cry out, I told you so. He had heard the cheers of the people, conferred with bishops and archbishops, sat with the king and queen, and guided the conduct of international politics.

Let the fanfare for his shining hour echo through the ages, for he would not hear its like again. The celebration at Barcelona was to be the summit of his celebrity in his lifetime.

Never again would Columbus have the sure grip on his destiny that had been his in the years of striving alone to win approval for the undertaking or in the months of the voyage itself. In an important sense he could not have recognized, he had already surrendered control over his destiny to history. To the forces of history, in that the maneuvering among the mighty for political and economic advantage, as well as his own incompetence as a leader of men in the new lands, would conspire to ease Columbus off center stage. To the opinion and judgment of history, in that the telling of his story would presently fall to others.

3

Witnesses to History

Among the courtiers at Barcelona was an Italian-born cleric and diplomat, Peter Martyr d'Anghiera. He was a diligent letter-writer whose correspondence with prominent friends in Italy in the months after Columbus's return provides a contemporary record of reactions to the news of discovery and of interpretations given to these events. His letters, collected and preserved, are indispensable raw material for the history of Columbus.

An impressionable young page in the court who also saw the returning Columbus was Gonzalo Fernández de Oviedo. As a grown man, after a classical education in Italy and a spell of soldiering, he lived most of the rest of his life in the new lands and wrote an encyclopedic history of the early discoveries and colonization.

Likewise, the young Bartolomé de las Casas, who had been in the welcoming crowd at Seville, was inspired to make his life in the new lands, first as a planter, then as a priest and an apostle of the Indians. His attacks on the Spanish treatment of the Indians made him a controversial and heroic figure in his day and throughout history. But his contribution to the writing of history is the comprehensive account he left of the first and third Columbus voyages and the early colonial period. This is, Morison opines, "the one book on the discovery of America that I should wish to preserve if all others were destroyed."

And there was Ferdinand Columbus, who was not yet five years old when his father returned from the voyage of discovery. He grew up to serve his father's memory as archivist and biographer. The scholarly Ferdinand had access to many of the books Columbus is thought to have studied in planning the enterprise and many of the papers known to have been written by Columbus himself. With these materials at hand, Ferdinand wrote the first definitive biography of Columbus, a primary source of knowledge about the discoverer and particularly about his first and fourth voyages.

The story of Columbus that comes down to us over the span of five centuries derives in large part from the accounts of these four witnesses to history. We would wish to know more. If only Columbus's own writings were not so fragmentary and riddled with contradictions and ambiguities. If only Ferdinand could be fully trusted on the subject of his father's origins and on the genesis of his father's historic vision. Nonetheless, the story is better documented by contemporary writers than that of any previous voyages of exploration, or of many to follow.

Peter Martyr was born on the shores of Lake Maggiore and named for an assassinated Dominican inquisitor whose martyrdom was venerated in the principality of Milan. After studies in Milan and then Rome, he left Italy for Spain in 1487, at the age of thirty, in the company of Inarcho López de Mendoça, the count of Tendilla, whom he had met in Rome. Through the count's influence, the learned and sophisticated Italian became a member of the Spanish court as a teacher of the young nobles, but his charm and talent were to assure him wider opportunities. He went on to lecture at the University of Salamanca, soldier against the Moors, and undertake some diplomatic missions for the monarchs. He also took holy orders, which apparently did not include vows of poverty, and to which he must not have felt bound regarding celibacy.

With a substantial income from his church offices, Martyr could afford to be a generous host at his spacious house in Valladolid. A visitor in 1514 was impressed by the home's gold and silver, finely bound books, and polished furniture. The bedroom was decorated with "silk and purple stuffs," and the dining table groaned with partridge, pheasant, quail, and other rich fare. Martyr was known to have children. As Henry R. Wagner, an American businessman and independent scholar, wrote of him in this century: "We can easily visualize him as a typical Italian churchman of his day, a bon vivant, fond of entertaining his friends and including no doubt a 'niece,' married or not, somewhere in his home."

Still, Martyr found time to write long, fluent, gossipy letters to his friends and mentors. His first known letter about Columbus, dated May 14, 1493, was written from the court in Barcelona and addressed to his wealthy friend Count Giovanni Borromeo in Milan. The diffident tone gives the impression that Martyr at first had only a passing interest in the discovery. He opened the letter with news of the attempted assassination of the king sometime before, and finally got around to the news of discovery. "A few days after," he wrote, "there returned from the Western Antipodes a certain Christophorus Colonus, a Ligurian, who with barely three ships penetrated to that province which was believed to be fabulous; he returned bearing substantial proofs in the shape of many precious things and particularly of gold which is a natural product of these regions. But, Illustrious Count, we must pass over foreign matters."

On September 13, Martyr wrote to Count Tendilla and the archbishop of Granada: "Attention, you two most wise and venerable men, and hear of a new discovery. You remember Colonus, the Ligurian, who persisted when in the camps of the sovereigns, that one could pass over by way of the Western Antipodes to a new hemisphere of the globe; it is important you should recall it. Because the deed was in a measure due to you both. And I hold it true that without your counsel the thing would not have been done. He is returned safe and declares he has found wonderful things."

Martyr had so far confined his letters to a digest of what Columbus had written in his missive to the court and had told the assembled noblemen in Barcelona. He seemed to accept Columbus's claims. By October 1, however, skepticism crept into the correspondence. Perhaps the monarchs, too, were beginning to have second thoughts. In a letter to the archbishop of Braga, he wrote:

> A certain Columbus has sailed to the Western Antipodes, even, as he believes, to the very shores of India. He has discovered many islands beyond the Eastern ocean adjoining the Indies, which are believed to be those of which mention was made among cosmographers. I do not wholly deny this, although the magnitude of the globe seems to suggest otherwise, for there are not wanting those who think it but a small journey from the end of Spain to the shores of India. . . . It is enough for us that the hidden half of the globe is brought to light and that day by day the Portuguese go farther and farther beyond the equinoctial circle itself. Regions hitherto unknown, as if they were all so many thoroughfares, will soon be explored.

Despite rising skepticism about certain claims, Martyr was awaking to the potential significance of the events, which promised knowledge about the unknown half of the earth, and was warming to the subject of world navigation, which he would devote the rest of his life to describing for his correspondents, and for posterity. A year later, he wrote Count Borromeo: "I have begun to write books about this great discovery."

And so he did, becoming the first historian of the Americas. From 1494 until his death in 1526, he concentrated on gathering and disseminating information about the transoceanic voyages. He had the instincts of a good journalist and the insights of a good historian. At every opportunity, he interviewed Columbus and listened to the stories of succeeding navigators and colonists. His writing has been characterized as journalistic, for he selected the more interesting and important details, to avoid being boring, and related them as vivid stories dispatched to distant readers. The historian in him glimpsed earlier than most people the greater import of the discoveries. It also informed his writing, as Morison has said, with a "critical intelligence which pierced some of the cosmographical fancies of Columbus."

Martyr was well aware that he was writing history, even if it took the form of letters about current events. As he said, "the material for my immortality was provided by the new worlds discovered by the Spaniards." He may even have coined the expression "the new world"—a part of the world he never visited. He was the only one of the four early historians never to go there.

Martyr's importance to the history of Columbus and his achievements is twofold.

First, his letters informed the educated public of Iberia and Italy about the unfolding events. Much of what contemporary Europe knew of the discoveries came from Martyr. And he saved copies of more than 800 of these letters, all in Latin, and collected them as a series of eight books under the title of *De Orbe Novo.* The first *Decade de Orbe Novo*—each of the volumes was called a decade—was finished by 1501, and an unofficial, paraphrased book based on it was printed in Venice in 1504. The authorized volume came out in 1511 (the first edition of the complete eight decades was printed in 1530) and has survived as the one book, except for Columbus's journal extracts, that tells the story with a freshness undiminished by the passage of years. Martyr wrote of the moment at the moment. The other witnesses would write their books dozens of years—as much as half a century—after the events they described.

Second, the published letters of Martyr seem to have influenced history's neglect of Columbus over the next two or three centuries. The letters give few details about Columbus himself and increasingly overlook him in the rush of subsequent exploits. One reason history—and, of more immediate importance, the mapmakers—largely ignored Columbus for so long may be because Martyr also had. For all the significance he imputed to the discoveries, he "buries the discoverer under the event," as Justin Winsor wrote in 1891. This may have been a reflection of the waning interest in Columbus in the years following the homage paid him at Barcelona, and of his vanishing fame immediately after his death in 1506.

An English translation of Peter Martyr's first three decades would be published in 1555, to inspire Elizabethans in their own excursions into the New World. The revival and magnification of Columbus's reputation would come even later, through the discovery and publication of other contemporary writings, particularly those of Las Casas.

Bartolomé de las Casas, born in Seville, was a youth of eighteen years when he witnessed Columbus's arrival there. His father and uncle went to the New World as colonists with Columbus's second expedition. After his studies at Salamanca, he followed in 1502 with a fleet led by Nicolás de Ovando. He was, at first, much like other fortune seekers in Española.

Las Casas became a planter with many Indians working under him through the *encomienda* system. By law, native families were "commended" to a colonist, the *encomendero,* who was responsible for their conversion to Christianity and their assimilation into the new colonial economic order. In practice, they were subjected to a form of slavery. The colonists were entitled to use the people as laborers, which they did with little regard for their health and well-being. The *encomiendas* were run as if they were landed estates in a society of masters and slaves.

In 1510, a Dominican convent was founded and Las Casas became the first priest to be ordained in the New World, though this did not alter his attitudes and practices as a typical *encomendero.* But soon he experienced a more fundamental conversion. As a missionary to Cuba, he grew increasingly appalled by the massacres and other outrages committed against the Indians. He returned a changed man.

From 1514 on, Las Casas gave himself unsparingly to the cause of the Indians. Forsaking his *encomienda,* he became the protector of the

Indians and their "universal procurator" in dealings with the church and the state in the colonies and back in Spain. He made five or six journeys to Spain to advocate more humane treatment of the Indians. Finally, he returned to Spain for good in 1547 and engaged in a sharp polemical exchange with Juan Ginés de Sepúlveda, a respected translator of Aristotle. Sepúlveda upheld "the just causes of war against the Indians." Las Casas did not win the debate—indeed, he was denounced to the Inquisition, though never prosecuted—but the attention to his arguments led to stronger reform laws for the colonies and the abolition of the *encomienda* system.

On his retirement to the Dominican College of San Gregorio at Valladolid, Las Casas continued to defend the Indians in the Council of the Indies and occupied himself writing his major work, *Historia de las Indias.* The book, begun in the 1520s, was a narrative of the first discoveries and the early colonial experience. In the prologue to *Historia,* he said: "I am moved to write this book only by the very great and extreme need in all of the Spanish kingdom for trustworthy information and enlightenment about this Indian world, information which I have observed to be lacking throughout Spain for many years."

Even though Las Casas wrote many decades after the discovery, he was able to recount in detail and with awe "the most outstanding feat man has ever seen." He admired Columbus as a navigator and a man of unswerving faith in God. But his admiration did not blind him to Columbus's failings, particularly concerning his role in the brutal and repressive handling of the Indians. It was Las Casas who left history the firmest evidence on which to judge the dark side of Columbus and the tragic consequences of the discovery.

The book, however, would not have wide circulation until late in the nineteenth century, in part because its indictment of Spanish colonial practices made it a political embarrassment. Las Casas had kept editing and revising the manuscript until close to his death in 1566, at the age of ninety-two. There was no thought of immediate publication. It was his stipulation that the fathers of San Gregorio not let the manuscript be seen by laymen for another forty years. Even though unpublished, his *Historia* exerted an influence in the writing of American history, starting with Antonio de Herrera. Appointed official chronicler of the Indies in 1596, Herrera acknowledged that he relied heavily on his close reading of the Las Casas manuscript. So, too, did other writers through the centuries. But not until the 1870s, more than three centuries after his death, would Las Casas's *Historia* be published, and the complete book has yet to be translated into English.

History's debt to Las Casas extends to his role in preserving much of Columbus's journal of the first voyage. It is the first such day-by-day account known to be kept by an explorer. Soon it would become so common for mariners to prepare diaries that in 1597 Francis Bacon would marvel that diaries were kept for sea voyages where there was nothing to see but the water and the sky, whereas, generally speaking, diaries were never kept for land journeys, "wherein so much is to be observed."

Be that as it may, the Columbus journal is the most complete record of the discovery. How the substance of the journal, if not the document itself, has come down to us is a story unto itself, with all the ingredients familiar to history: human foible, immediate need outweighing concern for posterity, neglect and oversight, then a surprising discovery that vivifies the past.

Columbus delivered the original journal to Ferdinand and Isabella on his arrival at Barcelona. It has not been seen since the death of Isabella in 1504. But a court scribe prepared an exact copy that was handed to Columbus before his departure for the second voyage. This copy is known to have survived at least until 1554. Ferdinand Columbus used it as a source for his father's biography. Las Casas must have borrowed it from either Ferdinand or Diego, the elder son. In his *Historia,* Las Casas wrote at the end of the section on the first voyage that he had taken the discoverer's words "from the book that Columbus made for the Kings of his first navigation to and discovery of the Indies." But after 1554 the copy dropped out of sight.

Robert H. Fuson, professor emeritus of geography at the University of South Florida, has reconstructed the outlines of the journal's checkered history. In *The Log of Christopher Columbus,* published in 1987 with a new translation of the journal, Fuson notes that the scribe's copy was among the papers, charts, and books Diego inherited after his father's death in 1506. When Diego died in 1526, the inheritance passed to his son, Luis. Since he was a minor, control over the papers was held by Diego's widow, María Álvarez de Toledo. Even she may not have possessed all of the documents until after the death of Ferdinand in 1539. As the family scholar, Ferdinand would have been the one with the greatest interest in his father's writings. María eventually had most of the material placed in the Dominican monastery of San Pablo in Seville (later to be transferred to the cathedral), and on her death in 1549, any papers that had remained in her possession were inherited by Luis. As Fuson observes: "This was one of the greatest tragedies that could have befallen future scholars."

If Luis had any praiseworthy qualities, they have eluded historians. Henry Vignaud found him "devoid of morality." Fuson called him "the dimmest star in the Columbus constellation." This grandson of Columbus was a wastrel who went through money and women with reckless abandon. "In later years," Fuson writes, Luis "was imprisoned for having three wives (at the same time!) and managed to acquire a fourth by bribing his jailers for overnight passes. His only fondness for books or family papers was the price they might fetch in the marketplace, thereby providing the means to support his debauchery."

This must be what happened to the copy of the Columbus journal. In 1554, Luis was authorized by the crown to publish it, but there the trail grows cold. The journal was never published. Instead, he probably sold it to some wealthy nobleman, and the manuscript may survive in a private library somewhere in Spain. Though finding "lost" Columbus documents is increasingly unlikely, a few have been uncovered from time to time, as occurred in 1790.

With the approach of the 300th anniversary of the discovery voyage, Martín Fernández de Navarrete, a retired navy officer in Madrid, was granted permission to search all the libraries of Spain for documents on Columbus and the explorations. His quest led to the previously overlooked archives of the duke of the Infantado. Buried there was a manuscript in the hand of Las Casas that he had titled *El libro de la primera navegación, The Book of the First Navigation.* This was a lengthy abridgment of the Columbus journal. When he had had access to the manuscript, Las Casas obviously copied many of the admiral's own words and paraphrased other long passages as reference material for the book he was writing. The abstract was written in Spanish on both sides of seventy-six large folio pages. Las Casas left clues in his book, Fuson notes, indicating that the section derived from the journal was written after 1527 and before 1539. So this is presumably when the priest abstracted the document.

Although Navarrete recognized the importance of the journal abridgment as early as 1791, his edited version was not published until 1825, as part of a collection of other documents related to the fifteenth-century discoveries. The authenticity of the journal as extracted by Las Casas has never been seriously doubted. There were omissions, of course, and some obvious errors that could have been the fault of Columbus, the court copyist, or Las Casas. Even so, Fuson concludes, "the abstract must be accepted as an excellent synopsis of the copied original."

Publication of Navarrete's discoveries set in motion a wave of scholarly interest in Columbus that rolled through the nineteenth century. Alexander von Humboldt, the great German geographer and polymath, drew on the new information in writing his influential interpretations of Columbus and the New World explorations. Samuel Kettell, a New England editor, translated the Las Casas text into English and published it in Boston in 1827. The excitement of the Navarrete publication lured Washington Irving, the American author, to Madrid with the idea of translating the entire collection of what he called "the most complete body of facts hitherto laid before the world, relative to the voyages of Columbus."

A student of Spanish literature, Irving felt this was the major project he needed to revive his flagging career. Faced with the voluminous material, however, Irving recognized that he was not equal to the translation task and decided that writing a biography of Columbus would be more interesting, and more profitable. Irving's *The Life and Voyages of Christopher Columbus,* published in 1829, was read avidly in the United States and contributed to the idealized image of the discoverer that dominated literature for more than a century and has not been entirely expunged. His soaring fancy produced a romance, more than a judicious biography.

Beyond his value as a primary source of the Columbus story, Las Casas has also figured in the making of history long after his death. One motive behind the authorization of Navarrete's search of the archives was the political unrest spreading through Spain's colonies in America. In *Bartolomé de las Casas: Bookman, Scholar and Propagandist,* written in 1952, the American historian Lewis Hanke points out that the Spanish monarch, fearing the loss of his American dominions, ordered the investigation of historical materials on the conquest, as Hanke says, "to demonstrate to the world the lack of substance in the charge that [Spain's] New World realms had broken away because of [Spain's] bad treatment of them." Historians benefited from the discovery of illuminating documents, including the journal abstract. But for Spanish politicians the ploy had backfired. The Las Casas material on the Indians was incendiary.

Navarrete himself, in an otherwise remarkably objective analysis of the writings of Las Casas, felt obliged to excoriate those authors who are always "sowing hatred and discord between brothers." Once unloosed, though, the long-ignored fulminations of Las Casas against the abuses heaped on the Indians only fanned the flames of revolt. For Simón Bolívar, the liberator of much of Spanish South America, Las Casas became gospel in justifying the revolutions between 1810 and 1830. The insurgents held him in such esteem that it was suggested at one time that the capital of Colombia should be named Las Casas.

The first biography of Columbus was what today would be called an "authorized" version. Despite the limitations of such an uncritical work, it is another valuable primary source of the history, and for almost three centuries it was, in addition to Peter Martyr's letters and the Columbus Letter to Santángel, the most accessible and respected contemporary account of the discoveries.

The biography was written by his son Ferdinand, who was known as Don Fernando or Hernando and is so referred to by writers wishing to avoid confusion with his father or with the king. Hernando was born in 1488 in Córdoba to a young woman of humble station who was Columbus's mistress. Once his father returned in triumph, he was appointed a page in the Spanish court, where he remained for many years and developed a passion for books and scholarship. He made two trips to the New World, with his father on the fourth voyage in 1502–4 and with his half-brother, Diego, in 1509, but this was adventure enough to last him a lifetime.

As a grown man with inherited money, Hernando settled down to the comfortable life of travel, study, and book-collecting. The library in his home by the river in Seville held one of the finest private collections in Europe. John Boyd Thacher, a historian and bibliophile writing in the early twentieth century, said of the library: "Here were gathered no less than 15,370 books and manuscripts, representing the classics, the gems of incunabula, the first fruits of the fecund press, the rarest editions of the poets and of those who had written enduring prose; the sermons and the teachings of the fathers of the Church, the works of the philosophers, the printed fabrics of countless dreams."

The biography Hernando wrote was only one of two significant services he rendered for history. He also acted as custodian of papers and books that had belonged to Columbus, some of which bear the admiral's marginal annotations by which scholars have inferred the likely progression of his thinking as he moved toward his Enterprise of the Indies. Hernando's stewardship thus saved many documents from the profligate Luis Columbus. In accordance with his wishes, on his death the library was eventually transferred to the cathedral of Seville. Unfortunately, through neglect and losses by vandalism, fewer than 2,000 volumes have survived in the Biblioteca Colombina adjoining the cathedral. But these include a number of the books Columbus read and presumably drew on as he prepared for his role in history.

Hernando did not get around to writing the book about his father until late in his own life. He had grown concerned for his father's reputation in history. The crown had reneged on its promise of sweeping grants of property and political rights to Columbus and his heirs. A legal battle over these rights had seen credible witnesses testifying that the idea for the voyage may not have originated with Columbus and that, in any event, others had been instrumental in its success. Indeed, historians have extracted from this testimony several tidbits about the crews and Columbus in the days before he set sail. Insofar as defense of his father was the motive behind Hernando's labors, the book must be read with due attention to possible bias. Discerning scholars have found in the biography compelling evidence that Hernando resembled his father in more than physical appearance; he could be vain and boastful, sensitive to slights, and artful in building the legend that has sometimes beclouded the reality of Columbus.

In the preface to his annotated translation of the biography, *The Life of the Admiral Christopher Columbus by His Son Ferdinand,* Benjamin Keen wrote in 1959 that Hernando might have also felt impelled to defend his father because of two publications. One was Oviedo's book, published in 1535, which advanced the fanciful view that the Indies had once belonged to ancient rulers of Spain and so Columbus could not be the discoverer—which must be the first of countless arguments disputing the primacy of the achievement. In another book, a bishop in Genoa, Agostino Giustiniani, dropped a casual reference to Columbus's lowly origins—"a truthful observation," Keen comments, "but most damaging to the pride of his aristocratic descendants." Hernando devoted "disproportionate space" in the beginning of the biography, Keen notes, to a polemical response to the two chroniclers. It is also revealing that Hernando never mentions his own humble mother anywhere in the book, though, as Keen points out, he "repeatedly alludes to his father's high-born Portuguese wife."

Most historians, nonetheless, agree with Morison's judgment that Hernando's book "needs no more discounting than does any biography of a distinguished father by a devoted son." The book's merits include its richness of detail about Columbus's pre-voyage life and insights into his personality and the sources of his inspiration. Also, it often reads like a gripping adventure story set in tumultuous times. As Keen writes, the book "vividly re-creates the moral and intellectual atmosphere of Columbus's world and the swirling passions of which he was the center."

Keen's one serious reservation concerns Hernando's "intellect and heart." Hernando lacked what might be called a social conscience. Even though this was not a common trait among men of that time, Keen points out that it "was manifested in such generous men among his contemporaries as Sir Thomas More or Bartolomé de las Casas." Hernando, though, was unmoved by the misfortunes of the Indians, ascribing the ravages of disease and famine after the conquest to God's avenging hand. To read Hernando's account of the discoveries is to understand what Las Casas was up against. Las Casas, who knew Hernando, wrote that the son of Columbus "understood very little about the rights of the Indians and the injustices that his father began against the natives of [Española]."

Hernando's biography did not go to press for years. The crown may have proscribed publication because of its criticism of the monarchs' treatment of Columbus. After Hernando's death in 1539, at the age of fifty-one, the manuscript languished among the family papers. Since he had not married—it is believed that he led a celibate life, though he never took holy orders—the manuscript passed to Diego's widow and thence to the irresponsible Luis, who did with it what he had apparently done with the journal copy. Luis sold it to an Italian physician, Baliano de Fornari of Genoa. It is to him that history is indebted for the preservation of Hernando's biography. Fornari took the manuscript to Venice and personally supervised its translation from Spanish to Italian, by Alfonso Ulloa, and its eventual publication in 1571. Well that he did, for the original manuscript is lost.

In the foreword to the book, Ferdinand Columbus said that he assumed "the burden of this work" in part because the labors and illness of his father had "left him no time for the writing of memoirs." He further promised "to tell the story of the Admiral's life only from his own writings and letters and what I myself observed." The result, accordingly, is as close to the story of Columbus by Columbus himself as we are likely to get.

The fourth contemporary source for the story of Columbus and the early discoveries is Gonzalo Fernández de Oviedo. His contribution has been overshadowed by the writings of the other three witnesses, for which Oviedo himself must bear some responsibility. His major work, *Historia general y natural de las Indias,* the first volume of which was published in 1535, is so comprehensive and rambling as to intimidate readers and researchers then and ever since. But in recent decades, until his death in 1976, the Italian scholar Antonello Gerbi drew attention to the value of Oviedo's *Historia* as a wide-ranging record not only of the voyages of exploration but of life in the colonies, including for the first time in any detail the flora and fauna. Gerbi's painstaking research, elaborated in his book *Nature in the New World,* has reminded historians of why Oviedo has been called the first sociologist of the Americas and why Humboldt extolled Oviedo's scientific inquisitiveness and considered him a founder of "what is today called physical geography."

A hidalgo of Madrid, Oviedo was only fourteen years old when he first met Columbus outside Granada. He was a page at the court there on the eve of victory over the Moors and the decision to back Columbus. He saw Columbus again the next year at the celebration in Barcelona. The young Oviedo, perhaps impressed by the great events, was already inclining toward a vocation as chronicler. Writing of himself at the time, he said: "Therefore I do not write about any of these . . . things from hearsay, but as an eyewitness. Although I write of them from this place [America], or, more properly speaking, according to my memorandum books, wherein they have been written since the time itself."

After his experience as a court page, Oviedo traveled in Italy between 1498 and 1502, acquiring a Renaissance education in the classics and fine arts. Gerbi believes this formed the man who would go to America in 1514 and become the official chronicler of the Indies, beginning in 1532. "The future historian of the Indies, if a Spaniard by birth, language, and office," Gerbi writes, "is an early sixteenth-century Italian in his mentality, his scientific curiosity, in his lofty concept of his office of historian, and finally in the subtle humor which not infrequently filters through and lights up the enormous farrago of his writings."

From the time Oviedo first stepped ashore in America, at Santo Domingo, when he was thirty-six years old, he diligently entered into his "scribbling books" everything he saw and heard. He arrived to be an inspector of gold mines and remained for the greater part of his life, serving in various capacities as a tax official, an administrator, and the commander of a small military garrison. (Although he tried to give the contrary impression, writing of taking part "in the conquest and pacification" by arms of some regions of the New World, he was not a conquistador.) His official duties gave him the opportunity and left him the time to interrogate seamen, soldiers, and missionaries who came to Española and duly record their tales. Oviedo's account of the Columbus voyages, though not extensive, benefited from information he gleaned from the memories of surviving participants.

But Oviedo's forte was natural history. He was a perceptive observer of the trees, plants, and animals. He cultivated a botanical garden with specimens he collected in his travels through the Caribbean; there he also performed an autopsy on a seven-and-a-half-foot snake, extracting "thirty and some eggs" for study. He filled notebooks with descriptions and his own sketches of hundreds of plants, including tobacco ("I cannot imagine what pleasure one can derive" from smoking it), rubber (and rubber balls made by the Indians), coca (the chewing of which was practiced then as today by Indians in Peru), and kapok (which he discovered and praised for use in cushions and pillows).

Oviedo complements the other contemporary historians with his emphasis on cataloguing and describing the people and nature of the New World, which the others slighted. As Gerbi writes: "Since sixteenth-century America is almost a silent world as regards history, almost entirely lacking in any written past, but abundantly endowed with new forms and unknown creatures, it is immensely fortunate for Oviedo and for us that his mind was this way inclined."

Oviedo's descriptions emphasized the differentness of life in the New World, but he was shrewd enough to reject emerging ideas that it was either inferior or superior to life elsewhere; he seemed to recognize that nature in the two worlds is all one. He also cast an appraising eye on the Europeans who came to the New World, describing the political organization of their communities and recounting their problems with the Indians. In this, Gerbi writes, Oviedo is "revealed to us as the first 'sociologist' of America." His "social types"—the adventurer, the cacique, the priest, the captain, and so on—are forcefully delineated, Gerbi says, "almost as if they were so many zoological species."

But Oviedo could be tiresomely querulous. "Certain cunning historians, who talk of the Indies without seeing them," were the object of frequent complaints; Peter Martyr was a specific target. At one time or another he found much to criticize in just about everybody: Indians, Spaniards, priests, lawyers, conquistadors, foreigners, and even, on occasion, the sovereign himself. He did not especially condone harsh treatment of the Indians, but his accounts of them were sufficiently disparaging to draw the undying wrath of Las Casas, who branded Oviedo as a "deadly enemy of the Indians." If Las Casas tended to idealize the Indians in defending them, Oviedo often accentuated their faults. Alberto Mario Salas, an Argentine scholar, writes: "His Indians are not the gracious unclothed natives that Columbus saw, nor the exotic beings of Peter Martyr, nor the mild and ingenuous folk of Las Casas. To Oviedo Indians are dirty, lying, cowardly people who commit suicide because they are bored or because they wish to molest the Spaniards, a people who neither know how to work or wish to."

Of course, Oviedo lived long enough in the colonies to find much to criticize. He saw and described the melancholic decline of Santo Domingo and the importation of hordes of black slaves. In one of the last things he wrote, Oviedo in 1554 informed the prince who would become Philip II of the ruin of Española. He minced no words in assigning the blame to bad government, corruption, and outright robbery. "This poor city is a prey of vultures," he concluded.

Through the years, Oviedo acquired a reputation among historians as being anti-Columbus. One reason, which incensed Ferdinand Columbus, was his identification of the West Indies with the islands that had been owned by Hesperus, the mythical king of Spain, and were known in legend as Hesperides. It was pure fantasy, displeasing to Hernando, as we have seen, but pleasing to the current monarch, Charles V, who began to look with favor on Oviedo's historical efforts.

Another reason for suspecting Oviedo's attitude toward Columbus was his apparently innocent but mischievous telling of the story of the unknown Portuguese pilot. As the story goes, a caravel sailing from Spain to England was blown off course and after many days came upon "one or more of the islands of these regions and the Indies."

After many months, the ship returned, and only the pilot lived to share the secret of the winds and course leading to the western discovery. Oviedo wrote: "Moreover, it is said that this pilot was a very intimate friend of Christopher Columbus, and that he understood somewhat of the latitudes, and marked the land which he found, and in great secrecy shared it with Columbus." Columbus supposedly asked the pilot to make a chart and indicate on it the land he had seen. "It is said," Oviedo continued, "that Columbus received him in his house as a friend and sought to cure him, as he too landed very weak; but that he died like the rest, and thus Columbus was informed of the land and navigation of those regions, and he alone knew the secret."

If there was any truth to the story, it showed that Columbus had misled people into believing that the idea of the Enterprise of the Indies had been his alone and that the waters he proposed to cross had never before been sailed. "Whether this was so or not, nobody can truly affirm; but so the story ran among the common people," Oviedo added. "As for me, I hold it to be false."

Such stories assume a life of their own. Las Casas repeated it, and even Hernando mentions it as a "curiosity," but without contradicting it. From time to time, historians have seized on the unknown pilot's tale in questioning the singularity of Columbus's vision. Defenders of Columbus thus charge Oviedo with malice toward the discoverer. Humboldt, though deploring the pilot "calumny," acknowledged that it was unfair to consider Oviedo an enemy of Columbus, for he had praised the admiral's deeds and rights and had expressed the wish to be buried in the cathedral of Santo Domingo, near Columbus's tomb.

Oviedo died in 1557 at the age of seventy-nine, probably in Santo Domingo, though some accounts give Valladolid, in Spain, as the place of death. In his last years, he was white-bearded and deaf but could look back with satisfaction on his life and work. He wrote warmly of his three successive wives (the first two had died) and the institution of matrimony. "I was not accustomed to the concubines that my neighbors kept (and some of them two)," he wrote. At his death, however, only the first part of his history had been printed. The complete book, in four volumes, was finally published in Madrid in the middle of the nineteenth century.

A few other contemporaries left lesser contributions to the Columbus record. Perhaps the first published biography was produced by the Genoese bishop Agostino Giustiniani. In his *Polyglot Psalter,* a collection of the Psalms in four languages, Giustiniani included a sketch of Columbus's humble origins in Genoa. His account is believed to be closer to the truth than Hernando Columbus, in his heated objections to it, wanted to concede. But Giustiniani's book, printed in 1516, must have had few readers other than Hernando. Saying that he had hoped to "acquire great praise and not indifferent gain," Giustiniani complained that "my credulity was deceived, because the work was praised by every one, but left to repose and sleep as scarcely the fourth part of the books were sold."

Another Genoese author, Antonio Gallo, had written an earlier account giving details of Columbus's life and personality, which may have been the source of much of Giustiniani's information. But Gallo's manuscript remained unpublished until the eighteenth century, a not uncommon fate for many documents pertaining to the discoveries.

This happened also to the chronicle of Ferdinand and Isabella that was written by Andrés Bernáldez, a priest of Seville and friend of Columbus. The navigator had lived in the priest's house for a time following his second voyage. Bernáldez devoted four chapters to Columbus, giving important details about the second voyage that he must have heard from the admiral himself. In addition, he had access to an account of that voyage prepared by Diego Álvarez Chanca, a physician, as a report to the church officials in Seville. The informative Chanca letter was not published until it was turned up by Navarrete. The Bernáldez manuscript was not published until later in the nineteenth century.

The true dawn of Columbus scholarship broke with the publication, begun in 1825 and concluded in 1837, of the manuscripts and documents uncovered by Martín Fernández de Navarrete. Soon after Washington Irving availed himself of these materials, Humboldt also brought his formidable intelligence to bear on the Navarrete documents in his work, *The History and Geography of the New Continent,* published in 1836–39. Through Humboldt, according to Justin Winsor, "the intelligence of our own time may indeed be said to have first clearly apprehended, under the light of a critical spirit . . . , the true significance of the great deeds that gave America to Europe."

On the occasion of the 400th anniversary of the discovery, the Italian government commissioned Cesare de Lollis, a classical scholar, to compile a monumental collection of documentary and narrative sources pertaining to Columbus. This was published in 1892–94 as fourteen volumes known as *Raccolta di documenti e studi pubblicati della R. Commissione Columbiana.* Even more definitive than the Navarrete works, the *Raccolta Columbiana* has been the bible for scholars ever since. The Italian National Quincentennial Commission is preparing an updated edition, *Nuova raccolta,* and the Center for Medieval and Renaissance Studies at the University of California at Los Angeles is publishing a series of English translations of such documents under the title of *Repertorium Columbianum.* One of the most important contributions to Columbus scholarship in this century is a critical edition of the mariner's writings collected and annotated by Consuelo Varela, published in 1982 as *Cristóbal Colón: Textos y documentos completos.*

By the end of the nineteenth century, ninety-seven pieces of writing by Columbus had been tracked down or were known to have existed. Precious as the surviving documents are, their ambiguities, contradictions, omissions, and emphasis on Columbus's rights more than his accomplishments perplex as often as they enlighten historians. Many other documents are undoubtedly lost forever. The nineteenth-century scholar Henry Harrisse offered one explanation. "The fact is that Columbus was very far from being in his lifetime the important personage he now is," Harrisse writes, "and his writings, which then commanded neither respect nor attention, were probably thrown into the waste-basket as soon as received."

Harrisse was born in Paris but grew up in the United States, where he practiced law and devoted his spare time to translating and annotating the works of Descartes. Next he turned to Columbus, compiling a bibliography of Americana from 1492 to 1551. He returned to Paris in 1869 to live the rest of his long life and wrote most of his carefully researched books on Columbus in French, notably *Christophe Colomb,* published in 1884. His scholarship corrected some errors and misinterpretations and set higher critical standards for those who would follow. Harrisse also called attention to an aspect of the Columbus historiography that will probably come as a surprise to most people today. For several decades after his death, Columbus was virtually ignored by historians. In the early sixteenth century, Harrisse found, the standard chroniclers of the world's history failed to mention Columbus or his achievements. He could find no reference to Columbus by the German chroniclers before 1531, and in England it was not until about 1550 that Columbus achieved some measure of historical standing.

Columbus may have made history in 1492, but it was a good three centuries before history, reclaiming knowledge from the archives and reappraising earlier accounts, began welcoming him into the pantheon of the world's great figures. Then he became a symbol of the adventuring human spirit and an avatar of the Western faith in progress ascendant in the nineteenth and early twentieth centuries. The real man was lost in soaring myth.

Controversies over this or that aspect of Columbus and his four voyages did not cease. If anything, the newly discovered documents have provoked more arguments than they settled. John Larner, a University of Glasgow scholar, gives three reasons. One is that the creators of Columbus as an icon, exemplar of courage, virtue, and various political or religious agendas, have contaminated the literature and very image of the man. Another reason, Larner says, are "those lacunae in the sources so typical of whatsoever study conducted on any fifteenth-century character." In some cases the gaps are intentional, covering up less exemplary motives and aims. Even when unintentional, they open the gates to legitimate questions and wild surmise. A third reason for "unrelenting battles," Larner writes, is that "There is virtually no primary or near-contemporary source whose authenticity has not at some time been questioned." Since the original manuscript has disappeared, Hernando's biography has been viewed with suspicion. The translator Ulloa was known to be careless and was once sentenced to death (though later reprieved) for forgery. The biography, some scholars have contended, could be flawed with undetectable errors or may even have been cobbled together from an early manuscript of Las Casas and so may not be the work of Hernando. The accuracy of the Las Casas excerpts of Columbus's papers has also been questioned. The bishop could have been careless, or, in his zeal in arguing the case for rights of the Indians, he may have selected and interpreted occurrences that exaggerated Spanish brutality and cupidity and Columbus's involvement. Even if Hernando's biography is authentic and the works of Las Casas reasonably balanced and complete, as most scholars now believe, much room is left for dispute over nearly every aspect of Columbus.

His magnified reputation, beginning in the late eighteenth century, also made him a larger target for historians and others who sought to justify or debunk the myth. They have exploited every gap in the contemporary record and arranged the few established facts to suit their ends. Now, as a consequence, the idealized Columbus has run into heavy seas.

The known facts of his life and voyages have not changed much in recent decades. But succeeding generations of historians, and not a few people in other walks of life, have recounted the familiar events from changing points of view. They have been interpreting the same materials, mostly the accounts of four contemporary witnesses and the few Columbus writings, in the peculiar light of their own age. History is said to be the child of the times. Just as the possibilities of history change through time—more so and more rapidly since Columbus's exploits changed the world—the perceptions of past events are forever in flux.

4

The Many Faces of Columbus

Nothing better illustrates history's changing image of Columbus than the succession of portraits of him that have appeared over the centuries. They show a man of many faces, only a few of which bear much resemblance to the man described by those who knew him. History, it seems, can no more agree on what he looked like than on how to assess the many other disputed aspects of his life and deeds. If his physical characteristics are unclear, consider the formidable odds against ever being able to sift fact from fancy about who Columbus was.

There should be little confusion over the man's physical appearance. His son, who should know, gave a concise description in his biography. "The Admiral," Hernando wrote, "was a well-built man of more than average stature, the face long, the cheeks somewhat high, his body neither fat nor lean. He had an aquiline nose and light-colored eyes; his complexion too was light and tending to bright red. In youth his hair was blonde, but when he reached the age of thirty, it all turned white."

On this Ferdinand Columbus had no apparent reason to mislead, and other contemporaries provided confirming descriptions. Las Casas: "His form was tall, above the medium: his face long and his countenance imposing: his nose aquiline: his eyes clear blue: his complexion light, tending toward a decided red: his beard and hair were red when he was young, but which cares then had early turned white." Oviedo: "He was of good stature and appearance, of more than medium height and with strong limbs, his eyes bright and his other features of good proportion: his hair very red and his face somewhat burned and freckled."

Hernando went on to describe his father's character in words an artist could be expected to find revealing of the man behind the countenance. "In eating and drinking, and in the adornment of his person, he was very moderate and modest," he wrote. "He was affable in conversation with strangers and very pleasant to the members of his household, though with a certain gravity. He was so strict in matters of religion that for fasting and saying prayers he might have been taken for a member of a religious order. . . . And so fine was his hand that he might have earned his bread by that skill alone." Elsewhere in the biography, Hernando added: "The Admiral was a learned man of great experience and did not waste his time in manual or mechanical labor, which did not comport with the grandeur and immortality of the wonderful deeds he was to perform."

Granting the son some possible excess in this character analysis, one certainly does not get from Hernando the impression of his father as a rough seaman. But Columbus could not be too gentle and modest if he was to promote his vision so persistently in Spain and if he could control a group of tough seamen who suspected they might be headed to the edge of the world. Washington Irving, who examined all the descriptions with a novelist's eye, summed up Columbus as "tall, well-formed, muscular, and of an elevated and dignified demeanour" and as one whose "whole countenance had an air of authority."

No portrait of Columbus was drawn, carved, or painted from life, or by anyone who had known him. Contrary to the assumption of some historians, portrait painting was in fashion in fifteenth-century Spain, and contemporary paintings exist of Ferdinand and Isabella—but none of Columbus. This could indicate that in his lifetime he was not considered so important as afterward, or that the Columbus family had other uses for their money than paying artists.

No fewer than seventy-one portraits of Columbus, mostly from the eighteenth and nineteenth centuries, were exhibited at the Columbian Exposition in Chicago in 1893. They are all interpretations of the man and vary as much as do the many portraits of Jesus. Thacher, in his 1904 book, discussed thirty-nine of these portraits as representative of the many artistic renderings of Columbus. On canvas and on wood, there is a Columbus for every taste. He is seen as heroic, contemplative, and mystical; godlike to hard-nosed; confident to conniving. He is lean-faced with an aquiline nose; fat-faced and jowly; blond, swarthy, olive-skinned; clean-shaven, bearded, mustachioed; dressed in the robes of a courtier or in plain monastic raiment.

The earliest known portrait was commissioned by Paolo Giovio, a wealthy historian better known by his Latin name, Paulus Jovius, for a gallery in his villa on Lake Como. The date and artist are unknown, but both Justin Winsor and Samuel Eliot Morison believe the portrait,

Woodcut based on the portrait commissioned by Paulus Jovius

though not executed from life, has the greatest claim as an authentic likeness of Columbus. It shows a man in vaguely monastic robes. His curly gray hair is thin and receding. The nose is long, and the mouth firm, with a protruding lower lip. But the face is full, not lean, and the eyes are brown, not blue. The most striking feature is the downcast eyes, which Morison affirms to be the countenance of "a chastened Columbus after his Third Voyage." What is believed to be the original of this painting is in the Galeria Gioviana in Como. A woodcut based on the portrait appeared in a posthumous edition of a book by Jovius, published in 1575, and this apparently influenced many later artistic representations of Columbus.

A long line of round-faced Columbus portraits followed the example of the so-called De Bry Portrait, an engraving of which appeared in 1595 in *Collection of Voyages* published by Theodore de Bry, the Flemish engraver and editor. De Bry claimed that it was painted by order of King Ferdinand, though he offered no convincing proof. Whoever the artist was, he must not have read Hernando's or Oviedo's books, which had been published years before. The face of Columbus is heavy and stolid. Thick curls spill out from under an Italian peaked cap. The eyes are large and dull. Nothing about the portrait suggests the strength and authority of the man. But, as Thacher observes, probably no other picture of Columbus has been so often reproduced, with certain modifications, in histories of the discoveries. The De Bry type can be seen in museums throughout the world.

As time passed and historians and hagiographers of the nineteenth century brought into being a more heroic Columbus, artists reflected this changing view. They painted their vision of strength and greatness. Morison chose one such ideal portrait of Columbus for the frontispiece to his biography. Painted for the Naval Museum of Madrid, the portrait, Morison writes, "follows closely the personal descriptions of Columbus, and gives an impression of force, dignity and integrity." Likewise, Paolo Emilio Taviani, the historian from Genoa, selected for the cover of his book, *Christopher Columbus: The Grand Design,* another painting from the Madrid museum that shows a man of long visage, ruddy complexion, reddish hair turning to gray, and eyes that seem to be focused far into the future.

This was the Columbus of the nineteenth century, the embodiment of that age's faith in progress and avatar of the New World's emergence as a promised land of human fulfillment. Few artists in the twentieth century, however, have felt inspired to depict Columbus in any shape or guise. Either they believed there was nothing new to portray, or they had slight interest in the man, progress and heroes not being what they used to be.

In 1910, the Spanish artist Joaquín Sorolla y Bastida decided that the next-best thing to a contemporary portrait would be one based on the likeness of a Columbus descendant. With the duke of Veragua as a model, the artist painted *Columbus Leaving Palos,* which can be seen at the Mariners' Museum in Newport News, Virginia. Sorolla's Columbus, following the nineteenth-century tradition, is the image of daring and determination in the face of the unknown.

One of the few newer portraits shows a Columbus of dark visage

Cristoforo Colombo, by Leonardo Lasansky, 1984

that seems to reflect the image of the man in an age that is hard on heroes and given to a less optimistic vision of the human potential. The portrait, commissioned by the James Ford Bell Library of the University of Minnesota, a repository of literature and maps of European exploration, is a color intaglio by Leonardo Lasansky, completed in 1984 and entitled *Cristoforo Colombo.* After a study of the Columbus literature, Lasansky, a professor of art at Hamline University in St. Paul, Minnesota, decided to execute what he calls a psychological profile of the mariner. "What fascinated me was all the things we don't know about the man," he says. "I wanted to deal more with the mythology and the mysterious aspects, rather than rely strictly on physical descriptions. Portraits of him, since his death, have been very stylized. They show the generic explorer, with Columbus virtually interchangeable with a Cortes or Pizarro." In any case, Lasansky created a Columbus antithetical to the strikingly handsome hero portrayed a century ago that, he remarks, is still the cinematographer's image of the generic explorer.

Lasansky's Columbus is a study in gray against a pink background. As the artist fashioned the copper engraving, the face of his Columbus grew darker and more shadowy, the rather gentle aspect imagined in the original concept undergoing a metamorphosis into the somewhat sinister look of a waterfront tough. Lasansky explains: "Columbus had to have been very strong, tough, and single-minded. He did not have to look like a handsome yachtsman, as he's sometimes shown. I wanted him to look like he was a real tough son of a bitch." The square face and stout body are reminders of the De Bry school of Columbus portraiture. One side of the swarthy face is in focus, and the other is in complete shadow. The flat black cap he wears, the artist points out, is an inversion of the lower face. Every facet presents a view less of the man as he was than of the Columbus enigma projected across the centuries.

With even less certain results history has sought to delineate the man behind the face. His family and country of origin have been the subject of much dispute, especially since the eighteenth and nineteenth centuries. Neither Columbus nor his son Hernando, deliberately or otherwise, offered many clues, and the vacuum they left has been filled with a rush of conjecture and tall tales.

Even though contemporary witnesses wrote of Columbus the

Christopher Columbus, undated engraving

Ligurian, the man from Genoa, partisans of many countries have grasped at straws of evidence to seize a part of the famous mariner, fomenting endless debate. In a 1986 review of recently published Columbus biographies, Tim Radford was impelled to write in the Manchester *Guardian Weekly* that "what we don't know about Christopher Columbus would fill a very large number of very fat books." As Radford points out, the absence of definitive knowledge has resulted in a string of assertions that he was, in origin, "Castilian, Catalan, Jewish, Corsican, Majorcan, Portuguese, French, German, English, Irish, Greek, Armenian, Polish, Russian and (wait for it) American; the descendant of a Vinlander who sailed back, changed his name to Colon and then set off to 'discover' his own continent."

Every verifiable historical document, however, indicates that he was born in the independent Italian republic of Genoa—in the city or nearby—sometime between August and November of 1451. One notarized paper from Genoa in 1470 is the acknowledgment of a small debt owed by "Cristoforo Colombo, son of Domenico, an adult nineteen years of age." Another notarized document in 1479 concerns testimony by Columbus, then a resident of Lisbon, who had been called back to Genoa in connection with litigation over a trip he had made to Madeira for Genoese shipowners; the witness was stated to be "about twenty-seven years old."

Domenico, the father, was a wool-weaver, as his father, Giovanni, had been. He was a sometime tavern keeper and warder of the Porta dell'Olivella, the eastern gate of Genoa. He seems to have dabbled in real estate and politics. City records tell of his business dealings, occasional indebtedness, and at least one brief imprisonment (he was freed and declared innocent). He and his wife, Susanna Fontanarossa, a weaver's daughter, were known to have lived in Genoa from 1452 to 1455 and at other times lived in nearby Savona and then back in Genoa. Christopher was their eldest child, as far as can be known. Bartholomew, the chartmaker who would share many of Columbus's adventures, was a year or two younger than Christopher. The other children who grew to adulthood were a sister named Bianchinetta and a brother Giacomo, better known by the Spanish equivalent, Diego, who joined Christopher on the second voyage. All in all, the Columbuses of Genoa were fruitful and humble tradespeople, like many others, and nothing for a young man to be ashamed of.

Columbus was, if not ashamed, especially reticent about his family and origins. They are never mentioned in any surviving documents prior to 1492; afterward, he acknowledged Genoa as his native city but continued to withhold any details of his family. Taviani believes that Domenico's politics—in dealings that split Genoa, he had sided with France against Aragon—may have caused Christopher's wariness. As Taviani suspects, this could explain his failure to invite his father to Spain before or after the discovery. The father was still living in Genoa in 1494, but died sometime before the turn of the century. But it is doubtful that Domenico was important enough to have made an impression in Iberia.

A more plausible explanation may lie in Columbus's own ambitions. His need for royal support and his yearning for aristocratic standing probably drove him to conceal his modest origins. Once he had achieved titles and an impressive coat-of-arms, and soaring fame, he could not suddenly admit that he was only a weaver's son; by then, indeed, he may have believed his own fantasy. If he did not, at least his family felt the need to maintain the conceit. Hernando probably could have cleared up matters, but he could not accept the family's humble background. Accordingly, much of the continuing confusion over Columbus's heritage can be laid at the door of his son.

In the opening chapter of his biography, Hernando wrote:

> Two things which are important to know about every famous man are his birthplace and family, because men generally accord more honor to those who were born in great cities and of noble parents. Therefore some wished me to tell how the Admiral came of illustrious stock, although misfortune had reduced his parents to great poverty and need; and how they descended from that Colonus of whom Cornelius Tacitus tells in the twelfth book of his work, saying that he brought King Mithridates a prisoner to Rome, for which exploit the Roman people awarded Colonus the consular dignities, the honor of bearing the standard, and a place among the tribunes. They also wished me to make a great story of those two illustrious Coloni, his relatives, of whom Sabellicus tells that they won a great victory over the Venetians.

With this obfuscating paragraph, all too typical of him, Hernando muddied the waters of history and stocked them with red herrings. It is unlikely that the son did not know or suspect the truth of his father's modest beginnings; he allowed only that Columbus "chose to leave in obscurity all that related to his birthplace and family." It is unlikely that he really believed the family descended from the illustrious Colonus. Hernando betrayed his motives in noting that "men generally accord more honor to those who were born in great cities and of noble parents." His biography was nothing if not a devoted son's effort to see that Columbus received his due in history.

On the matter of the family origins, Hernando demonstrated, to the despair of succeeding historians, that even contemporary witnesses are not invariably reliable sources. Indeed, the son was here engaged in one of the first historiographic controversies over Columbus. Responding to Giustiniani's book telling of Columbus's humble parents in Genoa, Hernando sought to replace this "false account" with one to his liking. Never offering documentation, he affirmed that the Columbuses "were persons of worth who had been reduced to poverty by the wars and factions of Lombardy."

But even Hernando conceded that family background was irrelevant in the case of Columbus. His greatness had other sources. Hernando believed "that the Admiral was chosen for his great work by Our Lord, who desired him as His true Apostle to follow the example of others of His elect by publishing His name on distant seas and shores, not in cities and palaces, thereby imitating Our Lord himself, who though his descent was from the blood royal of Jerusalem, yet was content to have his parentage from an obscure source."

Hernando's father would have been pleased with this rationalization of his origins as being immediately humble but distantly noble and with the pointed associations with the lowly birth of Jesus Christ. Hernando may have even heard this explanation from Columbus's own lips. It accords with the admiral's prophetic writings late in life.

In any case, if the son could take liberties with Columbus's origins, what was to stop future historians, chauvinists, and storytellers? The vast historiography of Columbus is thus filled with a bewildering number of hypotheses about who he was and where he came from.

Most of the hypotheses are founded on little more than the preponderance of Colombos in Italy, Colóns in Spain, Coloms in Portugal, and Coullons in France. From these threads any number of fanciful genealogies have been woven to give one nation or another a claim to Columbus. Some claims had even less foundation; a footnote in a book published in London in 1682 affirmed, without explanation, that the "famous Columbus" was "born in England, but resident at Genoa." One of the most enduring hypotheses, based on some interesting deductions and suggestive associations, is that Columbus was a converted Jew of Spanish origin whose family had been forced to emigrate to Genoa. The arguments for and against the Jewish Columbus point up the difficulties historians face in developing a clear picture of the man's origins.

Conjecture about Columbus's Jewish background, Taviani writes, arose because of the presence of the surname Colombo among Italian Jewish families and gained a foothold in history with the theory that Columbus was born in Galicia. In the late nineteenth century, Celso García de la Riega produced documents—later exposed as forgeries—to show that Columbus was born at Pontevedra in Galicia. He then decided that Columbus must have been Jewish, which would explain his refusal to discuss his family and early life. Supporters of this theory also noted such characteristics of Columbus as his aquiline nose, his devotion to the writings of the Old Testament, and his interest in gold and money. These were given as indications of a Jewish background, but Taviani says these are "just as much Genoese characteristics." As for the fascination with gold and money, Taviani adds, "if we are to go by popular prejudice alone, one might as well argue that Columbus was a Scotchman!"

The most elaborate and fascinating attempt to prove that Columbus was a "*converso*" Jew was made by Salvador de Madariaga in his vivid biography, *Christopher Columbus,* published in 1939. He contends that the family was Catalan Jewish. They first Latinized the surname "Colón" into "Columbus," then adopted the Italian form of "Colombo." In Genoa, the family converted to Christianity.

Columbus's Jewish origins, in the view of Madariaga, explained at once his silence about his family and also the ease with which he insinuated himself among the powerful of both Portugal and Spain, where *conversos* held positions of influence in finance, the church, and even the court.

By the end of the fifteenth century, Spain's population included upward of 300,000 *conversos.* They were active in commercial affairs, and their educated elite married into Spanish aristocracy, assuming a significant role in the arts and in government administration. Ferdinand's treasurer, Luis de Santángel, who interceded in Columbus's behalf, was a member of a prominent family of converted Jews. Others were eminent ecclesiastics, including some who would be canonized and also the worthy Bartolomé de las Casas. Even the infamous

Tomás de Torquemada, first leader of the Spanish Inquisition against heretics, mostly Jewish, was himself from a *converso* family.

The evidence Madariaga advances to establish Columbus's Jewish ancestry begins with his habitual use of the Castilian language in speaking and writing, even before he reached Spain and even in correspondence with people back in Genoa. To Madariaga this indicates that Columbus had probably grown up knowing Spanish, and "there is only one reasonable way of explaining this: the Colombo family were Spanish Jews settled in Genoa, who, following the traditions of their race, had remained faithful to the language of their country of origin."

Authorities on Columbus point out that it was more likely that Columbus learned Spanish in Portugal, where it was the language often used among the upper class, into which Columbus married. He was definitely writing in Spanish at that time, for the notations in his books are in that language, with an admixture of Portuguese. Examining these and other writings, a Spanish philologist, Ramón Menéndez Pidal, determined that Columbus never used Hebraic Spanish or Italo-Spanish but Spanish with some Portuguese spellings. Experts further argue that the absence of Italian in his writing actually testifies to his Genoese origins. Growing up in Genoa, a young man of his circumstances would have known only the Genoese dialect and not Italian, the more literary language. Morison believes Columbus probably was illiterate until after he left home.

Madariaga asks other questions by way of suggesting support for his thesis. Why did Las Casas write: "In the matters of the Christian religion, no doubt, he was a Catholic and of much devotion"? Was there some doubt? Could his piety have been a diversionary tactic? Also, why the name changes? Other Genoese in Spain retained their Italian names, and besides, "Colombo" is a perfectly good Spanish form. Madariaga concludes: "May we point out how Jewish this all is? The men of the wandering race are so often bound to shift the conditions of their existence that, with them, change of name has become a habit, practically unknown though it is to the rest of mankind."

If Columbus was Jewish, though his family had long before converted to Christianity, it could account for some of the mystery surrounding his early life. Even if it might give him a bond with influential *conversos* in Spain, his Jewish ancestry, were that the case, might be better kept a secret in a country that was becoming increasingly intolerant of heterodoxy.

Years before 1492, the year Ferdinand and Isabella expelled the Jews who refused to be baptized, the position of *conversos* in Spanish society was growing precarious. Their wealth created jealousy. Their embrace of less conventional forms of Christianity, predating the humanism of Erasmus, raised suspicions that their conversions were not entirely sincere. Responding to this sentiment, the king and queen in 1478 obtained a papal bull establishing the Spanish Inquisition. By the time of Columbus's arrival, the Inquisition under Torquemada exerted terrifying power. *Conversos* were denounced for secretly practicing Judaism, tortured, tried, and condemned to death at the stake. Their property was confiscated and portioned out to the Inquisition, the crown, and their accusers. Several thousand converted Jews were put to death, and many thousands of others fled the country.

If Jewish blood indeed ran in his veins, Columbus was wise to keep quiet about it, as he did concerning so much of his life before reaching Spain. But there is no proven substance to the Jewish hypothesis, and even less support for the related conjecture that his real purpose in undertaking the voyage was to find a homeland for Jews.

Given the dearth of genealogical information, Taviani takes what seems to be the only reasonable position on the issue. Christopher's father must have been a baptized Catholic. Otherwise he could not have been a warder of the city gate or allowed to own property. The same would hold for his mother—though with the name of Susanna and with a father whose name was Jacopo (Jacob), she could have been of Jewish origin, but not necessarily. The name Susanna was popular among Italian Christians, and many Christians had Old Testament names, then as now. She, too, would have been a practicing Christian, if the family was to be landowners. Likewise, Taviani notes, Christopher's grandfather Giovanni and his grandfather's father were surely Catholics, or they could not have settled in a country village; in fifteenth-century Italy, Jews were not permitted to live in rural areas.

"The problem," Taviani concludes, "is therefore one of ancestry and not of religious faith; and it is hard to establish anything certain. Is it, after all, so important? Jews have produced so many great minds, so many geniuses, that it would not be all that strange if Jewish blood flowed through the veins of history's greatest discoverer. But there is nothing to confirm the hypothesis."

Experts on Columbus do not disagree with Madariaga on one point. Discussing the admiral's habit of concealing more than he revealed of his life, Madariaga writes: "Like the squid, he oozes out a cloud of ink round every hard square fact of his life. This ink, multiplied by the industry of his historians, has made but blacker and thicker the mystery which attaches to him."

There is much less doubt among historians over his birthplace. It was in the republic of Genoa that Columbus was born, most likely in 1451. There he grew up by the sea, and at a "tender age," as he once wrote, cast his lot with those who go to sea. At first, he probably made short voyages, and between them worked in his father's shop in Savona, where the family had moved in 1470. Columbus tells of experiencing his first long voyage four years later. This took him all the way to the Genoese colony of Chios, an island in the Aegean and entrepôt for trade with the Orient. Chios was also a major source of mastic, resin from an evergreen that is now an ingredient of varnishes but then was taken as a painkiller, the fifteenth-century equivalent of aspirin. He made a second trip to Chios the next year, and sometime, probably that same year, he took part, as Hernando related, in a minor naval campaign in the continuing war between Genoa and Aragon, sailing for Genoa's ally, René d'Anjou of France.

This may be all that will ever be known for sure about the early Columbus. It is sufficient for understanding his choice of careers, but not the many other faces he assumed in life and in history.

Even more crucial than his ancestry or place of birth may be its timing. Fourteen fifty-one was two years before the fall of Constantinople to the Ottoman Turks. The loss of Christendom's eastern capital was felt most acutely in Genoa. Not only did it threaten the republic's eastern commerce, but a garrison of 400 Genoese was engaged in the climactic battles. The returning remnants of the garrison brought home the horror of war and an alarming sense of loss that must be avenged. Young Columbus was to grow up hearing of the scourge of Islam, the blockage of regular trade routes to the spices of the East, and the parlous times for Christendom. Priests and popes issued calls for a new crusade to retake Constantinople and Jerusalem. All this could have nourished dreams of a great adventure in the mind of an ambitious young man with nautical experience.

5

Genesis of the Idea

Call it chance or providence, but the arrival of Columbus in Portugal in 1476 brought him to the right place at the right time for transforming any dream he might have harbored into the scheme that would lift him out of obscurity. How he came to be in Portugal is a story with mythic resonances: the hero, near death, emerges from a misty nowhere to recognize the destiny he must pursue, against all odds.

The story, related vividly by Las Casas and in a garbled version by Hernando, is probably true, at least in its bare essentials. In the summer of 1476, Columbus shipped out with a Genoese fleet of five vessels bound for Lisbon and then England with a cargo of mastic from Chios. The fleet passed through the Strait of Gibraltar, where for the first time Columbus faced an Atlantic wind. On August 13, off the southern coast of Portugal, the fleet was attacked by French-Portuguese warships. Since both Portugal and France were at peace with Genoa, the motive is unclear. The warships must have been given some cause for suspicion, or the attackers simply had booty in mind, distinctions between war and piracy not always being respected. In the ensuing battle, three of the Genoese ships caught fire and sank. Many men drowned. Clinging to an oar, Columbus saved himself and struggled to shore, exhausted and possibly wounded. He came to land near the village of Lagos, a few miles east of Cape St. Vincent.

The people of Lagos dried, fed, nursed, and sheltered the survivors. After a few days, Columbus was well enough to make his way to Lisbon and into the community of Genoese merchants and shipowners who lived in the labyrinthine Alfama section of the city, hard by the Tagus. He was about twenty-five years old.

The idea of sailing west across the ocean to reach the East seized his imagination at some point in the eight or nine years Columbus lived in and sailed out of Portugal. Exactly when or how he conceived of his plan is another of the Columbian mysteries. The thought presumably did not come to him immediately or all at once, but he must have evolved a fairly complete plan sometime before 1484, when he appeared before John II seeking the ships and financial support for his undertaking. As in everything else, Columbus's own words on the subject obfuscate more than elucidate. It was his practice, Taviani writes, "never to tell everything to everyone, to say one thing to one man, something else to another, to reveal only portions of arguments, clues, evidence accumulated over the years in his mind." Perhaps Columbus told so many partial stories in so many different versions that, as Morison suspects, he himself could no longer remember the origins of the idea.

In all likelihood, the inspiration sprang from no single source, but from all around him. He heard the stories of westering seamen and of exotic flotsam washing ashore on islands under Portuguese control. Some of the stories were pure fantasy; others, supported by a modicum of fact, had grown more alluring in the many retellings. On voyages to these islands, and north perhaps as far as Iceland and south along the coast of Africa, he gained a taste for Atlantic sailing. He and his brother Bartholomew, who had come to Lisbon as a chartmaker, must have been intrigued by the mythical islands sprinkled on the maps. A 1424 mariner's chart by Zuane Pizzigano showed several hypothetical islands in the western Atlantic at locations corresponding to the West Indies and America, raising unsubstantiated speculation of a Portuguese prediscovery. There may even have been something to the story of the unknown pilot from whom Columbus supposedly obtained secret knowledge of lands across the ocean; historians can neither accept the hypothesis nor lay it to rest. But as far as anyone can determine, and volumes have been written on the subject, there was no one blinding flash of inspiration.

Nor did Columbus derive his plan from a careful reading of scholars. He was not then, and never became, a man who read to learn; he read to gather support for what he already thought to be true. He may have perused the accounts of Marco Polo (at least he was familiar with them, and those of Sir John Mandeville), but it is likely that this reading did not so much inform his concept as it inflamed a mind stoked with the dry tinder of desire. He did study some of the more respected compendiums of geographic knowledge, but apparently only after his idea of the western voyage was well developed through hearsay, observation, and a keen intuition.

From what he did read and the knowledge readily available to him in Lisbon, Columbus made some calculations of global distances. He conveniently managed to constrict the unknown he proposed to challenge. Had he unwittingly deceived himself on the size of the world? Or had he deliberately contrived calculations to deceive others? All that can be said with assurance is that Columbus was a man consumed by an enthusiasm that willed away obstacles and brooked no doubt. He not only invented a great scheme, but also more or less invented the necessary supporting evidence. In his receptive and creative mind the idea of sailing west to the Indies, though not original with him, became an obsession to be acted upon with vigor and persistence. This made all the difference and secured for him an exalted place in history.

Columbus may have seemed to come out of nowhere, but his idea did not. Ideas do not emerge from a vacuum. Even a man of his intuition, zeal, and self-assurance could not have conceived of such a scheme in a time much earlier or in a place much different from Portugal in the late fifteenth century.

Portugal was perfectly situated to embark on the rising tide of oceanic exploration. Camoës, the bard of Portugal's grand epoch, wrote:

> *Behold her seated here, both head and key*
> *of Europe all, the Lusitanian queen;*
> *where endeth land and where beginneth sea. . . .*

To landbound minds the country's rugged coasts might seem to be the end of the world. On a trip to Cape Finisterre in 1466, a member of the party traveling with a Bohemian nobleman expressed this gloomy feeling: "One sees nothing anywhere but sky and water. They say that the water is so turbulent that no one can cross it and no one knows what lies beyond. It is said that some had tried to find what was beyond and had sailed with galleys and ships, but not one of them has returned." One can share the prospect today when standing at Sagres, next to Cape St. Vincent, the jutting southwestern terminus of the Eurasian landmass. Winds sweeping the bleak promontory drive back the scent of oregano in May, as if pushing back and marking a boundary to the sea's domain, which no one of the land should dare to enter.

But in the fifteenth century, the Portuguese had been venturing into those waters and, with ever-increasing boldness, going farther west and south. They learned from experience that the currents and winds were especially favorable for voyages in those directions, out to islands they found and settled one by one (the Madeira group before 1420, and the Azores beginning in 1427) and down the African coast ever closer to the equator, the forbidding torrid zone of medieval lore. They learned, moreover, not to fear the sea and to imagine discoveries yet to be made. All this was the talk of every dock and street corner, as the young man from Genoa must have noticed.

Except for its geographic position, Portugal was not obviously suited for great undertakings. It was a small country, then as now, with fewer than one million inhabitants. Their land was poor, and so were they. This was, however, all the more reason for the Portuguese to value the sugar and wood from the Madeira Islands and to sail in search of gold in Guinea. Portugal had other things going for it as well. Situated on the Atlantic near the outlet of the Mediterranean, the country stood on the "street corner of Europe," in Parry's phrase, where commerce from northern Europe came into increasing interaction with that of such trading powers as Venice and Genoa. Merchant bankers from Italy and cosmographers from Majorca were drawn to the bustling port of Lisbon. Portugal at the time, unlike other countries, was enjoying a long period of peace and political stability. And its leaders, seeing the need and opportunity, also had the foresight to foster the first national program of planned oceanic exploration.

The organizing and guiding force behind this program was a legendary figure known in history as Prince Henry the Navigator. The third son of John I, he had little chance of ever occupying the throne, and spent his entire adult life in the pursuit of exploration. Although he himself made no voyages of discovery, Henry established himself in 1419 as governor of the Algarve, Portugal's southern province, and at Sagres assembled an entourage of cosmographers and navigators. It is fanciful to describe this as an oceanographic institute, the way some accounts would have it. But his planning and determination, in collaboration with his brother Prince Pedro, launched many a far-ranging expedition that returned with new knowledge and wealth. Exploration has been called planned discovery, and in that sense, says J. R. Hale, a historian of Renaissance exploration, Henry was "the first rational organizer of exploration as an expanding reconnaissance based on cooperation between pilots at sea and experts at headquarters." As such, Hale adds, this was "the first example of a program of discovery being put into effect."

The western coast of Africa was the most alluring goal for Henry. He was drawn to it by a mixture of the same religious, economic, and political factors that energized the entire Age of Discovery. One motive was a crusading zeal against the Muslims, who, aside from being to Christians the despised infidel, controlled much of known Africa and had expanded their power by vigorous and threatening measures. Another motive was the gold from Guinea. Henry also felt it his Christian duty to make contact with Prester John, a king of legendary wealth rumored to reside somewhere in darkest Africa; the existence of such a Christian monarch was only a myth, but such a powerful one that medieval Christendom pinned its desperate hopes on Prester John to help counteract the spread of Islam. A fourth motive was the search for new routes to the spices of the East, circumventing the usual ones in the Levant, which were blocked by the menacing Turks. All were considered sound reasons for the Portuguese and then other European Christians to take the risks and bear the expense of maritime exploration. Europe, more than any other civilization in the fifteenth century, more than Islam or China, felt the need to reach out into the beyond. Inasmuch as a full consideration of the motive behind Europe's expansion is beyond the scope of this book, Braudel's succinct observation will have to suffice: "Perhaps the merit of the West, confined as it was on its narrow 'Cape of Asia,' was that it 'needed' the rest of the world, needed to venture outside."

It is not certain whether Henry consciously sought to reach India and the spice islands by sea around the tip of Africa. No one had given serious thought to the proposition since the Vivaldi brothers of Genoa had set out in 1291 with the evident intention of rounding southern Africa, and were not seen again after they passed Cape Nun on the Moroccan coast. All Henry's efforts were directed instead toward exploring the Atlantic along the western-African coast. His first objective was to explore beyond Cape Bojador to see what lay below Africa's bulge. If he was seeking a way to India, more than likely he thought it would be a new caravan route or waterway to be found across the continent to the Indian Ocean.

After several unsuccessful attempts, the cape was rounded in 1434, and in another ten years Senegal was reached. Henry's captains proceeded cautiously in the face of the medieval superstition that anyone who tried to cross the equator would run into boiling waters and certain death. They also ventured farther west into the ocean, finding the westernmost islands of the Azores and colonizing the Cape Verde Islands. It is not known whether Henry or his contemporaries ever contemplated sailing west across the Atlantic to reach Asia, any more than rounding southern Africa with that objective in mind. Nonetheless, their explorations would nourish the Asia-seeking dreams of another generation.

By the time Prince Henry died, in 1460, Portuguese ships had charted the African coast as far south as Sierra Leone, past the site of modern Dakar, only ten degrees above the equator. Over the previous two decades, regular shipments of gold, ivory, and slaves had whetted Portuguese appetites for maritime adventure. Their recognition of means and ends grew more specific. A papal bull in 1456, issued at the request of Alfonso V and Henry, conceded to the Order of Christ, of which Henry was governor, the spiritual jurisdiction of all regions conquered by the Portuguese now or in the future, "from Capes Bojador and Nun, by way of Guinea and beyond, southwards to the Indies." By this one can see clearly that people had now begun to think of circumnavigating Africa.

In his study of the Portuguese seaborne empire, Charles R. Boxer writes: "The cumulative effect of these [three] Papal Bulls was to give the Portuguese—and in due course the other Europeans who followed them—a religious sanction for adopting a similarly masterful attitude towards all races beyond the Pale of Christendom." Not only the geographic but the religious foundations were being laid for Europe's global expansion.

Even if Henry has been mythologized in history, he was real, and his dynamic leadership must have been decisive, for in the decade or more after his death little progress was made in extending Portugal's southward drive along the African coast. Then, in 1472, a trading center known as São Jorge da Mina was established in the gold country of present-day Ghana and was fortified a decade later. In 1473, Lopo Gonçalves safely crossed the equator, laying to rest superstition.

John II ascended the throne in 1481 and resumed with vigor the work of his great-uncle Henry. He sent emissaries by land to try to make contact with Prester John and sought a navigable waterway across the African continent. Finding a way through or around Africa to India had now become state policy. Travelers' reports, new maps, and informed geographical theories by early-Renaissance humanists, particularly in Florence, made India—the lands of the East—more desirable and seemingly more achievable. The Portuguese court had even been advised by a Florentine cosmographer that it should be possible to reach the Indies by sailing west. Such was the atmosphere Columbus breathed in Lisbon.

If Lisbon was the center of action in Europe's oceanic expansion, Florence was the intellectual nexus of the Renaissance out of which emerged a new world-view that would encourage further action. Jacob Burkhardt, the nineteenth-century Swiss historian, credits the Italians with the intellectual "discovery of the world." The Crusades, he writes, "had opened unknown distances to the European mind, and awakened in all the passion for travel and adventure. It may be hard to indicate precisely the point where this passion allied itself with, or became the servant of, the thirst for knowledge; but it was in Italy that this was first and most completely the case."

In his study of geographical thought in fifteenth-century Florence, Thomas Goldstein, a scholar of the Renaissance, says the synthesis of this new knowledge led to the expression of a major theoretical premise that had never been clearly stated before. "What it involved was nothing less than a complete revision of the basic concept of the earth; the theory, that is, that the ocean could be used as an intercontinental waterway," he writes in 1965. "Added to this was a second equally revolutionary premise—equally subversive of the entire medieval tradition of geography: that the navigable Ocean Sea included the Southern Hemisphere. Taken together these premises meant the decisive abandonment of the traditional (ancient as well as medieval) concepts of the orbis terrarum—the idea that a severely foreshortened three-continent land mass (Europe, Asia, and Africa) was forever confined within its own limits by an all-encircling Ocean Sea, conceived of very much as we today look upon outer space, as another orbit, believed to be by its very nature inaccessible to the efforts of man."

This revolutionary concept, which Goldstein describes as the "intellectual conquest of the earth," had far-reaching psychological as well as practical implications. And it began to emerge in Florence more than half a century before Columbus's first voyage.

On the maps of this period, the world was portrayed as three connected landmasses—Europe, Asia, and Africa—surrounded by an unnavigable ocean and an uninhabited torrid zone in the Southern

Hemisphere. This was the Orbis Terrarum, the traditional conception of world geography that had gone unchallenged for centuries.

Then the rediscovery of Ptolemy stimulated thinking about the size and configuration of the world. In 1410, a Florentine humanist completed a Latin translation of Claudius Ptolemy's *Geography,* a second-century compendium of ancient geographical knowledge and theory. This served as a textbook for debate and conjecture by a group of learned men who began meeting regularly as the Council of Florence. Given their consuming interest in spice-growing regions, the Florentines were attracted to Ptolemy's descriptions of the many Southeast Asian spice islands. In the Renaissance, classical writings carried an authority second only to the Bible and Christian dogma, and here was Ptolemy lending confirmation to Marco Polo's reports.

Ptolemy also gave the Florentines reason to expect that these islands might be accessible by long-distance sea routes. His descriptions and maps showed that the African continent extended south of the equator, and might be inhabited. He raised the possibility that the Southern Hemisphere might be navigable. This was encouraging news to Prince Pedro, Henry's brother, who visited the Council of Florence in 1428 in the first of presumably many contacts between the theoreticians of Florence and the explorers of Portugal. But Ptolemy seemed to rule out any hope of getting to the Far East by rounding Africa. Like the medieval scholars, he assumed that the Indian Ocean was landlocked, with southern Africa merging with an unknown southern land, Terra Incognita, that extended east and wrapped around the Indian Ocean.

The Florentines, however, did not accept Ptolemy's *Geography* uncritically. They also examined the writings of Strabo, another early Greek geographer. He had nothing to say about whether or not the Indian Ocean was landlocked, but he introduced the Florentines to the provocative idea that the Asian landmass as a whole, south as well as east, was washed by the Ocean Sea. And these waters, Strabo said, "extend out into the Atlantic Sea."

There it was, hinted at by Strabo and resurrected and recognized possibly as early as 1439, the ingredients for the concept of a single ocean sea, navigable as an intercontinental waterway.

At approximately this time, a Venetian merchant, Niccolò de' Conti, returned from twenty-five years in the East, and his accounts expanded on the knowledge first reported by Marco Polo. Conti had traveled "almost at the furthest end of the world," as far as Sumatra,

Borneo, and Java. He brought back detailed accounts of what he had learned of a group of islands beyond, the much-sought Spice Islands, the Moluccas. On his return, Conti was interrogated closely by a representative of the pope and by the Florentine scholars. In a departure from medieval practice, Conti's information concerning many islands far off the Asian mainland soon found its way onto world maps.

Of no little importance was the influence of the rediscovered Ptolemy on cartography. More than a millennium before, Ptolemy had enumerated principles of scientific cartography and had prepared maps with a framework of coordinates. For all their shortcomings, attributable mainly to a lack of knowledge, Ptolemy's maps offered a much more realistic and useful representation of the world than did any of their medieval successors, which were not works of geography in the modern sense so much as philosophical statements based on Christian dogma. The typical medieval *mappaemundi,* for example, portrayed a round landmass of the three-continent Orbis Terrarum, with Jerusalem at the center. These were called T-O maps, because the land was divided by a "T" of water (the Mediterranean, the Nile, and the Don) and encircled by an "O," which was the Ocean Sea as the encompassing boundary of existence.

The earliest map known to include Conti's information and also reflect the new theoretical thinking was drawn in Genoa in 1457. The map showed for the first time the Spice Islands and many other details from Conti. It also showed a sea passage around the southern tip of Africa. Two years later, Fra Mauro, the period's foremost cartographer, was commissioned by the Portuguese monarch to prepare a map incorporating the new knowledge. Fra Mauro drew a continuous ocean to the south of Africa and Asia. The Portuguese consulting this map were no doubt reassured in the correctness of their aim in finding a sea route to Asia by the south of Africa. But the Florentines insisted that there could be an alternative route.

A prominent member of the Council of Florence was Paolo del Pozzo Toscanelli, a physician, mathematician, and geographer. Through Portuguese on occasional visits and the Italian bankers operating in Lisbon, the ideas flowering in Tuscany had spread and aroused increasing interest back in Lisbon. In 1474, by then an old man of some seventy-five years, Toscanelli summarized his thinking—and that of his confreres—in a letter to an acquaintance, Fernão Martins, who was canon of the Lisbon cathedral. Alfonso V had requested an elaboration of the Florentine's particular theory that the shortest sea route to Asia lay to the west, straight across the Ocean Sea.

Toscanelli's proposal was to sail west across the ocean to Antilla, the legendary islands the Portuguese believed to exist and that Toscanelli apparently assumed to have already been discovered. These islands would serve as a convenient way station en route to Cathay. Toscanelli included a world map (since lost) and some calculations of the distances from Portugal to Antilla to Cathay. Like Ptolemy, only more so, he had made the world smaller than it really is.

The ideas fundamental to Toscanelli's proposal represented the gradual replacement of medieval geography with a more modern world-view. Another Florentine, Lorenzo Buonincontri, postulated in 1476 the existence of a fourth continent, reflecting not new knowledge but an openness to the possibilities that the ends of the earth were not yet known. The Florentines were providing the theoretical underpinning for Columbus's inchoate ideas of sailing across the ocean.

The foregoing sets the larger stage onto which Columbus was stepping and reveals that, in arriving at his grand scheme, he had not come into the possession of a singular idea that had eluded others. Historians for generations have been under no such illusions, though this recognition of converging contemporary influences has sometimes been overshadowed by the Olympian image of the man as created by hagiographers and popular writers. But if his idea was not as extraordinary as often portrayed, it does not follow that this was no extraordinary man.

Why was it Columbus, and not someone else, who seized upon the idea and pursued it with such tenacity? Of all the questions about Columbus, this is the most important and most mystifying. What happened in his years in Portugal that inspired the man and gave him such supreme confidence in his perceived destiny?

Historians have examined the sparse record of Columbus's activities in Portugal from every possible angle, seeking answers to these questions. Perhaps he began to entertain the idea in 1477. Early in that year, he accompanied a Genoese fleet on a voyage to England. After visiting the port of Bristol, he may have taken a ship to Iceland and beyond. Hernando quoted from his father's letters: "In February

1477, I sailed my self an Hundred Leagues beyond Thule," the ancient name for Iceland. Could he have heard there stories of the Norse voyages to Vinland? Columbus never mentioned it, nor did Hernando. They may not have wanted to share the credit, or, perhaps more likely, Columbus had learned nothing of the early Norse adventures. Some scholars, citing his tale of incredible tides, even doubt that Columbus went to Iceland. And there seemed to be no reason for him to have been journeying into the open winter sea beyond Iceland.

But on that trip Columbus had begun to learn the ways of Atlantic sailing and to pick up intriguing stories. In Galway, which he apparently visited, he recalled seeing "a man and a woman of extraordinary appearance in two boats adrift." Morison suspects they were Finns or Lapps, not Asians. But in a marginal note to a book he had read, Columbus recorded: "Men of Cathay which is toward the Orient have come hither." It was the first of many such exotic clues.

In 1478, Columbus gained more Atlantic experience by sailing to Madeira to purchase sugar as an agent for Italian merchants. A lawsuit stemming from this voyage was what caused Columbus to return to Genoa in 1479 to testify, the record of which helps establish his Genoese origins.

When he came back to Lisbon from Genoa, never more to return, Columbus married Felipa Perestrello e Moniz. He met her at the chapel of a convent in Lisbon where the daughters of Portuguese nobility were schooled, and where young men went courting. As Hernando wrote: "For as much as he behaved himself honorably, and was a man of a comely presence, and did nothing but what was just; it happened that a lady whose name was Dona Felipa Moniz, of a good family and pensioner in the Monastery of All Saints, whither the Admiral used to go to Mass, was so taken with him, that she became his wife."

It may well have been a love match, as Hernando suggested. Never once did Columbus himself describe his wife or their marriage. But a man of ambition might also have been swayed by her family's social standing. Her mother's lineage was noble. Her father, Bartolomeo Perestrello, came from Italian ancestors who had migrated to Portugal a century earlier. He had been a seagoing man, and was appointed by Prince Henry as the hereditary governor of Porto Santo in the Madeiras. He was dead by the time Columbus met his daughter, and the family was relatively poor, but they had connections. Columbus needed connections.

Taviani believes Columbus conceived his plan between the last months of 1479, the presumed time of his marriage, and the last months of 1481. There are compelling reasons to accept this interpretation.

Soon after the marriage, Columbus moved to Porto Santo to live with his wife's widowed mother and his wife's brother, who had inherited the governorship. There he heard many of the stories going around. Of the pilot who saw, far west of Cape St. Vincent, a strange piece of wood that had not been carved by iron and that had been blown by the west wind from unknown islands across the ocean. Of people in the Azores who found unfamiliar tree trunks washed ashore and the bodies of two dead men, very broad-faced and, as Hernando related, "differing in aspect from Christians." Of mariners venturing beyond the Azores and Canaries who had seen islands on the horizon. These were among the clues Hernando said had influenced his father's thinking. Of course, just being on a small island in the Atlantic could have filled him with curiosity and longing.

Columbus was one husband who seems to have had more reason than most to bless his mother-in-law. While on Porto Santo, she recognized Columbus's restless interest in everything about oceanic voyaging and distant lands. Hernando reported that she "gave him the journals and sea charts left by her husband," and as a result, Columbus's passion was "still more inflamed." Hernando concluded that it was the papers of Bartolomeo Perestrello, who had sailed for Prince Henry, and the information from Portuguese seamen that fixed Columbus's mind on the westward ocean crossing. "Of all things he made such good use," Hernando wrote, "that he concluded for certain that there were many lands West of the Canary Islands and Cape Verde, and that it was possible to sail to, and discover them."

In late 1481 or the next year, Columbus shipped with a Portuguese fleet to El Mina on the Guinea coast. It must have been no earlier, because he wrote, in later years, of "the castle of Mina of the most serene king of Portugal, which we have seen." The fortress was erected in 1481. He was impressed with the abundance of gold, which he was also to mention in future writing. And he studied closely the currents and winds and took note of the habitation of the torrid zone. But by then, it would seem, he already knew what he had to do.

Hernando, being a bookish type, emphasized the importance of "the great authority of learned men" to his father. He cited geographical measurements of Ptolemy and Marinus of Tyre, the descriptions of Asia by Marco Polo and Mandeville, and the pronouncements of Aristotle and Seneca on the possibility of sailing west to the Indies. Copies of books Columbus read and annotated, preserved by Hernando, included *Historia Rerum* by the man who would become Pope Pius II and *Imago Mundi* by Pierre d'Ailly, a French cardinal in the early fifteenth century. No doubt Columbus consulted these respected sources, but probably a few years later, when he used them not in the conception of his plan but to confirm and document it.

Historians convinced of the man's exceptional genius give the impression that the idea sprang solely from Columbus's intuitive powers. Putting together what he saw and heard and learned about the ocean and the rumored distant lands across it, he got the idea of a westward crossing and invented the plan. But this discounts the importance of the Florentine world-view. Some awareness of it was current in Lisbon, and this must have come to Columbus's attention no later than 1480, when historians suspect he first got access to Toscanelli's 1474 letter and map. His wife's connections presumably facilitated this.

"That map set Columbus's mind ablaze," Las Casas wrote. Columbus, wanting to know more, is believed to have written Toscanelli that same year or the next, certainly before 1482, the year the Florentine physician died. The old man replied mainly by enclosing a copy of his previous letter. In the covering note, Toscanelli wrote:

> To Cristobal Columbo, Paul the Physician, greeting:
>
> I observe thy great and noble ambition to pass over to where the spices grow, Wherefore in reply to thy letter I send thee a copy of another letter which some time ago I wrote to a friend of mine, a servant of the most serene king of Portugal, before the wars of Castile, in answer to another which by command of his highness he wrote to me on this subject; and I send thee another sea-chart like the one which I sent to him, wherewith thy demands may be satisfied.

In response to a request for additional information, Columbus received a second letter from Toscanelli. He praised Columbus's "high courage," but offered him nothing more than a repetition of ideas he had sent to Martins in 1474.

The Toscanelli correspondence, Hernando wrote, "encouraged the Admiral much to go upon his Discovery," an interpretation that went unchallenged until early in this century. In 1901, Henry Vignaud, an American diplomat in Paris and a Columbus scholar, provoked controversy by raising doubts about the authenticity of the Toscanelli letters. His suspicions were aroused by the fact that no original texts or copies of the letters to Martins or to Columbus have ever been found, only the copies made by Columbus himself in the blank pages of a book. Vignaud cited errors in the letter and geographic conceptions that a man like Toscanelli would presumably not make. Besides, he pointed out, there is no person by the name of Fernão Martins known in history. And why did Columbus never mention the correspondence in his writings before or after the first voyage?

The letters, Vignaud contends, were forgeries. They were invented by Las Casas and Bartholomew Columbus, he charges, to contradict the story of the unknown pilot that was current after the first voyage and had left the impression that Columbus had exploited another mariner's knowledge. The forgers were thus seeking to establish a scientific basis for the enterprise. But the only extant copies of the letters are in Columbus's own hand, in pages bound in his own edition of *Historia Rerum,* which today is in the library at Seville. If anyone was the forger, the finger would seem to point at Columbus himself.

Nearly all historians dispute Vignaud's charges. It proves nothing that the original texts are lost; most documents from that period were destroyed in the 1755 Lisbon earthquake. A Fernão Martins has since been authenticated. And Taviani writes: "Only a madman would actually forge three documents in order to take credit away from himself. Only a simpleton would fabricate a document between two other people, introducing the Canon Martins. Sooner or later the forgery would have been unmasked." The Vignaud hypothesis, John Larner observes, "was ultimately to strain the goodwill of even the most credulous Columbian scholar."

A few historians who accept as authentic the letter from Toscanelli to Martins regard the two to Columbus with more suspicion. Why would he write to an unknown mariner, and with such fulsome praise? It could be supposed that Columbus prepared these letters to cover up the possibly illegal means by which he came into possession of the original Toscanelli letter and map. In any case, the two letters to Columbus, genuine or forged, add nothing to what Toscanelli had said in his original correspondence.

Even though Vignaud's attack on the credibility of the Toscanelli letters has not persuaded most historians, his reasons for pursuing the investigation—to counter conventional wisdom to the effect that Columbus's researches were founded on scientific data—now draw widespread acceptance. Serious historians, particularly those who set themselves the goal of questioning accounts of venerated heroes, should sympathize with Vignaud's observations in introducing his 1902 book. "There is nothing harder to overturn than an opinion which has in its favour time and numbers," he writes. "The belief that Columbus was a man who had, as a result of his own unaided studies and investigations, arrived at the conclusion he should find Asia to the west has become so embedded in history, and is supported by evidence at once so ancient and respectable, that it seems something little short of sacrilegious to cast a doubt thereon, and as though a storm threatened to overwhelm the bold innovator."

From Toscanelli and other authorities, it is generally agreed, Columbus drew his notions about global distances that underlay the calculations supporting the feasibility of his idea. Since it could not be claimed that anyone's calculations were infallible, derived as they were from so much conjecture, Columbus chose estimates of distances so as to give his proposal the benefit of every doubt. He was a man inspired and not about to let arithmetic stand in his way. He thus made a number of gross errors.

On the authority of Marco Polo and others, Columbus exaggerated the length of the Eurasian continent from Ptolemy's already inflated 177 degrees and Marinus of Tyre's 225 degrees to a full 253 degrees. He stretched it another 30 degrees to encompass the reported distance from China to the eastern coast of Japan. He had now accounted for 283 degrees of land out of the earth's 360-degree circumference.

Next, Columbus estimated that circumference to be 10 percent smaller than Ptolemy had reckoned and 25 percent smaller than it actually is. Not until the eighteenth century would scientists and surveyors be able to arrive at a sure knowledge as to the length of a degree of longitude. So Columbus chose estimates for a degree at the equator of 52 statute miles. At the higher latitudes where he intended to cross the ocean, the estimated length of a degree would be even less—45 miles.

Using these numbers, Columbus figured that there lay only 2,760 miles of open water between the Canaries and Japan. This was 700 miles less than the Toscanelli estimate, and more than 9,500 miles less than the actual distance. Columbus's enthusiasm was so great that his mind seemed to will the world to be more congenial to his plan of action. He then defended his mistake stubbornly and blindly.

If Columbus had been a more rational man, he would never have achieved greatness. If his calculations had been closer to the truth, he might never have pursued his vision. If he had heeded the experts, who quite correctly doubted his estimates, he might never have weighed anchor. Is the Columbus example thus an argument favoring a stubbornly irrational approach to exploration and life? Not at all—unless one believes luck will always save the day. If America had not existed, and at the approximate location of Japan in his calculations, Columbus would almost certainly have sailed into oblivion, never reaching land and perhaps never returning to Europe.

Armed with these miscalculations and consumed by ambition, Columbus took his case to the court of Portugal, probably in late 1483 or the beginning of 1484. He had reason to hope that John II, knowledgeable in oceanic exploration and eager to extend Portugal's global reach, would be receptive.

The Portuguese historian João de Barros, writing in 1539, provides history's most authoritative account of Columbus's first formal presentation of his plan. He said Columbus had determined that one could sail west to the Indies and "came to demand of the king D. João that he give him some vessels to go and discover the Isle Cypango by this Western Ocean." John listened intently but, Barros says, was put off by Columbus: "The King, as he observed this Cristovao Colom to be a big talker and boastful in setting forth his accomplishments, and full of fancy and imagination with his Isle Cypango . . . , gave him small credit. However, by the strength of his importunity, it was ordered that he confer [with experts] to whom the King had committed these matters of cosmography and discovery."

In view of the suspect distance calculations, the king's experts acted reasonably in recommending against approval of the plan. "They all considered the words of Christovao Colom as vain, simply founded on imagination, or things like that Isle Cypango of Marco Polo," Barros concludes. And so John II rejected Columbus.

The account by Barros makes it fairly clear that Columbus sought ships to sail west to Japan, proving this was a goal of his as early as 1483. Since John would shortly license an expedition to seek the legendary Antilla, it is likely that he would have granted the same to Columbus, if such had been the destination he had in mind. In that event, Columbus might have discovered America eight years earlier, and for the Portuguese. Or he might have failed utterly. For, if he had sailed from the Portuguese outpost of the Azores, instead of the Spanish Canaries to the south, he would probably have been driven back by contrary winds at the higher latitude. History's might-have-beens are countless.

John's reasons for dismissing Columbus have never been spelled out. He may have been put off by Columbus's excessive demands for noble rank and a share of the discovered wealth; these would be his demands of the Spanish monarchs, and could have been those he made of John. The king may have wanted to keep oceanic discovery a Portuguese monopoly closed to foreign adventurers. Or it may be that he simply did not like or trust Columbus. Why take a chance on him? John had also put his money on finding a route to the Indies via the south of Africa—reason enough perhaps to turn down Columbus.

Columbus refused to be denied the chance to risk his life proving himself right, and he seemed so sure that he was right. The basis for this certainty continues to perplex historians and inspire conjecture that Columbus, while in Portugal, had come upon some "secret" knowledge. This has led to the revival of variations on the theme of the unknown pilot, who, real or not, continues to cast a long shadow over Columbus history.

In the version recorded by Oviedo, a Portuguese helmsman who showed up in the Madeiras while Columbus lived there was the sole survivor of a ship that was returning from the West Indies when it was blown off course. Before dying, the helmsman drew a chart and gave it to Columbus, who had befriended him. Vignaud accepted the truth of the pilot's prediscovery as the reason, he asserts, anyone would want to forge the Toscanelli letters. A new version of the story has been suggested by Juan Manzano, a historian at Seville University. In a 1976 book, Manzano tells a story about a ship sailing from Guinea to Iberia in the 1460s that got caught in a storm and the trade winds and was carried west to the islands now known as the West Indies. These seamen could have been the source of tales told by Cuban Indians, as recorded by Las Casas, about the arrival years before of "other men, white and bearded like us." Eventually, according to this story, a few survivors of the voyage made it back across the ocean, arriving in Madeira and meeting Columbus. After he heard their accounts, Columbus began reading d'Ailly and other authorities and making his calculations. He became convinced that the storm-swept seamen had reached not the West Indies but Cipangu—Japan.

In this context, Manzano suggests that the words of Ferdinand and Isabella in a letter to Columbus in 1494 take on a possibly new meaning. "It seems to us that all which at the beginning you told us that you could find has, for the greater part been true," they wrote, "as if you had seen it before you spoke of it to us."

The pilot's prediscovery makes a satisfying story, identifying a single moment of inspiration and revelation and giving a plausible explanation for why Columbus fixed his sights on Cipangu and was unswerving in his pursuit of the goal. He could be certain that there were lands where he calculated Asia to be, because he had been told by someone who had been there. The story has only one weakness: there is not a shred of evidence, other than the hearsay reported by Oviedo and Las Casas. Manzano cites the Portuguese historian Jaime Cortesão, who found two examples of ships in the eighteenth century being blown west across the Atlantic in much the same way. But could fifteenth-century ships have survived the ordeal? Historians also wonder why no one in the Madeiras ever left a record of the unknown pilot. Surely Columbus was not the only person who knew of the pilot's presence on the island. In the absence of evidence, the story of the unknown pilot remains one more Columbian mystery. There could be some truth to it, though probably not, and, in all likelihood, we will never know.

Nor will we ever establish exactly what Columbus knew and how he learned it. But, once he had developed his plan, it was the force of his personality and his driving ambition that set him apart from any others who, under the influence of the expansive world-view developing in Portugal and Florence, might have entertained ideas of sailing west to reach the Indies. When the king of Portugal would not give him the ships, the obsessed Columbus decided there was nothing left for him but to pick up his dreams nurtured in that country and try elsewhere to win royal support.

6

The Road to Palos

Three images, arrayed in our minds like faded panels of an epic fresco, evoke the pre-voyage years of Columbus in Spain.

He is the engaging, assertive petitioner standing before Ferdinand and Isabella at the Alcazar in Córdoba. He unrolls a map of the world and recites a plan of startling simplicity that could bring untold wealth to Spain and spread Christianity to the ends of the world. They are impressed, especially the queen, but are preoccupied with the final campaign in their war against the Moors. They are intrigued by this foreigner with big ideas, yet circumspect. How can he be so sure of himself? A commission of eminent scholars is instructed to weigh the merits of the proposal.

He is the man with an enlightened vision explaining and defending his plan before those benighted scholars and clerics, the personification of medieval ignorance. In the cloistered chambers of the University of Salamanca, he has to endure their derision and their repeated objections based on thc classics and the saints. It is not proved that the world is round. The ocean is too vast to be navigated. St. Augustine had denied the existence of the Antipodes, and even if there are lands in the other hemisphere, they would be uninhabitable and one would never be able to return from them. It is unlikely that, given all the years since Creation, there are still lands undiscovered. After long deliberation, the commission renders its judgment against Columbus.

And he is again, in January 1492, after the fall of the Moorish stronghold of Granada, making one more plea to the king and queen, and once more being turned down. Dejected but resolute, he rides away from the court, thinking he will now have to try to win over the French king. At this moment, however, Luis de Santángel, a man of much influence in the court, entreats Isabella to take a chance on Columbus. The investment would be small, and the potential reward tremendous. A court bailiff is dispatched on horseback to bring back Columbus. After weeks of bargaining, a contract is drawn up between the crown and Columbus, who then sets out on the road to Palos and his destiny.

The whole truth has suffered in the repeated telling of these stories. The one about the confrontation with ignorance at Salamanca is largely fiction, inspired by Hernando and perpetuated by Washington Irving. Historians recognize the false notes, but the legend lives on. The other two stories, in their popular versions, overlook crucial influences on Columbus between his arrival in Spain in 1485 and his departure on the voyage. Contrary to legend, in those years he was not a man alone and without notable support. "Columbus's ability to thrust himself into the circles of the great was one of the most remarkable things about him," Parry writes. In his later, tormented years, a self-pitying Columbus would dwell on the doubters and scoffers he had faced, seldom acknowledging those who had offered him kindness and the opportunity to present his case to the crown. The truth is that he had the good fortune to meet and enlist the aid of several men who were willing to believe in him. Without them, for all his stubborn persistence, Columbus could not have realized his burning ambition.

The intent here is not to review all that is known and debated about Columbus's struggle to win royal support. Instead, the facts and fictions of only a few key issues will be considered: Who were the people who enabled him to pursue and win the monarchs' patronage? Why did the commission reject his proposal? What finally persuaded the king and queen to back him? Did Isabella have to pawn her jewels? What was Columbus's real objective?

Columbus had left Portugal secretly, Las Casas tells us, "fearing the King would send after him and hold him." Why the fear we do not know. Perhaps he had left unpaid debts or was absconding with a purloined copy of the Toscanelli letter and map, the kind of knowledge the king might consider a state secret. Perhaps it was only one more example of his suspicious, secretive nature.

His wife had died earlier that year, according to Hernando (or did he walk out on her, as Henry Harrisse supposes from an interlinear reading of a letter Columbus wrote in 1500?), and he was accompanied by their son, Diego, four or five years of age. They made for the little port of Palos de la Frontera, in Andalusia, not far from the Portuguese frontier. This choice of destinations is easily explained.

Palos was one of the closest ports across the border, and the only people he knew in Spain were his wife's relatives who lived nearby in Huelva.

Yet a tenacious legend has grown up around Columbus's arrival in Spain, less dramatic than his washed-ashore appearance in Portugal but much more touching. Tradition has it that Columbus and little Diego, weary, penniless, and hungry, got off the ship at Palos and trudged along a dusty road a few miles out of town, climbing the hill to the Franciscan monastery of La Rábida. He knocked at the portal of red and pale-yellow stone to beg for water and bread. A painting hanging in the monastery today depicts the scene, rich in pathos, of the tattered father and son standing at the door.

The truth of this legend, which originated with an account in 1513 by García Fernández, a physician in Huelva, is unknowable. After landing, Columbus might have gone to the monastery to pray, as was his practice at the end of a voyage. But he could have fulfilled this obligation at the church in town. The two could well have been hungry and destitute and knew they would be cared for at the nearest monastery. It might be more reasonable, however, to assume that he had already settled in Huelva with his sister-in-law and her husband before he decided to visit La Rábida. Columbus probably was taking Diego there to be a boarding student, freeing himself to pursue his dream.

Whatever the circumstances, Columbus's arrival at La Rábida proved to be a fortunate turn of events. He met Antonio de Marchena, an official of the Franciscan order and a man knowledgeable in cosmography. (In his account, given years later, the physician Fernández left the impression that Marchena and another friar, Juan de Pérez, were one and the same person. The confusion is responsible for a mistake common to many historians; Winsor, as a typical example, refers to the friar at La Rábida as Juan Pérez de Marchena.) Of Marchena, Columbus once wrote, in a rare moment of generosity: "I never received anything from anyone, except from Fray Antonio de Marchena, besides what came from the eternal God."

The two must have hit it off from the start. Columbus took this friar into his confidence, something he rarely did, and Marchena in turn probably directed the mariner's attention to the writings of scholars and church authorities that would fortify his case for the ocean crossing. It is certain that most of his scholarly research on the subject was done after he reached Spain. In the books he studied, Columbus made notes of his developing thoughts and supporting evidence: "The earth is round and spherical." "Pierre d'Ailly agrees that the sea is entirely navigable." "The end of Spain and the beginning of India are not very far apart, indeed they are close, and it is known that this sea is navigable in a few days' time with favoring wind." "Aristotle says that between the end of Spain and the beginning of India there is a brief sea, navigable in a few days." "Esdras says that six parts of the globe are habitable and the seventh is covered by water. Observe that Saints Ambrose and Augustine and many others consider Esdras a prophet."

If Columbus had had reservations before, he was now emboldened by the confirmation of his concept from such revered authorities—particularly the Books of Esdras in the Hebrew Bible, parts of which appear in the English Bible in its Book of Ezra. Taviani writes: "References to Esdras crop up continually, both before and after the discovery, to such an extent that he appears to take on more significance than Ptolemy. If Toscanelli supplied the scientific support, Esdras furnished the religious." And it was in Spain that he began to rely more and more on religious considerations as a motivation and an argument for his scheme.

Though we know little about Marchena the Franciscan cosmographer, much can be inferred as to his role in shaping and encouraging Columbus's plan. Through Marchena, moreover, Columbus was introduced to one of the most powerful and richest grandees of Spain, Enrique de Guzmán, the duke of Medina Sidonia. Columbus's ideas and eloquence must have made a strong impression. The duke considered financing the expedition himself, which he could afford to do, but for some reason the crown squelched the plan. Through either the duke or Marchena, Columbus was next introduced to another nobleman, who owned a large merchant fleet. This was Luis de la Cerda, the count (later duke) of Medina Celi. He, too, was tempted to underwrite Columbus, and so informed the monarchs. They seemed receptive, but may have felt that, if done at all, the voyage should be launched under royal auspices. It was around this time that Columbus took his case directly to the monarchs. Influential friends cleared the way for his first audience with the king and queen.

Columbus was presented to the court in Córdoba early in 1486, but had to wait several months for the return of the monarchs before he could see them in person. The meeting occurred at the

Alcazar in Córdoba, fact for once according with legend, and it ended inconclusively. Despite a personal appearance by Marchena to endorse the plan, Columbus was told that his ideas would have to be examined by a group of experts headed by Hernando de Talavera, who was the queen's confessor and head of a monastery near Valladolid.

All in all, the initial reaction to Columbus had been mixed. Francisco López de Gomara, writing half a century later, says: "Since he was a foreigner, and was poorly dressed, and with no greater support than a friar, he was not believed or listened to by anyone; from this he felt a great torment in his spirit." This, however, must have overstated the court's response. After all, Columbus's plan was not rejected out of hand, and arrangements were made to put him on a modest retainer while he awaited the Talavera commission's verdict.

Historians are not certain how long the commission deliberated. Taviani says six months; Morison, four years. But they are agreed that the pivotal issue in the debate was not whether the earth is round. "Pure moonshine," says Morison. How the popular notion originated is perhaps the most straightforward example of Columbian mythbuilding, with clear sets of fingerprints.

In the biography of his father, Hernando described the confrontation between the geographers, who "were not so well informed as the business required," and Columbus, who did not "wish to reveal all the details of his plan, fearing lest it be stolen from him in Castile as it had been in Portugal." This being undoubtedly true, the proceedings were probably fated to be contentious and clouded with mistrust. The experts raised numerous objections about the world's being too large for anyone to sail across the ocean to Asia, about the habitability of the Antipodes, and about the unlikelihood of any undiscovered lands. "The Admiral gave suitable replies to all these objections," his son reported, "but the more effective his arguments, the less these men understood on account of their ignorance; for when a man poorly trained in mathematics reaches an advanced age, he is no longer capable of apprehending the truth because of the erroneous notions previously imprinted on his mind." There was some truth in this as well, though Hernando was often unreasonably harsh in denigrating those who opposed his father. The men on the commission were cautious and suspicious of new ideas, but they, like most educated Europeans then, held no lingering attachments to the belief in a flat earth. And some of their objections were well taken.

But when Washington Irving wrote his popular biography of Columbus in 1828, the novelist in him embellished the accounts of Hernando and others. Irving's version fostered the image of Columbus struggling alone against the forces of "ignorance and illiberality"—the hero as underdog:

> The greater part of this learned junto, it would appear, came prepossessed against him, as men in place and dignity are apt to be against poor applicants. There is always a proneness to consider a man under examination as a kind of delinquent, or imposter, upon trial, who is to be detected and exposed. Columbus, too, appeared in a most unfavorable light before a scholastic body; an obscure navigator, member of no learned institution, destitute of all the trappings and circumstances which sometimes give oracular authority to dullness, and depending upon the mere force of natural genius. . . . The hall of the old convent presented a striking spectacle. A simple mariner standing forth in the midst of an imposing array of clerical and collegiate sages; maintaining his theory with natural eloquence, and, as it were, pleading the cause of the new world.

Who would not look with sympathy on Columbus in these circumstances? Such calcified pedantry is not uncommon, and was likely much in evidence among the commissioners. In the medieval manner, they did not always make distinctions between opinions and observed facts; the more venerable the opinion, the more weight it often carried. Many of them no doubt deserved Irving's condemnation as a "mass of inert bigotry."

But Irving's story is misleading. He has the experts tossing off contradictory objections. They cite scripture to oppose the notion of a spherical earth. But they also argue that the circumference of the earth must be so great as to require at least three years to reach India, for they properly observe that the world must be larger than Columbus maintained. Finally, Irving has them saying that the "rotundity of the earth was as yet a matter of mere speculation." Magellan's expedition had yet to circumnavigate the globe, true, but the scholars of Columbus's day generally accepted the early-Greek idea of a spherical earth.

Irving notwithstanding, the central issue was the size of the earth and the width of the ocean. The learned experts were right on this, and Columbus wrong. The recommendation, announced either in

1487 (Taviani) or some three years later (Morison), was that the monarchs should reject the proposed venture.

Irving does acknowledge, and most historians affirm, that Columbus managed to win some converts among the savants, which could account for the length of time it took for the commission to report its findings. Indeed, the commission may have come close to ending with a hung jury. Some writers, Taviani notes, even believe that Talavera himself supported Columbus. One of the men favorably disposed to Columbus was Diego de Deza, a professor of theology. Columbus had found another friend who would come to his aid at a decisive moment.

The record of Columbus's activities while awaiting the decision is, as usual, spotty. Sometime during his sojourn in Córdoba, he took to frequenting a pharmacy run by Genoese compatriots. Physicians, surgeons, and others with a scientific bent met there regularly for conversation, and Columbus must have found their company congenial. It was at the pharmacy that Columbus struck up a friendship with a young man named Diego de Arana, who introduced him to an orphaned cousin and ward of his family. Diego would become an officer on Columbus's first voyage. The cousin, a peasant woman of twenty, was Beatriz Enríquez de Arana. She and Columbus became lovers, and in August 1488 she gave birth to their son, Ferdinand.

Her love must have sustained Columbus in those years of uncertainty and rejection. Her adoptive family, with a prospering wine business, may have given Columbus some financial assistance. But the widowed mariner never married Beatriz, and probably never intended to. As staunch as he was in his religious beliefs, these could not lead him to the altar; besides, bishops seemed to live comfortably with their religion and the mistresses they kept and freely acknowledged their bastards. Columbus probably felt that a peasant's daughter would be an unsuitable wife for a man of his ambition. And after his successful voyage, it would have been unthinkable for an admiral to take a wife who could not be presented at court.

How long the relationship lasted is another unknown. Columbus provided Beatriz with a modest annuity after the first voyage, but by then, or shortly thereafter, the two seem to have gone their separate ways. Still, she remained in his thoughts—more through feelings of guilt, however, than of longing. In his last will, Columbus said, "she weighs heavily on my conscience."

While Columbus was falling in love and soliciting support in Spain, his brother Bartholomew was acting as his agent in Portugal. If only Bartholomew had left accounts of his dealings, we might have a clearer understanding of both the genesis of the enterprise and the protracted negotiations to carry it out. Bartholomew's own role has been unfairly slighted. As a chartmaker, he may have made crucial contributions to the plan's conception, and he proved himself to be a loyal and tireless advocate on his older brother's behalf.

Bartholomew was perhaps instrumental in securing for Columbus an invitation and safe-conduct credentials for a visit to Lisbon to revive his appeal to John II. The king encouraged the visit, writing to Columbus as "our special friend," but historians can find no record showing that Columbus actually made the trip. In any event, the appeal to Portugal came to naught. By this time, Bartholomeu Dias had returned in 1488 from rounding the Cape of Good Hope, and John thus felt vindicated in his African strategy. He was no longer interested in a westward route to Asia.

Bartholomew Columbus, meanwhile, looked to England and France for support. By the accounts of Hernando and Oviedo, Bartholomew secured an interview with Henry VII in England, but came away empty-handed. In 1490, he went to France and, though turned down again, at least found a patron in Anne de Beaujeau, elder sister of Charles VIII. With a retainer from her, Bartholomew lived in France several years, making maps and sending letters to his brother that encouraged him to believe that, if Spain refused, France might yet back his enterprise. Bartholomew was still in France when Christopher crossed the Atlantic.

Columbus had had at least one more audience with Isabella, in the summer of 1489 at Jaén. Some historians assume that this was when he learned of the commission's negative verdict, but others believe he had been informed much earlier. In either case, Isabella offered Columbus little more than the counsel of patience. "Once the matter of Granada was settled," she told Columbus, then the plan could be considered again.

On this visit, if not before, Columbus gained another influential friend. According to Oviedo, Alonso de Quintanilla, the court treasurer, "ordered that [Columbus] be given goods and all that was necessary to alleviate him from his poverty."

Another two years passed, and Columbus, his patience running out, was disheartened when, in 1491, he made another journey to La

Rábida. He wanted to see his son Diego. He needed the comfort and advice of the friars. There he found a new ally, Juan de Pérez, who was a former confessor to the queen. Like Marchena, whom Columbus had met on the first visit, Pérez took an interest in Columbus's idea and dissuaded the mariner from packing up and going to France. It was Pérez who orchestrated the final and ultimately successful appeal to Ferdinand and Isabella.

In an upper room at the monastery with a commanding view of the estuary flowing out to the Atlantic, Pérez passed many hours in planning sessions with Columbus, reviewing details of the enterprise and rehearsing the most effective arguments to overcome royal doubts. Fernández, the local physician and an authority on cosmography, was brought in as a consultant. Pérez apparently introduced Columbus to the most prominent sea captain in Palos, Martín Alonso Pinzón, who could offer advice on the practical aspects of planning and equipping long voyages. Pinzón presumably paid for the mule on which Pérez rode to appeal personally to the king and queen to grant Columbus just one more audience.

For a man who was essentially a loner, rootless and untrusting, Columbus had managed to gain a number of friends and allies, and their efforts in his behalf seem to have been instrumental in overcoming royal reluctance to back the enterprise.

Juan de Pérez applied his familiarity with the intricacies of court politics and the queen's way of thinking to telling effect. His eloquence before the queen may have been decisive, but it was not his influence alone that brought the matter to a head. Pérez could not help noticing an undercurrent of support among many members of the court. Diego de Deza, the Dominican from Salamanca who had been on the Talavera commission, sought to sway the queen to give Columbus a chance; the inscription on his tombstone in the Seville cathedral notes that he was the generous and faithful patron of Columbus. Santángel seemed to be open-minded. Like other courtiers, he was looking ahead to the expansion of Spanish power once the Moors had been disposed of. It is only conjecture, but Pérez may have sensed these stirrings and shaped his arguments to appeal to the monarchs' ambitions for post-Moorish Spain. Isabella must have been impressed. In a short time, she sent a letter to Columbus commanding him to appear at the court at Santa Fé, the royal camp outside

Granada. She included money for new clothes for his court appearance, which took place in August 1491 or shortly thereafter.

Columbus was not immediately successful. The proposal was again submitted to a committee for review, but Las Casas wrote that this time experts in navigation and cosmography were consulted. They seemed to be more favorably inclined to Columbus than the previous commission had been. Still, the proposal was rejected by the court. Hernando and Las Casas suggested that the stumbling block this time was Columbus himself. As far as most historians can determine, this was the first time Columbus had laid out in detail the compensation he expected. His excessive demands for titles, revenues, and other rewards to follow his success shocked the king and queen. What possessed this man? First he pleads for support. Then he dictates absurd demands and conditions. He insists upon being accorded a title of nobility at the outset and, upon success, must be given a rank of admiral equal to that of the grand admiral of Castile; that is, he must become admiral of the Ocean Sea. In addition, he must be empowered as viceroy and governor general of the lands he might discover; the titles must be hereditary; and he and his heirs must receive a commission on the proceeds from all commerce with the newfound lands. Though stunned, court officials did not turn Columbus out on his ear.

For several months, through the surrender of Granada on January 2, 1492, Columbus remained with the court, entreating and negotiating. He was unrelenting in his demands. No one has ever developed a satisfactory explanation for his display of obstinacy. Other petitioners might have been so intent on winning approval that they would have been willing to bend a little and reduce their terms—but not Columbus. Had his allies given him some reason to hold out? But he could not be sure the monarchs would agree to support his plan, much less his demands. Was he encouraged by some special liaisons in the court? Novelists and imaginative historians have so speculated. He is said to have had the ardent support of the marquise de Moya, the wife of an important adviser to the court, and that her interest was quickened by the mariner's amorous attentions. Another woman, Beatriz de Bobadilla, the governess of one of the Canary Islands and an intimate friend of the queen, also took a deep interest in Columbus's plan, for reasons that have been similarly suspect. In neither case is there any supporting evidence, however. Nor is there anything to substantiate stories that Isabella saw more in Columbus than a charming, insistent supplicant. Like some other writers, the Cuban novelist Alejo Carpentier describes an uninhibited sexual union between Columbus and the queen. In *The Harp and the Shadow* (1978) he describes their seduction of each other and the pillow talk in which she promised him all the ships he needed, only to renege at daybreak. Finally, after a lovers' quarrel in which both call each other pigs, Carpentier's Isabella gives in to Columbus's plea for three caravels. Such speculation, Taviani says, is "a sheer fairy-tale, rejected by all serious historians."

For a while, it appeared that Columbus had overestimated his support. After the fall of Granada, when he had been led to believe the sovereigns would be free to agree to his proposition, Columbus was called before Ferdinand and Isabella at Santa Fé. They informed him in no uncertain terms that they had no intention of backing his voyage. He was dismissed from the court with finality.

As Columbus rode away on his mule, Luis de Santángel (perhaps accompanied by Quintanilla) rushed in to see Isabella. He respectfully told her, as Hernando reports, that "he was astonished to see that her Highness, who had always shown a resolute spirit in matters of great pith and consequence, should lack it now for an enterprise of so little risk, yet which could prove of so great service to God and the exaltation of His Church, not to speak of very great increase and glory for her realms and crown." Santángel's reasoning was irresistible. Isabella was persuaded to change her mind. Perhaps it was her instinct all along—which would explain her agreement to give Columbus repeated hearings over six years—to believe there was something to what this foreign mariner proposed with such resolute confidence. Subsequent analysis of Columbus's writings suggests that his appeal to her deep religiosity might have turned her around.

In a melodramatic turn of events, Isabella dispatched the messenger to order Columbus back to the court.

Santángel's intercession was a turning point also because he assured the queen that financing the expedition need not be an insurmountable obstacle. As Ferdinand's chief financial adviser, he could speak with authority and knew how to arrange the wherewithal.

But Santángel's involvement at this critical juncture has also inspired conjecture in this century that he was part of a Jewish cabal at the court whose ulterior motive in supporting Columbus was to seek a New Israel for the world's Jews. The only indisputable evidence that proponents for this view have been able to muster is the fact that Santángel was a Jew who had converted to Christianity, like many others in influential positions. Even if Columbus also had a Jewish ancestry, a contention that was discussed earlier, there is absolutely no evidence that this had any known bearing on his ambitions.

A more endearing legend has grown up around the story of how the Columbus voyage was financed. Isabella certainly did not have to pawn her jewels to raise the money. The fiction that she did, Morison says, dates to the seventeenth century, but has found a secure niche in legend. A statue in front of the viceroy's house in Santo Domingo shows Isabella with jewel case in one hand while with the other she is pulling a necklace out of the case. Reflecting the longevity of the legend in idiom, if not in absolute belief, the American ethnographer John Wesley Powell said in 1890 that the American Indians were just passing from savagery "into barbarism when the good queen sold her jewels." After the launching of Sputnik in 1957, President Dwight D. Eisenhower resisted appeals for an immediate American response in kind, saying he would not "hock my jewels" for extravagant adventures. But there is some truthful basis to the story. With the royal treasury largely depleted, owing to the long campaign to reconquer the land from the Moors, Isabella despaired of financing Columbus and suggested she might put up the crown jewels as collateral on a loan.

In those final deliberations in 1492, however, Santángel assured her that something else could be worked out. He and Francisco Pinello, a Genoese banker in Seville, would arrange a loan from the ample coffers of the Santa Hermandad, the powerful police force of which they were joint treasurers. No wonder Columbus made his first announcement of discovery in a letter to this most valuable member of the court's inner sanctum.

The financial arrangements, drawing on a combination of royal and private money, were typical for voyages of exploration then and for generations. The port of Palos, as we shall see, was ordered by royal decree to provide two of the three ships. That accounted for only a fraction of the costs. As far as historians are able to determine, Santángel and Pinello delivered 1.14 million *maravedis,* out of the estimated 2 million for total expenses. The loan was eventually repaid. Columbus himself arranged to put up half a million *maravedis,* which he apparently borrowed from another Italian financier in Seville, the

Florentine Juanoto Berardi. Indeed, as Consuelo Varela, a modern Seville historian and authority on Columbus, points out, Berardi so overextended himself in backing the venture that he was driven to financial ruin.

The role of foreign money was not exceptional. Many of the Iberian merchants and bankers were émigrés from Italy and northern Europe, who had access to capital from the older commercial centers. The 2 million *maravedis* presumably did not include the crew payroll, which was a royal responsibility. Taviani, updating calculations made in 1903 by Thacher, reckons that the 2 million *maravedis* spent on the enterprise was the equivalent in modern terms of about $7,000.

An agreement between the monarchs and Columbus—known as the Capitulations of Santa Fé—was struck after three months of hard bargaining and signed on April 17, 1492. Juan de Coloma, secretary of Aragon, represented the king and queen. (Despite the general impression that most of the dealings with Columbus were conducted by Isabella, nearly all of the key figures in the court responsible for agreement, notably Santángel and Coloma, were confidants of Ferdinand.) Pérez apparently acted as Columbus's attorney in the final negotiations, and a shrewd and firm advocate he must have been. Nearly everything the mariner had demanded was granted to him in the agreement. In the first sentence, the document addresses Columbus as "Don," indicating that he had been accorded noble status—the first of his many conditions.

The following is the text of the document that set in motion Columbus's voyage of discovery:

> The things prayed for, and which Your Highnesses give and grant to Don Cristóbal Colón as some recompense for what he is to discover in the Oceans, and for the voyages which now, with the help of God, he has engaged to make therein in the service of Your Highnesses, are the following:
>
> Firstly, that Your Highnesses, as actual Lords of the said Oceans, appoint from this date the said Don Cristóbal Colón to be your Admiral in all those islands and mainlands which by his activity and industry shall be discovered or acquired in the said oceans, during his lifetime, and likewise, after his death, his heirs and successors one after another in perpetuity, with all the pre-

eminences and prerogatives appertaining to the said office, and in the same manner as Don Alfonso Enriques, your High Admiral of Castile, and his predecessors in the same office held it in their districts. —It so pleases their Highnesses. [signed] Juan de Coloma.

Likewise, that Your Highnesses appoint the said Don Cristóbal Colón to be your Viceroy and Governor General in all the said islands and mainlands and in the islands which, as aforesaid, he may discover and acquire in the said seas; and that for the government of each and any of them he may make choice of three persons for each office, and that Your Highnesses may select and choose the one who shall be most serviceable to you; and thus the lands which our Lord shall permit him to discover and acquire for the service of Your Highnesses, will be the better governed. —It so pleases their Highnesses. Juan de Coloma.

Item, that of all and every kind of merchandise, whether pearls, precious stones, gold, silver, spices, and other objects and merchandise whatsoever, of whatever kind, name and sort, which may be bought, bartered, discovered, acquired and obtained within the limits of the said Admiralty, Your Highnesses grant from now henceforth to the said Don Cristóbal, and will that he may have and take for himself, the tenth part of the whole, after deducting all the expenses which may be incurred therein, so that of what shall remain clear and free he may have and take the tenth part for himself, and may do therewith as he pleases, the other nine parts being reserved for Your Highnesses. —It so pleases their Highnesses. Juan de Coloma.

Likewise, that if on account of the merchandise which he might bring from the said islands and lands which thus, as aforesaid, may be acquired or discovered, or of which may be taken in exchange for the same from other merchants here, any suit should arise in the place where the said commerce and traffic shall be held and conducted; and if by the pre-eminence of his office of Admiral it appertains to him to take cognizance of such suit; it may please Your Highnesses that he or his deputy, and not another judge, shall take cognizance thereof and give judgment in the same from henceforth. —It so pleases their Highnesses, if it pertains to the said office of Admiral, according as it was held by Admiral Don Alonso Enriques, and others his successors in their districts, and if it be just. Juan de Coloma.

Item, that in all the vessels which may be equipped for the said traffic and business, each time and whenever and so often as they may be equipped, the said Don Cristóbal Colón may, if he chooses, contribute and pay the eighth part of all that may be spent in the equipment, and that likewise he may have and take the eighth part of the profits that may result from such equipment. —It so pleases their Highnesses. Juan de Coloma.

These are granted and despatched, with the replies of Your Highnesses at the end of each article, in the town of Santa Fé de la Vega de Granada, on the seventeenth day of April in the year of the nativity of our Saviour Jesus Christ, one thousand four hundred and ninety-two. Juan de Coloma. Registered, Calcena.

Beyond its authorization of royal support, the document's significance lies in the insight it affords into Columbus's paramount interests and intentions. He had struck a business deal. He can be seen here as a grasping merchant with an eye to securing a monopoly on the riches he expected to find in lands he intended to exploit, much as he had witnessed the Portuguese doing on the African coast. An exploitative attitude toward America and native Americans was thus fixed at the outset. And this attitude was normal for the times. Exploration, more often than not, is motivated not by scientific and geographic curiosity but by the quest for wealth and power; it would be anachronistic to believe it otherwise in a society two centuries before the Scientific Revolution.

The terms of the agreement were never far from Columbus's thoughts for the rest of his life. They were the ambitious mariner's passport to the realms of power and influence and his guarantee of a fortune for himself and his heirs. Soon, however, exploration and colonization were thrown open to the highest bidder. The monarchs stripped Columbus of powers over the new territories, because of his manifest incompetence as a colonial administrator and their desire to establish their own undisputed power there. They also began to renege on the financial rewards, because they could not permit one subject such munificence at the expense of the entire kingdom. Columbus thus felt betrayed and slumped into the self-pity, anger, perhaps even paranoia that would grip him to his dying day. The contract he had fought for proved to be too generous for the crown to honor, and, it seems, was a source of Columbus's emotional undoing.

A curious omission in the document has given historians of Columbus one more reason for puzzlement and argument. The five articles of the agreement are written with extreme care in seemingly airtight legalese. The provisions are specific on Columbus's promised share in the proceeds and on the nature of the anticipated commerce—"pearls, precious stones, gold, silver, spices, and other objects and merchandise whatsoever. . . ." But the document makes no mention of Asia. The only reference to the expedition's geographic objective is the vague words about "those islands and mainlands which by his activity and industry shall be discovered or acquired in the said oceans. . . ." Because of the lack of a specific reference to Asia, or the Indies, some historians, beginning with Henry Vignaud early in this century, have suggested that Columbus never intended to go to Asia, but only to discover and exploit new lands, presumably the legendary islands far out in the Atlantic that were faithfully and alluringly depicted in contemporary maps.

In this context, the story of the unknown pilot again becomes a central issue. If the story is true, as Vignaud has argued, Columbus not only got his idea and instructions for the voyage from the dying pilot but had as his objective those same islands found by the pilot. To support this line of thinking, it is noted that Columbus did not begin to write specifically about seeking the Indies until he had sailed past the presumed position of these islands and found others that were closer to where Columbus supposed Cipangu and Cathay would be situated. Reflecting this point of view, E. G. R. Taylor, the British historian of navigation, contends that Antilla was Columbus's primary objective. When he could not find Antilla where it was marked on his navigation chart, he set his sights on Cipangu and then, on October 6, abandoned that goal and prepared to make the Asian mainland. This "resilience of mind," Taylor observes, showed that Columbus "had a fixed idea of a great discovery to be made by himself, while leaving to Divine Providence what that discovery would be."

Pieces of circumstantial evidence have been cited to support suspicions of a non-Asian objective. The expedition seemed poorly equipped for a voyage to the fabled Indies of the Great Khan. Columbus carried no trade goods other than cheap trinkets, nothing for which the potentate described by Marco Polo might be willing to give up some of his gold. Although the rulers of Cathay had supposedly expressed an interest in Christianity (in the thirteenth century, Kublai

Khan had sent presents to the pope via the Polos and requested missionaries for the instruction of his people), no representatives of the Christian church sailed with the fleet.

Historians generally dismiss the idea that Columbus's objective was anything short of the Indies. In *The History of America,* William Robertson wrote in 1777 that Columbus was sailing in search of Asia but was always alert to the possibility that he might find other, intervening lands. His journal entry for September 19, paraphrased by Las Casas, revealed that Columbus "was certain that to the north and south were some islands . . . and he went through the midst of them, because his wish was to press on toward the Indies." Navarrete concluded from the documents he uncovered that Asia was the one and only objective of Columbus.

In the prologue to his journal, Columbus wrote that he was sent by the king and queen "to the said regions of India to see the said princes and the peoples and the lands, and the characteristics of the lands and of everything, and to see how their conversion to our Holy Faith might be undertaken." Of course, the prologue was not necessarily written at the outset of the voyage. But additional documents turned over to Columbus at Santa Fé included a letter of introduction to the Great Khan. The expedition's interpreter was knowledgeable in Arabic, a language used in many parts of Asia known to Europeans. It is suggested that the omission of Asia by name reflected Spain's caution not to appear to be encroaching on the Portuguese monopoly there, as established by papal edict.

The evidence of Columbus's Asian objective, Morison writes, is abundant. The phrase "islands and mainlands in the Oceans" in the agreement meant Japan, China, and neighboring islands. "This is sufficiently proved," he continues, "by the fact that when Columbus returned in 1493, insisting that he had discovered Cipangu and certain outlying dominions of the Grand Khan, nobody contested his right to be Admiral, Governor and Viceroy thereof, and the Pope freely conceded Spanish sovereignty over them." Moreover, Morison notes, the agreement of April 17 mentions pearls, precious stones, gold, silver and spices "among the products that the Admiral will be privileged to tithe, and these were of the Orient; there was no tradition or expectation that any such precious things were to be found in the Atlantic islands."

When Columbus took his leave of the king and queen at Santa Fé on May 12, he carried with him other documents regarding the preparation of the fleet of three ships. No more royal temporizing and vacillating. At last, his future was in his own hands. He was now probably forty-one years old, and it had been years since he last went to sea. He took the road to Palos, which he knew from his trips to La Rábida. In his mind, he must have already traveled the road to Palos, to the embarkation of his dreams, who knows how many times.

7

Masterpieces for Discovery

On Wednesday, May 23, 1492, the town fathers of Palos de la Frontera gathered at the Church of St. George, summoned for the reading of a royal proclamation. This church, on a hill at the edge of town, had been a mosque when the Moors held Andalusia. It had endured the passage of time and the changed circumstances that brought the country to the threshold of world power, and so it remains today as a monument to the day when unassuming Palos learned it had a rendezvous with history.

The church has changed little in five centuries. Except for a few inscriptions carved in stone, it has not yielded to anyone's temptation to promote the place as a shrine to history; the occasional tourist is welcome, but only at the regular hours established for worship. The humble edifice of yellow-and-tan limestone bears the Moorish stamp, but over the high altar, now as then, is the image of St. George and the dragon. The door facing the Río Tinto is still referred to as *la puerta del embarcadero,* the door to the pier. From the hill, the low white houses and narrow cobblestone streets of Palos extend along a ridge and down to where the harbor had been. The town of 6,000 people occupies a lesser place in world affairs now than it did in 1492, when the 600 people there looked to the sea for their livelihood and came to share in the making of history.

A bleak plain of silt deposited by the river buries the old port, where the Atlantic tides had coaxed many a caravel down the Tinto into the Saltes (now called the Odiel) and away from Europe. The sailors of Palos in the fifteenth century knew the open sea, and their ships made often for the Canary Islands and had ventured as far as the Azores and to the Guinea coast of Africa. Although other ports were larger and more impressive—Huelva across the river, Cádiz, or Seville—it was to Palos and its men of the sea that the crown had looked for service on that day in May.

The mayor and other officials, as well as ordinary townspeople, stood expectantly as the town notary, Francisco Fernández, unrolled and read the decree from Ferdinand and Isabella. The presence of the imposing visitor, his face ruddy and his hair white, may have given them a premonition of the business at hand.

People in Palos had seen Columbus before, on his visits to La Rábida. At his side in the church was Juan de Pérez, who had guided him through his successful appeal to the crown. Columbus is believed to have had some prior dealings with shipowners in the area, notably Martín Alonso Pinzón. If so, the people of Palos must have known something of this man's uncommon passion and of the likely purpose of the summons to the church.

The decree they heard read was like a sentence imposed in a court of law. "Know ye that whereas for certain things done and committed by you to our disservice," the notary intoned, "you are condemned and obligated by our Council to provide us for a twelvemonth with two equipped caravels at your own proper charge and expense." The people were further informed that Columbus had been commanded to go with three caravels "toward certain regions of the Ocean Sea, to perform certain things for our service, and we desire that he take with him the said two caravels with which you are thus required to serve us. . . ." Crews would be paid the customary wages, with advance pay for four months. All must be ready for a departure "within ten days of receiving this our letter."

We can only imagine the quizzical reaction that day in the church. Who will volunteer for such a risky venture? Whose caravels are to be chosen? How can we trust our lives and ships to this foreigner? Ten days? Impossible. Why should this burden fall to us? They presumably knew the "disservice" Palos had committed, some smuggling or piracy perhaps, though the particulars have gone unrecorded. Still, they must have left the church asking themselves: Why Palos?

Las Casas offered four possible reasons for the choice. The Palos area had many experienced seamen; Columbus had friends and relatives nearby; Palos, as the decree cited, had incurred a debt to the crown, and its repayment with two caravels would reduce the royal share of expedition costs; or Columbus simply wished to be near La Rábida, where he felt sympathy and appreciation. Spanish historians dismiss the first reason; capable sailors could be found at any number of Andalusian ports. They also doubt that Columbus could have known very many people in the area, except his Portuguese in-laws in

Huelva. The Spanish historian Juan Manzano favors the latter reason, claiming that most probably Columbus wanted to be near Father Marchena and Father Pérez. The assumption is that the sovereigns must have left the choice of the port to Columbus, for they would probably have preferred Seville, whose port they owned. As Manzano points out, Palos could have been required to supply the caravels and deliver them to some other, larger port for outfitting and manning. But Palos it was to be. After the decree was read, the crown purchased a half-interest in the town of Palos. This way, perhaps, they were satisfying Columbus, who wanted to be near La Rábida, and at the same time securing for themselves additional control over the site of embarkation.

Palos may have been chosen simply because its port was not preoccupied with the other seagoing enterprise of that momentous year. After the *reconquista,* which consolidated Christian rule in Castile, the king and queen had not only agreed to Columbus's proposition but, on March 31, signed an edict calling for the expulsion of all Jews. The exodus was tying up the major ports. Cádiz and Seville in particular were teeming with Jewish families trying to get aboard any available ship bound for North Africa or northern Italy or as far away as Turkey. Palos alone may have had the ships to spare.

About the ships, history once again presents us with some frustratingly blank pages.

As familiar as their names are—*Niña, Pinta,* and *Santa María,*—remarkably little is known about the three ships in the Columbus fleet. This state of historical ignorance extends to the whole class of exploring ships, the sturdy and highly maneuverable caravels, which were the major advance in seafaring technology that launched the Age of Discovery. Less is known about caravels, it is said, than about the more ancient ships of Greece and Rome.

"We do not know in any detail what these vessels looked like or how they were conceived and constructed," said Roger C. Smith, a nautical archeologist who specialized in studies of the caravel while at Texas A & M University's Institute of Nautical Archeology. No confirmed caravel wrecks have ever been found, though Smith and other archeologists have located two possibilities in the Bahamas and have been searching methodically for remains of Columbus ships off Jamaica and Panama. All estimates of caravel dimensions are conjectural. No

Drawing of the *Niña* by Hank Iken, 1986, based on archival evidence found by Eugene Lyon

architectural diagrams have survived; shipwrights worked from plans in their heads, not on paper. Besides, rulers considered these data, like sea charts, to be secrets of state, and so would probably not have permitted them to be committed to paper in any form. Contemporary drawings, such as there were, favored aesthetics over authenticity, and every modern picture of Columbus's ships, Morison writes, "is about 50 percent fancy."

Even the origin and meaning of the name "caravel" are uncertain. August Jal, a nineteenth-century pioneer of naval archeology, suggested that the word was derived from the Spanish words *cara,* for "face," and *bella,* "beautiful." These streamlined ships, he reasoned, had been pleasing to look at. Jal later gave a more likely interpretation, tracing the origin to the Latin word *carabus,* for a hide-covered wicker boat, or possibly to the Greek word *kapapos,* a light vessel. In his research, Smith uncovered references to ships built by the Moors in the fourteenth century that were called *caravos* and also to fishing vessels in the thirteenth century to which the word *caravela* was applied in a Portuguese manuscript.

The ships called caravels were products of a gradual evolution in European naval design and construction. They were hybrids—"a nexus of the technological development of the period," in the words of Carla Rahn Phillips, an authority on Spanish maritime history. They combined features of the sturdy, broad-beamed, square-rigged trading ships of northern Europe with the Mediterranean fishing and coastal-trading ships with lateen sails and a narrower hull.

The northern-European ships came out of the Norse tradition. For the Norse to make the transition from Viking raiders who prowled British and European coasts to traders and colonizers ranging the North Atlantic, they had evolved a new kind of ship. The Viking *langskip,* or longship, proved too small and narrow to be seaworthy for extended voyages on the open ocean. It was essentially a modified galley, propelled by oars and perhaps a supplemental sail, and as such was no match for the tempestuous North Atlantic. By the time the Norse were regularly venturing westward to Iceland and Greenland, they depended on a sailing ship known as the *knorr.* With a much broader beam than the longship, the *knorr* was reliably buoyant and could haul a good deal more cargo, as much as twenty tons and fifteen to twenty people. There was nothing sleek or majestic about these ships. They were less than ninety feet long and probably one-fourth to one-third as broad in beam. The hulls were clinker-built, with the planking overlapping. All in all, they were spartan and strictly utilitarian. Much of the ship was an open shell, without decking, and it must have taken on a deluge of water in rough weather. Without a rudder, steering was managed (not always well) with a large and awkward oar called a sternboard. Crews labored at the long sweeps in harbor or in doldrums. By hoisting a sail at sea, they could make a respectable six knots with a following wind.

Time passed, and the *knorr* was improved by English and German Hanseatic traders. With their breadth and rounded bow, Parry writes, these ships could ride over stormy seas rather than knife through them. The single mast and square sail made for easy handling by a small crew. A sternpost rudder was eventually introduced. A simple innovation, it had a liberating effect on navigators and shipwrights. With the larger rudders, helmsmen at the tiller could more easily turn a ship or hold her steady in a wind. It was thus possible to build larger ships and not worry about their maneuverability. Parry is certain that Hanseatic sailors in these round ships could have crossed the Atlantic if they had wanted to. But they were just as conservative as the Norse, who never once attempted to cross the ocean directly from Norway to America, or vice versa.

A different type of ship had come into use for the shorter hauls in the more protected Mediterranean waters. These vessels had the long, narrow shape of the Mediterranean galley, direct descendants of the Roman fighting craft that were powered by oarsmen. But the newer versions were enlarged considerably to accommodate more cargo. The planking of their hulls was carvel-built, or set flush, edge to edge, to form a smooth surface. And sails were added. They were lateen sails, unmistakably Arab in origin. To this day, east of Suez, the single triangular lateen sail extended by a long spar slung to a low mast is a common sight on the horizon.

The northern and southern shipbuilding traditions came together in the hands of the Portuguese and Andalusians. By the early fifteenth century, the Atlantic ports of Iberia had become a regular meeting place for ships from the North Sea and from the Mediterranean. Southern shipwrights had already adopted one important feature from northern ships: the sternpost rudder. They kept the more streamlined southern hull but for the larger craft used the northern square sails, which could be rigged as many separate sheets that added up to a much larger area of canvas and could be handled more easily by sailors. Lateen sails severely restricted the size of a ship. Only one sail could be rigged to one mast, and it had to be large, requiring a heavy boom. This made going-about in changing winds a slow and tricky maneuver. In the prevailing monsoons of the Indian Ocean, this was rarely necessary, but the Atlantic was another matter. Because square rigging provided more canvas for catching the winds, ships could be built larger, and large ships were much in demand in Iberia.

As Portuguese mariners in the fifteenth century returned from their explorations down the western coast of Africa, they made suggestions for improving the ships. The prevailing winds made the voyage south easy for a square-rigged ship; returning, against the wind, made sailors wonder if they would ever see Lagos or Lisbon again. It was then that they wished for a lateen sail, which could be set to catch the wind from different directions. Shipwrights, seeking a solution to the African problem, modified the vessels until, through trial and error, they arrived at the basic caravel design in use at the time of Columbus.

One of the most obvious results was a rigging arrangement of two or three or sometimes four masts for both square and lateen sails. The combination was a technological innovation of the first magnitude in seafaring. Ships were made fleet in all winds and, with a means for rigging more sails, could be expanded to larger, oceangoing sizes.

Although there was no single design, it was common for a caravel to have fore- and mainsails that were square and to have the mizzenmast at the stern rigged for a lateen sail. With such rigging, a ship could take full advantage of most wind conditions. The squares were more efficient in following winds, and the lateens were better suited for catching contrary winds. Even if the great lengths of the lateen yards made them cumbersome to handle in heavy weather, requiring larger crews, the advantages of the combined rigging became manifest. "Aerodynamically," Smith writes, "this grouping of sails allowed rapid maneuvering and increased speed, especially if the mizzen sail was trimmed to spill wind into the main." On Columbus's homeward passage, the *Niña* and the *Pinta* covered more than 200 miles in one day, making eleven knots in the gusts. Few sailing ships could do better until the racing yachts of the twentieth century.

From a few references in expedition accounts and some sketches on old maps, as well as a detailed mid-fifteenth-century Spanish caravel model (the Mataro model residing in the Prinz Hendrik Museum in Rotterdam), historians have been able to piece together other characteristics of the caravels. They were built on a massive straight keel, after the northern fashion. As for their dimensions, caravels were, as a rule, three times as long as they were wide, and they had a shallow draft of about six or seven feet, enabling them to move more safely in uncharted waters and to penetrate bays and rivers of new worlds. On most early caravels, the deck was raised at the stern and supported the captain's cabin. This superstructure, called the *tolda,* was later expanded to a full-fledged sterncastle as a raised platform for navigation and combat. Early caravels usually did not have a raised deck at the bow, a *tilda,* since it would have interfered with the long lateen main yard. But with the introduction of square sails, and in response to the need for a forward fighting platform, caravels were eventually redesigned with a substantial forecastle. The bow and stern were rounded in to a single post; the squared, or transom, stern did not come along until the end of the fifteenth century.

On most other details, historians must speculate from even less evidence and with less confidence. It is not known, for example, if any of the Columbus ships had a crow's nest or similar lookout atop the mainmast or if they had "rat lines," cross ropes in the standing rigging that served as a ladder for sailors. Models of caravels show that they had vertical timbers attached to the outside of the top of the hull. Their purpose is unclear. Did they act to reinforce the attachment of the shroud, or standing rigging, to the hull? Or were they used, like the rubber fenders on today's ships, to protect the hull while taking on cargo? Other questions concern the gunwales, the sides of the hull that rise above the main deck. Drawings and models show many round holes in the gunwales. Gun ports? Smith has questioned whether caravels could have mounted many guns: with their shallow draft, this might have made them dangerously top-heavy. Perhaps, instead, the holes were there for sweeps, the long oars that may have been used in dead calms, or merely as outlets for seawater draining off the deck.

As much as we do not know about these ships, one essential fact is beyond question: they were well made for their time and their crucial role in history.

Two other technological developments, besides the caravel, contributed to the ultimate success of Europeans in crossing the Western Sea and fending off would-be adversaries in strange lands. These technologies were the magnetic compass and guns.

The Chinese apparently were the first to understand magnetism and its application in navigation. They seem to have used magnetized needles in sailing at least a century before there is any record of their introduction in Europe. As early as the twelfth century, sailors out of the port of Amalfi are credited with the first European navigation by compass. This device became widely known when Crusaders to the Holy Land learned of its use from Arab seamen. The Arabs presumably had adapted the idea from the Chinese, although Parry maintains that there is no firm evidence that the magnetic compass was introduced into Europe, either directly or indirectly, from China. The record does show that Jacques de Vitry, a bishop, writing from the Near Eastern city of Acre in 1218, reported: "An iron needle, after it has made contact with the magnet stone, always turns toward the North Star, which stands motionless while the rest revolve, being as it were the axis of the firmament." Such a needle, he informed Europe, "is therefore a necessity for those traveling by sea."

Charts with compass bearings, an innovation in cartography that followed naturally, enabled sailors in the Mediterranean to make the next port with less guesswork at night and under darkened skies. Trade by ships could grow in reliability and frequency. By the middle of the fifteenth century, ships on the open and uncharted sea were using the compass to determine their latitude. The North Star is always aligned within a few degrees of the earth's axis, and its height above the horizon remains virtually the same at a fixed latitude. By observing the angle of the North Star above the horizon, a navigator could estimate his latitude. If the star appeared to go up in the sky, one was off course to the north; if it went down, one was too far south. The practice of "latitude sailing" was fairly well developed by Columbus's time.

The European armory for land warfare by then included increasingly powerful iron cannon, and more portable versions of the weapons were being installed on ships. Although Columbus carried a few bombards, and used them in a show of force on at least one occasion during the first expedition, cannon were not instrumental to his success. But European projectile and percussive weapons were decisive in subsequent operations. The balance of power between the explorer and the explored had changed considerably from the time of the Norse encounters with the Skraelings. Heavily armed Portuguese ships completely destroyed Arab navies in the Indian Ocean. As Albuquerque wrote to his king in 1513, "at the rumor of our coming the [native] ships all vanished and even the birds ceased to skim over the water." David B. Quinn, a modern British historian, writes: "while marine technology and navigational know-how brought Europeans to America and enabled them to carry out a long, discontinuous sequence of exploration, the fact remains that if the European arms had not been so overwhelmingly superior to those of the indigenous peoples, the European impact on North America—indeed, on any part of the Americas—would have been marginal only, as was the case in the sixteenth century in European relations with China."

But the compass and arms would have been of no use without the caravels and their command of the sea and wind.

Two of Columbus's ships, the *Niña* and the *Pinta,* were unquestionably caravels. Historians know this much, but they are less sure that the *Santa María,* the flagship, was a true caravel. She very likely was a *nao,* from the Greek word for "ship," which was a heavier and slower vessel used mainly for cargo. This would explain why the swift *Pinta* and *Niña* were always running ahead of *Santa María.* Columbus himself complained about the sluggish flagship's not being "suitable for the business of discovery," while heaping praise on the *Niña,* his favorite.

Columbus did not so much choose the three ships as accept what was available at Palos. The one we know as *Niña* was actually named *Santa Clara;* her more familiar nickname was derived from the name of the owner, Juan Niño of nearby Moguer. Not only was *Niña* Columbus's favorite ship, but Niño seems also to have won the admiral's special respect. After the voyage, on which he served as master of his caravel, Niño was singled out to accompany Columbus to Barcelona for the royal reception. The *Pinta* was owned by Cristóbal Quintero of Palos, and happened to be in port and ready for use.

Two equipped caravels were all that Palos was required to provide. When Columbus failed to negotiate a third ship out of the town fathers, he arranged to charter *La Gallega,* a ship built in Galicia and at the time anchored at Palos. This was the *nao* that Columbus renamed *Santa María.* Her owner was Juan de la Cosa, a name that, as we will see, has given historians no end of trouble.

Contemporary accounts are vague about the ships' sizes. Michele de Cuneo, an Italian gentleman who accompanied Columbus's second expedition, said *Niña* was "about 60 tons." Las Casas mentioned that *Santa María* was "somewhat" larger than the others. Modern scholars, notably José María Martínez-Hidalgo, former director of the Maritime Museum in Barcelona, have managed to arrive at somewhat more precise estimates of the ships' dimensions. *Santa María* apparently displaced 202 modern tons and had a length of 77 feet, a beam of 26 feet, and a draft of almost 7 feet. She was rigged with square sails on two of the three masts, with a lateen sail on the poop mast. *Pinta* was also three-masted, with two squares and one lateen sail. She was approximately 70 feet long, with a beam of some 22 feet and a draft of 7 feet. *Niña* was somewhat smaller, but not by much. Recent archival discoveries show that *Niña* was 67 feet long, had a beam of 21 feet, and a draft of just under 7 feet.

When the fleet sailed from Palos, *Niña* was rigged for lateen sails only. In the Canaries, after the shakedown cruise, Columbus had her refitted, replacing the larger lateens with square sails so that, as Ferdinand Columbus writes, "she might follow the other vessels more quietly and with less danger." This was the only major modification required to prepare the ships for the audacious voyage. Nothing more was necessary.

Seldom any more do the archives yield a new piece of illuminating evidence about the Columbus voyages, but this happened in 1977.

Eugene Lyon is research director of the St. Augustine Foundation, which supervises restoration of the oldest city in the United States, and is also an adjunct professor of history at the University of Florida. His specialty is archaic Spanish, and he was examining old documents in the Archive of the Indies in Seville when he came upon a bundle of papers. Called the *Libro de Armadas,* the 400 pages described the dispatch of several caravel fleets to the New World between 1495 and 1500. Lyon's eye landed on references in a faded script to "*Niña,* also known as *Santa Clara.*"

Careful analysis made Lyon realize that these were pages of contracts, bills of lading, and receipts for ship supplies. Accounts for *Niña* and her sister ship, *Santa Cruz,* were especially detailed because the two caravels belonged to Ferdinand and Isabella in partnership with Columbus. (He had bought a half-interest after the first voyage.) The papers documented for the first time the dimensions, armament, and rigging of one of Columbus's ships—*Niña.*

Niña not only brought Columbus home from the first voyage, but was one of the seventeen ships in the second expedition, from 1493 to 1496. She was badly damaged in a hurricane at Hispaniola in 1495 and had to be rebuilt. The documents mention "*Niña,* which was remade in the Indies." Lyon now felt certain that this was the Columbus *Niña.* After the second expedition, *Niña* hauled some cargo to Rome in 1497, without Columbus and possibly without his approval, and on the return was seized by French pirates. The crew managed to escape and bring her safely back to Spain, where she was made ready for the third Columbus expedition in 1498.

The *Libro de Armadas* tells of these preparations. The documents show that the third expedition was underwritten by two Italian traders who were in debt to the Spanish crown—another indication of how the voyages were financed. At this time, Columbus's own finances were apparently straitened. To pay his seamen in 1498, he used funds he was to have taken to the colony in Hispaniola, hoping to balance the books later with gold to be found there.

Before *Niña* set sail, her master, Pedro Francés of Palos, acknowledged receipt of the caravel's hull, masts, yards, rigging, and other itemized equipment, the list of which runs for pages and affords the first authoritative description of the ship. The Spanish, we see, were meticulous record-keepers. One surprise was that *Niña* had 4 masts, instead of 2 or 3, as had been thought. (The additional mast could have been installed in the post-hurricane reconstruction.) *Niña* had a bowsprit and 2 boomlets, one fore and one aft. The sails for the 4 masts were described as "worn" or "old," though she carried an extra set of new sails for the fore- and mainmasts. She had 6 shrouds, or lines, on each side of the mainmast; 4 on each side to support the foremast; and 3 on each side for the mizzen. In all, *Niña* carried 2,517 pounds of new hemp line for cables, sheet-ropes, tie-runners, bowlines, and lifts. She had rope ladders and 68 pulleys and blocks of various sizes. On deck was a small boat with 6 oars and a new 200-pound anchor, as well as 2 smaller anchors. For weaponry *Niña* carried 10 bombards, breach-loaded guns that were probably fitted on the gunwales. There were 80 lead balls for the guns, 54 long and 20 short lances, and 100 pounds of gunpowder.

As the day of departure approached, *Niña*'s hold was packed with provisions: 18 tons of wheat, 34 barrels of wine, some 7 tons of sea biscuit or unleavened bread, almost 2 tons of flour, more than a ton of cheese, barrels of water, jars of olive oil, and a supply of sardines, raisins, and garlic. To keep the stores from rolling and bumping, the barrels and jars were cushioned with vine shoots and olive wood, which also served as firewood. The record is especially detailed about the ton of salt pork. The meat was obtained from farms throughout southern Spain and washed with heated lye from the Triana soap works. The pieces were then rubbed with red clay and bran to create a protective crust, marked with an iron, and packed in baskets for loading aboard the caravels.

Calculations of the number of barrels required to hold the listed cargo led Lyon to what must be the most reliable estimate of *Niña*'s dimensions. In those days, a ship's tonnage did not mean her weight or displacement, but her cubic capacity in terms of wine casks, or tuns. Two casks equaled one Spanish *tonelada.* By Lyon's account, *Niña*'s cargo came to 52 tons, and her overall capacity was probably 58 to 60 tons, or slightly less than had been previously estimated. With this knowledge, Lyon and Martínez-Hidalgo determined that *Niña* must have been about 67 feet long, with a beam of 21 feet and a draft of just under 7 feet.

For the 1498 expedition, the records show, *Niña* and *Santa Cruz* carried more than 90 people on the royal payroll, including 18 farmers or stockmen, 50 crossbowmen, a priest, a locksmith, a miner, and a surgeon. Ten passengers, including two gypsy women, Catalina and

María, were convicted murderers freed on condition that they emigrate to the New World. Already, 6 years after discovery, America was a lure to those wishing to start life anew.

A list of medicines supplied to some of the caravels provides an insight into pharmaceuticals of the day. The 113 items on one list included a prune laxative, quince juice, violet conserve, rum, lard, rose water, lemon juice, lily root, arsenic, a compound of honey and opium, and a reddish resin of the dragon tree for the painful swellings of gout. (Columbus was afflicted with gout.)

A note in the margins of the *Libro de Armadas* discloses that on October 9, 1499, Columbus ordered Pedro Frances to turn *Niña* and its equipment over to Diego Ortiz, her new owner. "This may have been a forced sale," Lyon speculates. "Things had been going badly for Columbus. Two weeks earlier, colonists in Santo Domingo had revolted against his leadership and forced him to sign a humiliating settlement with Francisco Roldán, leader of the rebellion."

The marginal note is history's last record of *Niña,* but the documents give scholars the most authoritative picture of the Columbus ships they are likely to have—unless nautical archeologists can recover some well-preserved wrecks. *Santa María* was largely dismantled after she ran aground off Hispaniola; searches at the site have produced nothing save an anchor that might have belonged to the ship. *Pinta* made several more trips across the ocean. On her last voyage, in 1499–1500, under the command of Vicente Yáñez Pinzón of Palos, she took part in the discovery of the Amazon River, but went down in a hurricane off the Turks and Caicos Islands, south of the Bahamas.

In 1976, treasure hunters found a wreck on Molasses Reef in the Turks and Caicos waters and jumped to the conclusion that this was *Pinta.* Professional archeologists have serious doubts. Through analysis of Spanish ceramics and wrought-iron ordnance, they have dated the shipwreck between 1492 and 1525. The ship may have been a caravel or, because it seems to have been heavily armed, a small warship. In any case, the find is not very revealing of the ship's design and construction. The keel, endposts, and other diagnostic parts of the hull are missing. Divers, however, found evidence for one essential piece of equipment on the ships of discovery: the bilge pump. A lead valve was identified. Suction pumps had been used in European mines in the fifteenth century, but nautical historians said this was the first confirmation of their use also in ships of the era.

For several years in the 1980s, and again in 1990, divers and experts in remote-sensing technology from Texas A & M also probed the floor of St. Ann's Bay on the northern coast of Jamaica for signs of the *Santiago* and the *Capitana,* two caravels that Columbus scuttled there on his fourth and final voyage. But these and all other searches for caravel wrecks have so far proved to be unrewarding.

Caravels sailed on in history. They took Pedro Cabral in 1500 on a voyage toward the Cape of Good Hope that ended with the accidental discovery of Brazil. They took Ferdinand Magellan in 1519 on the expedition that circumnavigated the world. As exploration gave way to trade and colonization, caravels were gradually replaced by larger vessels with more capacious holds for cargo and heavier platforms for ordnance. These were variations on the design of the *nao,* the *Santa María* type. But it was the caravel that Victor Hugo would later hail as "one of the great masterpieces of man."

8

The Columbian Argonauts

The three ships rode anchor in a branch of the Tinto, down a dirt road from the Church of St. George. The men enlisted for the crews had filled the holds with provisions and taken on water from a fountain below the church. (The Columbus Fontanilla, with its original fifteenth-century brickwork, is the centerpiece of a roadside park in today's Palos.) They walked up the road to attend mass at midnight. Columbus himself had taken communion and boarded the *Santa María* in the hours of darkness. All was ready. Half an hour before sunrise, he issued the order to weigh anchor "in the name of Jesus."

By many accounts there were probably ninety men in all, who in the effusions of the World's Columbian Exposition of 1893 in Chicago would be hailed as the "Columbian argonauts." There were officers and seamen, a secretary and an interpreter, two royal officials, boatswains and carpenters and coopers, caulkers and "surgeons" and ship's boys. *Santa María* carried thirty-nine men; *Pinta,* twenty-seven; and *Niña,* twenty-four. It had taken Columbus more than two months to arrange for the ships and provisions and to persuade these men to take their chances on the Ocean Sea. For crews, as for ships, he had had to depend on what he could find in Palos and neighboring towns, and the seamen there were a practical lot not easily convinced to follow this stranger in pursuit of some golden fleece.

At first, he met stony resistance. A citizen of Moguer, testifying later, recalled that people "mocked" Columbus and "taunted" him in public, calling his enterprise "foolish." He might have his ships, but who would dare sign up to sail them? Three men seemed to turn this thinking around.

One was an old seaman called Pedro Vasques de la Frontera who was living in Palos at the time. People said he was "a man very wise in the art of the sea." Back in 1452, he would tell anyone and everyone, he had shipped with the Portuguese on a voyage in search of the legendary island of Brasil. They discovered the two westernmost islands of the Azores and, he was certain, were on the verge of a greater discovery when they decided to turn back. The idea of western discovery was in the air. When Columbus showed up in Palos, a witness said later, the old seaman "encouraged the people and told them publicly that all should go on that voyage, and they would find a very rich land." Poor old Pedro Vasques would not live to see Columbus return with the news of his prophecy's fulfillment.

If people might dismiss the rambling tales of an old salt, they would more likely heed a shipowner like Juan de la Cosa. He was a Basque who lived not far away, near Cádiz, and may well have become friendly with Columbus after a meeting some three years earlier. In any case, when this practical shipowner came forward with the offer to lease his ship and sail with Columbus, along with ten of his crew, the other seamen began to change their minds.

As previously noted, this man—or at least the name Juan de la Cosa—has played tricks on historians ever since. Was this the same individual who went on to become a prominent cartographer, whose 1500 map beautifully illustrates many of the new discoveries? The cartographer had the same name. The confusion is compounded by the fact that a seaman with that name went on the second voyage. Was he the Juan de la Cosa of the first voyage, or a different man? Many scholars have trouble believing that a shipowner would have enlisted as an ordinary seaman. If there were two Juan de la Cosas, which one became the mapmaker?

Justin Winsor was the first scholar to point out that the master on the first voyage and the mapmaker must have been different people. Morison cites witnesses in later legal proceedings who said the mapmaker had not been on the first voyage; others testified that the De la Cosa on the second voyage was the mapmaker. A document from that voyage, in which Columbus had crew members swear that Cuba was a continent, shows Juan de la Cosa signing and identifying himself as a master chartmaker and seaman. Alice Bache Gould, an American scholar, uncovered a document from 1494 leading her also to conclude that there were probably two different Juan de la Cosas. The shipowner who went on the first voyage could not have been on the second voyage, for the document authorizes a certain Juan de la Cosa to transport at that very time some grain from Andalusia as compensation for the loss of *Santa María.* Morison, accepting Gould's evidence, pronounced the two Juan de la Cosas to be different persons. After further analysis of early-sixteenth-century documents, some Spanish historians have recently concluded that the De la Cosa of the second voyage was a sailor who was not heard from again and declared that the man on the first voyage, the shipowner, did indeed become the famous mapmaker. Nonetheless, Roberto Barreiro-Meiro, subdirector of the Maritime Museum in Barcelona, insists that there was only one Juan de la Cosa, the master of the first voyage sailing as a seaman on the second voyage and then becoming the celebrated cartographer.

All of which leaves the issue as unresolved as ever. About the only certainty is that the Juan de la Cosa who became a cartographer was also associated with an expedition of Amerigo Vespucci in 1499 and was killed in Panama in 1509. But was this the man who had been the *Santa María*'s owner or the seaman on the second voyage, or someone else? This is but one of the many peripheral questions clouding the Columbus story that both delight and dismay scholars.

Another shipowner, Martín Alonso Pinzón, was even more influential in advancing Columbus's cause with the people of Palos. Controversy over his role would dog Columbus's heirs in the sixteenth century and exercise historians from then on. No historian, however, could dispute Pinzón's decisive role in those weeks at Palos. Without Pinzón, the historian Vignaud says, "it is conceivable that the enterprise would not have been carried out."

At the urging of Father Marchena, Pinzón agreed to join forces with Columbus. Pinzón seems to have taken charge of buying supplies for the fleet. An old seaman, Yáñez de Montilla of Palos, recalled that Pinzón "put much zeal into enlisting and encouraging seamen, as though the discovery was to be for his and his children's sakes." He volunteered to be captain of the *Pinta,* and one of his younger brothers, Vicente Yáñez, signed on as captain of the *Niña.* Two other brothers and a cousin also decided to go along. "Almost all the inhabitants of the town were under their influence," Las Casas would write of the Pinzóns, "for they were the richest and the best connected people there." Seeing these sensible men from a prominent local seafaring family step forward, as well as three Niño brothers from Moguer, others shook off their qualms and added their names to the crew list. This much is incontrovertible.

Columbus also needed someone like Martín Pinzón once the voyage was under way. Sure as he was of himself and his vision, Columbus must have recognized his inexperience as a navigator and a leader of men. He had been to sea often, but apparently never as the captain of a ship. And he must have known of the suspicions he, as a foreigner, aroused among the seamen of Palos. One man alone might succeed in promoting such an undertaking; executing it was another matter.

In an impressionistic biography in 1984, Gianni Granzotto, an Italian historian and journalist, draws a satisfying picture of the "mutual need" Columbus and Pinzón had of each other and the source of their mutual antipathy. The two men, he writes, "held each other in high esteem, though they may not have liked each other. Pinzón saw Columbus as a parvenu come out of nowhere, short on experience but endowed with an extraordinary amount of energy, drive and new ideas. Columbus considered Pinzón a first-rate seaman and nothing more." Sufficient though this was in forging an alliance, it was not enough on which to build a friendship. As Granzotto observes: "Columbus was afraid Pinzón might overshadow him. Pinzón envied Columbus's certainty of success. Their differences were irreconcilable. Friendship and candor might have been able to overcome them, but there was never any real friendship or candor between Columbus and Pinzón."

At a crucial moment in the voyage, when a discouraged Columbus supposedly entertained thoughts of turning back, Pinzón and his brothers urged him on. That is the story told years later by seamen of Moguer and Palos. At a strategy conference on *Santa María,* six days before landfall, Columbus was said to have asked Martín Alonso: "Captain, what shall we do? My people complain to me, what think you, gentlemen, we should do?" Martín Alonso responded: "Come, sir, we have hardly left the town of Palos and your honor is already discouraged." According to the story, related by witnesses, Pinzón then shouted: *"Adelante! adelante!"*—Onward! Translated as "Sail on! sail on!" this became the theme of Joaquin Miller's famous poem on Columbus, but if the rallying cry came from anyone, Morison notes, it was not from Columbus but Pinzón. That, at least, is the version of the story given by Pinzón partisans: other witnesses came forward to assert that it was the Pinzón brothers who had wanted to turn back.

Much of our knowledge about the Pinzóns and their contributions comes not from Columbus or Las Casas or Ferdinand Columbus, who have little to say on the subject, or from Oviedo, who dismissed the pro-Pinzón evidence as unworthy of consideration. We must depend instead on testimony in a protracted court case initiated in 1513 against the heirs of Columbus. At issue was a share of the Columbus inheritance, which the Pinzón family felt should come to them in recognition of Martín Alonso's pivotal role in the venture. Many documents of the testimony, the *Pleitos de Colón,* were published by Navarrete in 1825 and became an important source of historical study—and dispute.

In the years after the voyage, resentment built up among the Pinzóns and many of their neighbors. They felt that Martín Alonso, in part because of his death shortly after returning, had not received proper credit. Like many who become obsessed with the pursuit of their vision, Columbus could be ungenerous toward those who shared the risks and contributed to the success. "The voyage was his personal enterprise," Parry writes. "It was not surprising that he should tend to represent all ideas and initiatives as his own, and to deny credit to his companions; few commanding officers are exempt from this temptation, and Columbus had more excuse for it than most."

Columbus yielded to the temptation when he took for himself the reward for the first sighting of land, which by rights belonged to the seaman on lookout. He also could be suspicious of those around him, sometimes with justification. Some historians suspect Pinzón of having a hand in fomenting unrest among the crews in the last days of the outward voyage. At Cuba, the independent-minded Pinzón, an expert mariner in his own right, sailed off in the *Pinta* on his own gold-seeking reconnaissance. But a few scholars absolve Pinzón of blame in this incident, suggesting that the *Pinta* was running well ahead of the others and simply missed a signal from the flagship to turn back. Columbus, though, suspected insubordination. Relations between the two men, already strained, never improved. Columbus made no attempt to be magnanimous and share fame with anyone else, much less the recalcitrant Pinzón.

In the years immediately afterward, a legend grew among the people of Palos about Pinzón's contribution. This local man had not only helped Columbus enlist his crew, he had also supplied the admiral with the knowledge that proved crucial to success. The legend lay at the heart of the lawsuit. The Pinzóns contended that, before Columbus came along, Martín Alonso was making his own plans for transoceanic discovery. He and many others in Palos believed in the existence of lands across the ocean. Witnesses testified that, on a journey to Rome, Martín Alonso visited the Vatican Library and studied secret charts and documents describing a westward voyage by the queen of Sheba across the ocean to Japan. He was supposedly inspired by this to go and see for himself. At the court hearing in Seville, witnesses affirmed that this information, which Pinzón brought to Columbus's attention, encouraged the admiral to make the final, successful plea to Ferdinand and Isabella for support.

The lawsuit was eventually dropped in 1536. No such record of a Sheban voyage has ever been found in the papal archives, or anywhere else. Although Pinzón's role is still debated, most historians tend to dismiss the larger claims as another of the myths that cling to Columbus. The truth, Taviani asserts, is that Martín Alonso Pinzón was in Rome only to deliver a shipment of sardines, as he had done previously.

To this day, though, the people of Palos honor the native son more than Columbus. They celebrate Pinzón Day. Several streets bear his name, and at the plaza in the heart of the little town there stands a statue of Pinzón with cross and sword. Palos has no statue of Columbus.

Another myth can be dispelled without reservation. Contrary to popular notions, the crews of the three ships were not composed mainly of pardoned felons. Columbus did not have trouble raising a crew because all the experienced seamen believed the earth was flat and so feared they might sail off the edge; we have already seen the flat-earth canard exposed. The initial reluctance was due not so much to fear as to a well-founded skepticism regarding the expedition's likelihood of reaching the Indies. Only through the influence of Pinzón and others did the many regular seamen enlist for the voyage.

True, there was a royal decree offering a pardon to criminals who volunteered for the crew, which fed the legend that Columbus faced the unknown in the company of hardened criminals and misfits. True, four men wanted in connection with the murder of the Palos town crier took advantage of the amnesty. These four—Bartolomé de Torres, Alonso Clavijo, Juan de Moguer, and Pedro Yzquierdo—were the only criminals in the crews, and they were seasoned mariners who had sailed before with Martín Alonso Pinzón. They seem to have acquitted themselves well on the voyage, particularly Juan de Moguer, who would go on to become a pilot.

All in all, Morison concludes, Columbus was well served by the crews. "No one but real seamen could have sailed *Niña* and *Pinta* home safely," he writes in *Admiral of the Ocean Sea.* "And a considerable number of them are known to have accompanied Columbus on his later voyages."

But who were these men, and exactly how many did sail with Columbus on the historic voyage?

Establishing the names and details of the Columbus crews was, according to Morison, "the most important piece of original Columbus research yet done in the present century." It was the product of the labors of Alice Bache Gould. She epitomized the countless researchers who have spent careers deep in the Spanish archives in the lonely pursuit of a few more facts to document the Columbus story. Her meticulous researches appeared in a trickle of journal articles and never were compiled as a book. Her name and contributions have thus been relegated to the footnotes of the publications of more prominent scholars.

A Boston Brahmin, Gould was born in 1868 in Cambridge, Massachusetts, and grew up in an affluent and intellectual family. Her father, B. Apthorpe Gould, was a professor of astronomy, and her uncle Alexander Dallas Bache was a great-grandson of Benjamin Franklin and the distinguished superintendent of the United States Coast and Geodetic Survey. With her father's reluctant consent, she enrolled at the newly founded Bryn Mawr College and graduated in 1889 with a solid grounding in the classics and mathematics. She continued her education with two years of graduate studies in literature and science. In World War I, she served as an instructor in navigation at a navy training base. But it was her fluency in Spanish, acquired in childhood, that set the course of her career.

On her way to Rome in 1911, Gould's ship happened to be detained in Seville. To fill the time, she visited the Archives of the Indies in the former stock exchange, the Casa Lonja, near the port. Examining some old documents, she was annoyed by her trouble in deciphering the archaic Spanish script and determined that she would remain there until she had mastered it. For more than forty years, except for a brief period during World War I, she lived in Spain in a kind of self-imposed exile and diligently plowed through the Archives of the Indies and the national archive at the castle in Simancas, near Valladolid. Indeed, a bronze plaque honoring her is mounted there near where she died of a stroke in 1953, a frail, bent woman of eighty-five working on the Columbus archives to the end.

One task, above all others, had occupied Gould over the years. She sought to determine the number and track down the names and backgrounds of every single man and boy who sailed with Columbus in 1492. Most books today put the number at ninety, as did Las Casas and Hernando Columbus, but no one can be sure. Peter Martyr and Oviedo had written that the crews numbered 120. The best Navarrete was able to do was list the names of those crew members, forty in all, who had been left at La Navidad. Subsequent scholars could authenticate only seventy-one names, but sometimes drew up lists numbering as many as 100. Gould's research, published piecemeal from the 1920s through 1944, finally accounted for the names of eighty-seven completely authenticated crewmen and included fragmentary biographies of each one.

Ursula Lamb, a retired professor of history at the University of Arizona, has worked the Spanish archives herself and recalls from memory and legend the indefatigable efforts of Gould in ferreting out the crew list. Since the crown was paying their wages, most of the names appear on payrolls preserved in the archives. A few are mentioned in Columbus's journal, and some others, not documented on the payroll, are named in the lawsuit testimony. But Gould did not confine herself to these usual sources. She went to the jail in Moguer, where she had heard some documents were deposited, and had herself locked in with the prisoners each day so that she could read every line in search of clues. Into the cellars of the forbidding fortress of Simancas, complete with moat and drawbridge, the ninth-century structure that had once been occupied by Napoleon's cavalry, she descended and recovered valuable papers that had survived use as bedding for horses. From among dried Napoleonic manure, Gould pulled out a copy of the royal confirmation of the *mayorazgo* given to Columbus. Before Napoleon's troops had made a mess of things, Navarrete had found and published the *mayorazgo,* a will in which Columbus in 1498 had expressed his loyalty to Genoa and left several legacies there, and also the royal confirmation of it. But since then neither document had been seen, leading skeptical scholars to suspect they had been fakes to establish Columbus's Genoese roots. Gould's discovery vindicated Navarrete and established the authenticity of the document.

Gould was forever being drawn down such bypaths of research and thus never wrote the book she planned of the biographies of the Columbus crews. Her frustration was once vented in a letter. "If I ever get this book finished," she wrote, "I shall put on the title page the slave's inscription on his oar, 'oft was I weary when I toiled at thee.' . . . P.S. Damn."

At her death, Gould had at least finished a draft of what would be the most authoritative list of the crew ever compiled. José de la Peña y Camara, a former director of the Archives of the Indies, saw the list to eventual publication in 1984 by the Royal Academy of History. To the eighty-seven authenticated names were added those of other possible crew members studied by Gould, bringing the total to 118. Clearly, the true number remains unknown.

In a review of the Royal Academy's book, Rolando Lagarda Trias, a Spanish scholar writing in 1986, notes the limitations as well as the rewards of searches in the archives for more about the Columbus story. "The life of Miss Gould puts squarely before us the problem of whether it is ever possible to reconstruct the past completely," he writes. "The destructive action by time and man eliminates a good part of the documentation, and to this factor has to be added that many questions asked today were not felt to be important by contemporaries. In sum, archival research cannot give answers to all our queries, which is why we believe that the historian in his reconstruction of the past has to use his imagination in order to fill in the gaps in the documents by hypotheses which are consistent with the facts."

Historical imagination there has been aplenty, and too often the hypotheses and declarations of fact have stood on sand.

Despite various nationalistic claims, for example, no one from England, Ireland, or any other northern-European countries was aboard. All those who shipped out, except Columbus and four others (one Portuguese, one Genoese, one Venetian, and one Calabrian), were Spaniards, and most of them came from the environs of Palos. There was no room for more than a few supernumeraries. One was Luis de Torres, who was to be the expedition's interpreter in the courts of Asia. Rodrigo de Escobedo, secretary of the fleet, would write up accounts of diplomatic proceedings and the acquisition of new territories. Two representatives of the crown were on board: Rodrigo Sánchez de Segovia, comptroller, and Pedro Gutiérrez, a gentleman whose duties seem never to have been defined. Diego de Arana, a cousin of Columbus's mistress, had the title of marshal of the fleet. Each ship carried a surgeon, who was probably not an actual physician but a barber or an apothecary.

One of Gould's surprising discoveries was the correct name of the seaman who was the first to sight land. The man known in most histories as Rodrigo de Triana was actually Juan Rodríguez Bermejo.

According to the archives, the crew members were paid the going wage for long voyages. Masters and pilots received 2,000 *maravedis* a month; able seamen, 1,000; ship's boys, or gromets, 666. In an effort to translate the value of such wages, Morison notes: "A bushel of wheat in 1493 cost 73 *maravedis.* Sancho Panza's wages from Don Quixote were 26 *maravedis* a day . . . , a little better than that of Columbus's gromets."

Almost nothing is known about life aboard these ships, except that it could not have been easy. Only the captain and the pilot had anything like regular quarters, in the aft cabin. Everyone else slept on deck or below among the casks of water and wine, jars of olive oil, and stores of food. They ate biscuits, fatback, and beans or rice seasoned heavily with garlic. No amount of seasoning could disguise the often sorry state of their food's preservation and infestation. From his experience on his father's fourth voyage, Ferdinand Columbus recalled that seamen usually put off their meals until night, so as not to see the maggots in their bread. Cooking, when weather permitted, was done over a wood fire in a sandbox on deck. Absent any definitive accounts, Morison could only surmise that Columbus's seamen probably "fared quite as well as peasants or workers ashore, except during a storm, or weather so rough that a fire could not be kept."

Life on board these ships of discovery, in 1492 and for years thereafter, can only be imagined. Historians like Morison and Parry have had to settle for descriptions of conditions on a Hispaniola-bound ship almost a century later. In a 1573 letter to a friend back home, Eugenio de Salazar, a Spanish gentleman traveling to Santo Domingo, gave a lively account of a landlubber's introduction to the harsh reality of an ocean crossing. A new translation of the Salazar letter was made in 1987 by Carla Rahn Phillips, who described it as a "hilarious burlesque of life at sea" by a writer with a mastery of the Castilian language in all its nuances. Exaggerated it may be, but if one reads it carefully and is mindful of the writer's literary flourishes, the letter is a valuable part of the historical record.

Salazar likens the ship he was on to a city, "an elongated settlement" with "lodgings so closed in, dark and odoriferous that they seem to be buried vaults or charnel-houses." It is not hard to imagine the truth underlying his rank exaggeration. He goes on to describe the masts as the city's trees. They "run continuously with fish grease and stinking tallow." Filthy water washes the deck. Lice and rats are everywhere in evidence.

As a literary man, Salazar is enchanted by the language of the pilot's orders that send sailors scampering up the rigging like "cats chasing through the trees." Here are the cadences of a ship at work: "Hoist the topgallant; lower the fore-topsail; raise the foresail; don't stay it to the boom; give the spritsail a little sheer; raise the main course; lace the bonnet. . . ." And so, on through the day, the pilot's voice sounds in the wind. The echoes come back in the singing of shanties, as the men toil to raise the sails.

Marine language is infectious, Salazar notes, and is employed on every occasion. When he asks for a cup, he finds himself saying: "Let loose the common cup." Or a request for a napkin becomes: "Give here the big cloth." When someone else breaks wind (which, he says, often happens), the expression is: "Ah, wind from the stern."

Dining is an unappetizing ordeal. On the table are piles of "ruined biscuits" that on the tablecloths "looked like heaps of cow dung in a farmer's field." The wooden plates are filled with "stringy beef joints, dressed with some partly cooked tendons." Without waiting for grace, Salazar writes, the men take out their knives, "big and small of diverse fashions, some made to kill pigs, others to flay lambs, and others to cut purses," and separate the nerves and sinews from the poor bones. They drink a cup of wine that is "more baptized [diluted] than they want." Thus, he concludes, "they finish their meal without finishing their hunger."

In the close quarters, there is no escaping any element of daily life. Jammed together, he writes, "one belches, another vomits, another breaks wind, another discharges his bowels, all while you eat breakfast; and you cannot tell anyone that he is demonstrating bad manners, because the ordinances of this city permit everything." The ship has no proper head. "To relieve yourself," he explains, "it is necessary to hang out over the sea like some apprentice seaman's forecastle." The wooden seat on which one sits precariously for this purpose "is such that many times a turd that has begun to emerge, for fear of falling into the sea, retires and returns inside like the head of a tortoise, so that it is necessary to finish the job badly, forcing it with suppositories and other aids."

In the evening, the voice of a ship's boy is heard chanting: "Amen.

May God give us a good night and a good voyage, and a good passage for the ship, sir captain and master and good company." As the ship's boy tends the hourglass, he intones: "Blessed be the hour God came to earth, Holy Mary who gave him birth, and Saint John who saw his worth. The guard is posted; the watch-glass filling; we'll have a good voyage, if God is willing."

For the ninety or so men who shipped with Columbus, life on the uncharted ocean could not have been any more pleasant. But nearly all of them had been to sea before, and knew not to expect much in the way of comfort. They went to sea again, trusting Pinzón and, God willing, this man Columbus.

Out from Palos, at the end of the first day, Columbus made the first entry in the journal he would keep throughout the voyage. "We departed Friday the third day of August of the year 1492 from the bar of Saltes at the eighth hour," he wrote. "We went south with a strong sea breeze 60 miles, which is 15 leagues, until sunset; afterward to the southwest and south by west, which was the route for the Canaries."

These men were now collaborators in Columbus's vision. Whatever their opinion of him had been when he arrived in Palos, their destiny was to share with him a voyage west toward the Indies, "by which route," Columbus wrote in the journal's prologue, "we do not know for certain anyone previously has passed."

Part Two

9

Landfall—But Where?

October 12, 1492.* Two hours past midnight. The lookout at the prow of the *Pinta*, a sailor named Juan Rodríguez Bermejo, made the first sighting in the bright moonlight on the western horizon. *"Tierra! Tierra!"* he cried out. Land, yes, land. A line of low white cliffs shimmered in the distance. This time it was no illusion.

Columbus and the crew had been deceived by wishful thinking several times during the thirty-three-day crossing. They had left Gomera in the Canaries on September 6, were becalmed off shore, and did not finally get under way until the 9th, which is considered the beginning of the crossing. From September 16 on, hardly a day passed that Columbus did not note in his journal some supposed harbinger of land. Green vegetation floating in the water, "sure signs of land." A large cloud mass on the horizon, "which is a sign of being near land." A rain shower without wind, "which is a sure sign of land." But these promised lands never materialized.

By September 22, the mood of the crew had darkened with anxiety. The trade wind was a westering sailor's delight, but there had been too much of a good thing. On that day, to Columbus's relief, the wind changed for a while. "This contrary wind was very necessary to me," he wrote, "because my people were very worked up thinking that in these seas winds for returning to Spain did not blow."

Spirits soared, only to plummet again at the mistaken reports of land. On September 25, Martín Pinzón made the first false sighting from *Pinta*. Sailors climbed the masts and thought they saw land, too. This should be about the time and place where Columbus had ex-

*The celebrated landing date—October 12—is not correct. It is from the Julian calendar, used in the fifteenth century. Under the Gregorian calendar of today, the date is October 21.

pected to find the fabled Antilla. He veered from his due-west course and headed south-southwest for the land, but he was pursuing a mirage. Again, on October 7, men on *Niña* raised a flag and fired a bombard to signal a land sighting. Another illusion.

Unrest grew among the sailors and some of the officers, to the point of mutinous whisperings. There are conflicting accounts of what happened at this trying moment. According to some disputed versions, Columbus called a conference with the Pinzón brothers and other officers on October 6 and asked if they should turn back. This is when Martín Alonso supposedly shouted: "*Adelante! adelante!*" And so they did. On the 10th, steering west-southwest, Columbus wrote: "Here the men could no longer stand it; they complained of the long voyage." He urged the crews on, reminding them of the promised riches of the Indies. He told them, as his son Ferdinand relates, "that it was useless to complain, he had come [to find] the Indies, and so had to continue until he found them, with the help of Our Lord." In desperation, he finally vowed that they would turn back if land was not found in three days. But Columbus must have had his fingers crossed, for Las Casas has him concluding his journal entry for the day with a pledge to continue the voyage until he found the Indies.

About an hour before moonrise on October 11, Columbus thought he caught sight of an eerie light in the distance. "It was like a small wax candle that rose and lifted up," he wrote, "which to a few seemed to be an indication of land." Was it a campfire on shore? Possibly, but not likely, historians have concluded, for the fleet, it turned out, was still too far from land. But it could have been the bioluminescence of marine life. The tiny Bermuda fireworm gives off a blinking green light to attract a mate, a display often observed in these waters in the darkness just before moonrise. Or was the mysterious light only an apparition in the eyes of the wishful mariner? Columbus dared not let himself believe too much, but everyone on the three ships was alive that night to the prospect of land.

After the lookout's sighting a few hours later, seamen hauled in the canvas and the three ships stood off shore until daybreak. Then they proceeded around a tip of the island and came to a sheltered anchorage on the leeward side, which faced west. There Columbus and other officers went ashore in one of the small boats. Columbus took possession of the island in the name of Ferdinand and Isabella. He christened the place San Salvador.

But where was he? To this day, scholars are not sure where Columbus first set foot in the New World. It was a small island in the

Bahamas, far from the Asian mainland he was seeking, but which island?

The question of the exact landing site has little bearing on history or our assessment of Columbus. There is no reason now to amend the judgment of an American historian writing a century ago. "The problem well illustrates the difficulty in identifying any route without the help of persistent proper names, especially after the lapse of time has somewhat altered the landmarks," John Fiske wrote in 1892. "From this point of view it is a very interesting problem and has lessons for us; otherwise it is of no importance."

One would not know it, though, from all the heat the issue has generated, with mounting intensity in the years leading up to the quincentennial.

No fewer than nine different islands have been identified as candidates for the San Salvador where Columbus landed. All lie in the Bahamas, Turks, or Caicos groups, an archipelago stretching from near the southeastern coast of Florida to the eastern tip of Cuba. Columbus thought so little of these islands that he never returned to them on subsequent expeditions; hence the absence of any reliable historical or cartographic record that might have obviated the dispute. With the Spanish showing no interest in them, the islands eventually fell into British hands and retain post-colonial ties to Britain. In this regard, at least, national rivalries have not roiled Columbian waters.

But controversy rages among historians, geographers, navigators, archeologists, and an assortment of amateur investigators. They approach the question literally backward and forward: back from the northern coast of Cuba, the first place Columbus visited whose identity is beyond dispute, to the initial landfall; forward from the Canaries by trying to reconstruct the precise course of the ocean crossing. Their theories and conjecture are based on the same inadequate scraps of data. No map sketched on the voyage has survived, and the experts search in vain for unambiguous words by Columbus that might single out the place. Several islands answer to his vague descriptions. Undeterred, scholars have skillfully marshaled available evidence to make intriguing cases in favor of each of the candidate-islands. Each argument, however, suffers from some weak link, either an unsupported inference, a contested journal entry, or a critical omission in the record that may be missing forever.

Given the question's relative unimportance, considering all the other controversial issues about Columbus, why do so many people concern themselves with the landfall problem? It seems to be one of those geographical puzzles with sufficient clues to encourage the belief that the solution is within reach. One person just might be clever enough to arrange existing clues, or find new ones, and finally make a compelling case for one island or another. Besides, there is the embarrassment. Of all the things one would expect historians to know, it is where Columbus landed. "After centuries of doubt," said William F. Keegan, an archeologist at the Florida Museum of Natural History in Gainesville, who has dug for landfall clues in the Bahamas, "it would be satisfying to be able to point to the place where the first steps were taken."

John Parker, curator of the James Ford Bell Library at the University of Minnesota and a historian of discoveries, has noted that from 1492 to 1731 there was no landfall problem at all: "There was no discussion. There apparently was no interest."

It was in 1731 that the English naturalist Mark Catesby published the first volume of *The Natural History of Carolina* and dropped a casual reference to Cat Island in the northern Bahamas as "the first land discovered in America by Christ. Columbus." No supporting evidence was given. But over the years, other books repeated the claim, and in the nineteenth century it gained influential endorsements from Washington Irving and Humboldt.

At the same time, two other islands were being identified as the site. One was an island in the central Bahamas that the British called Watlings. In his history of the New World, published in 1793, the Spanish writer Juan Bautista Muñoz was the first to name Watlings as the landfall, but without offering an explanation. In 1825, Martín Fernández de Navarrete's first transcription of the Las Casas abstract of the Columbus journal contained a footnote identifying the landfall with Grand Turk Island in the southern part of the archipelago. Two years later, in the first English-language edition of the Navarrete transcription, Samuel Kettell defended the choice of Grand Turk, arguing that it best fit Columbus's description as a flat island surrounded by reefs and with a lake in the center, and further contending that the position of Grand Turk agreed with the course sailed afterward in passing other islands on the way to Cuba. Right or wrong, Kettell's explanation anticipated the approach taken in most future arguments over the question. Trying to match an island with Columbus's physical descriptions and with the bearings and distances traveled afterward toward Cuba—here, Parker writes, were "all of the ingredients of the future landfall controversy."

Even more islands would be proposed: Mayaguana (1864), Samana Cay (1882), Conception (1943), Caicos (1947), Plana Cays (1974), and Egg (1981). But from the middle of the nineteenth century on, it was Watlings Island that attracted the most influential champions. Reviving the idea of Muñoz, A. B. Becher, a captain in the British navy, wrote a book in 1854 on the question and made a case for Watlings that modern scholars find flawed in many respects. In 1884, an American admiral, J. B. Murdock, produced more persuasive arguments for Watlings and laid out the probable San Salvador–to–Cuba course that has many adherents to this day. His contention was that the three islands Columbus reported visiting and naming en route to Cuba are Rum Cay (the one he believes Columbus named Santa María de la Concepción), Long Island (Fernandina), and Crooked and Fortune islands (Isabela). Thacher adopted the Watlings landfall in his major biography of Columbus in the early twentieth century, as did Morison in 1942. Indeed, the magisterial Morison sought to settle the matter once and for all. He asserted that "there is no longer any doubt" that Watlings (which, to emphasize its claim, had been renamed San Salvador in 1926) was the landfall site. "That alone of any island," he writes, fits Columbus's description. And "no other island fits the course laid down in his Journal, if we work it backward from Cuba."

Morison had spoken, and not until the 1980s, soon after his death, did many historians and other experts muster the courage to challenge his judgment. San Salvador (Watlings) it may be, but no one could get away with presuming to say that the puzzle had been solved. The Society for the History of Discoveries reviewed the issue in 1981 at a special symposium, which had the effect of declaring open season on Morison's position. A few scholars scarcely disguised their glee in exposing Morison's occasional errors and flawed assumptions. The National Geographic Society weighed in with a comprehensive five-year study and in 1986 declared that the landfall had occurred at Samana Cay. In the November issue of the society's magazine, Joseph Judge, a senior associate editor who directed the investigation, asserted: "We believe we have solved, after five centuries, one of the grandest of all geographic mysteries."

One approach taken by the society was a new analysis, aided by computer simulations, of the course Columbus followed across the ocean from the Canaries. Such studies have always been fraught with hazards. Although Columbus's journal contained an almost complete daily account of the ships' movements, some errors (either by Columbus himself or in the transcription) are apparent in the record of compass headings and distances traveled. There is disagreement, for instance, about how far south the ships were driven by wind and ocean currents. It is not clear if, or to what degree, Columbus corrected his recorded course to account for this drift. Columbus may have been a great navigator, but from his record only a general course can be plotted for the crossing.

His plan was to sail due west along the twenty-eight-degree parallel. This was the latitude of Gomera, his starting point, and the presumed latitude of his destination, Cipangu, and a most fortunate choice it was. If he had proceeded much to the north, he would have missed the trade winds and, bucking head winds, might have sailed into oblivion, as must have happened to Dulmo and Estreito a few years earlier. His main instrument for maintaining this course was a magnetic compass. The compass gave him his direction, though not without some deviations caused by variations in terrestrial magnetism that were only then beginning to be studied. An inattentive helmsman also could allow a ship to edge off course; Columbus rebuked the helmsman several times on September 9 for straying off the heading. On a few occasions, Columbus seems to have checked his latitude to see if he had been veering to the north or south of the twenty-eighth parallel. As discussed earlier, in the practice of "latitude sailing" of the day this meant observing the height of the North Star to see if it had moved up or down in respect to the horizon; any such change meant a deviation in the course north or south of the chosen latitude. As for longitude, his east-west position, Columbus could only guess. Longitude could not be determined at sea with any precision until the invention of the chronometer in the eighteenth century.

To estimate longitude, the best Columbus could do was to plot his daily progress of distance traveled to the west through a method of navigation known as dead reckoning. This involved determining the ship's direction and speed and thus the distance covered from one point to the next. Time was measured with a thirty-minute sand-glass called the *ampolleta.* A ship's boy had the responsibility of turning the glass each time the sand ran down and announcing the passing of a half-hour with the ring of a bell. Then someone had to estimate speed. Seamen sometimes relied on their intuition, by observing how the vessel slipped through the water, how the waves rippled, and how the sails filled with the wind. Another method was to check the time it took for a floating object, like some flotsam or a wood chip tossed in for this purpose, to travel the length of the ship. At the start of the voyage, a fixed distance was marked along the rails. For estimating speed, a pilot would recite a rhythmical ditty (perhaps repetitions of "*miserere*" or "*mea culpa*") to count the seconds it took for the object to move the distance between the rail marks. Fifty palms, about forty English feet, in thirty-six seconds is one mile per hour, and so forth. From these estimates Columbus plotted his course and recorded in his journal the expedition's progress each day.

With all the possibilities for error, by a sleepy ship's boy, an errant compass, or a pilot whose timing was a shade off, it is not surprising that a reconstruction of the crossing course, as interpreted from Columbus's journal, can lead to any number of possible landfalls. Small errors accumulated and created larger ones of unknowable magnitude.

This brings up another controversial point in the Columbus story. From the outset, it seems, he had sought to allay fears of the crew through his reports of the distance traveled. For the September 9 journal entry, Las Casas stated that the fleet had made fifteen leagues that day and Columbus "decided to report less than those actually traveled so in case the voyage were long the men would not be frightened and lose courage." Subsequent entries include two figures, and the one he told the crew was usually three to seven leagues less than the figure Columbus had arrived at. So, ever since the Las Casas history came to light, a standard element of the Columbus legend has been that the wily explorer had engaged in double-entry bookkeeping, and historians have enjoyed pointing out the irony that the presumably false figures, underestimating progress, had been closer to the true value of the distances than Columbus's private calculations.

But the story is now suspect. Las Casas, in transcribing and summarizing the journal, may have misunderstood what Columbus was up to. James E. Kelley, Jr., an American mathematician and student of navigation, who collaborated with Oliver Dunn in preparing the recent and most definitive English translation of the Columbus log, concluded that the admiral never intended to keep the truth from his crew. Instead, he was recording distances in one kind of league and then relating progress in units of measure the crew could most readily understand.

References to a four-mile league turn up more than a dozen times in the journal, but what kind of miles were they? (Today's statute mile is 5,280 English feet long; a nautical mile is 1.15 times as long.) According to Kelley, Columbus was very likely charting the course in geometric leagues based on four miles of about 4,060 English feet each; the geometric league was a unit of measure common to Italian nautical charts of that period and was probably the measure he grew up with. Columbus then translated this to the Portuguese maritime league, with which the sailors were more familiar, the equivalent of four miles, but with each mile being equal to 4,888 feet.

Insofar as there was any deception, it seems to be more excusable than commonly thought. Concluding his analysis in 1986, Kelley writes: "Quoting his estimates in geometric leagues, which are numerically greater than the equivalent Portuguese maritime leagues, would both mislead and might unduly worry the crew on a long voyage. Eighty kilometers always seems further away than 50 miles, though these distances are equal. Considering the close quarters aboard those ships and the large numbers of people who knew something of the pilot's craft it is hard to see how the Admiral could have sustained a conspiracy even had he intended to."

Columbus did not significantly alter his course until the fifteenth day of the crossing. The fleet jogged to the north, in the face of their first westerly winds. Two days later, Columbus headed west-southwest, following up the first false sighting of land. He continued on a course that fell off slightly to the south the rest of the way. No one can be sure why he abandoned his original due-west heading. But, as Parry writes, this was "crucial for the outcome of the voyage."

If the fleet had stuck to the twenty-eighth parallel, Parry points out that "the first landfall would have been at the northwestern extremity of the chain of the Bahamas, on Eleuthera or Grand Abaco; the route west would have led between these two islands, through the Northeast Providence Channel; and that would have taken them into the Gulf Stream." Once in the power of that current, Parry contends, Columbus "would have returned to Spain without sighting the Greater Antilles and without finding gold, or any sign of gold. That, probably, for some years at least, would have been the end of western ocean exploring."

Looking at it another way, though, the twenty-eight-degree course could have carried him through the Gulf Stream, given Columbus's determination to press forward, and brought him to the Florida coast. He would have raised a mainland, not merely those disappointingly small islands. And it would have been in the vicinity of Cape Canaveral. This would have produced the supreme coincidence of history: Columbus's first arrival in the New World occurring at the very shore where, centuries later, people would make their first departures for other worlds in space.

Humboldt picked up on a reference in the Columbus journal suggesting that the admiral was diverted from his original heading by a flight of land birds he assumed were on their way to a nearby shore. "Never had the flight of birds more important consequences," he writes. "It may be said to have determined the first settlements on the new continent, and its distribution between the Latin and Germanic races."

At least one investigator of the landfall question, Arne B. Molander, an American aerospace engineer, has recently argued that a careful reading of Columbus's account can lead to the conclusion that he stuck closer to the twenty-eighth parallel than others have assumed. If so, then the northern course would have put him near Eleuthera for the landfall. In Molander's judgment, Egg Island, off the northern tip of Eleuthera, could well be the place.

Most studies of the crossing, however, bring the ships to a point at least 180 miles to the south, somewhere in an area about 12,000 miles square in the central Bahamas—room enough, still, to foster dispute. John W. McElroy, an American rear admiral, published in 1941 the results of what seemed at the time the most thorough analysis possible. By examining Columbus's dead-reckoning methods, he determined that the ships came to a point just south of the twenty-third parallel, or nine miles south of Watlings. McElroy's findings provided the underpinning for Morison's staunch advocacy of Watlings as the landfall.

But experts engaged by the *National Geographic* to re-examine the crossing called attention to an astonishing omission in McElroy's study. McElroy had conceded that "no allowance whatsoever is being made . . . for changes in course due to leeway or set of current." Leeway is the slow downwind adrift of a ship. So Luis Marden, a former *National Geographic* editor and an experienced transatlantic sailor, sought to correct the Columbus course to account for currents and leeway. He used detailed information from the best ocean charts about currents and prevailing winds and applied the appropriate adjustments to the day-by-day track. The result was a course that led straight to the Bahamas some sixty miles south of Watlings.

From this and other pieces of evidence the *National Geographic* decided that little Samana Cay was the site. The conclusion revived an idea advanced as long ago as 1882 and seemed to vindicate its author, Gustavus V. Fox, who had been Lincoln's assistant secretary of the navy. His identification of Samana with the landfall had been discounted by other experts, and then was completely ignored. In the vast Columbus literature on the occasion of the 1892 anniversary, one of the few historians to favor Samana Cay was Fiske, and he did so without conviction.

Two scientists from the Woods Hole Oceanographic Institution on Cape Cod, Philip L. Richardson and Roger A. Goldsmith, were quick to point out two flaws in Marden's case. His track, the oceanographers said, produces an end point about 300 miles too far west, farther west than Miami, and past so many islands that it is inconceivable that it could be the true end point. Marden, assuming Columbus had simply overestimated his speed, applied a corrective factor of 10 percent, which makes the end point come out in the right area, on the eastern edge of the Bahamas. McElroy had encountered a similar problem of overrun, presumably because he was using an incorrect length of a league. As for Marden's overestimate, however, Richardson and Goldsmith concluded that it may have been a consequence of the way he read the pilot charts, which gave him inflated current speeds.

By using what they considered to be a more accurate reading of data on prevailing currents, based on their long research in the Atlantic, as well as factoring in winds and magnetic variations affecting compass headings, the Woods Hole scientists made their own plot. They came up with an end point only fifteen miles from Watlings, or San Salvador—with no need for any arbitrary corrections. But Richardson and Goldsmith cautioned that such reconstructions of the crossing course are subject to significant uncertainties. A difference in the heading of only one degree would be enough to shift the track from San Salvador to Samana.

San Salvador or Samana Cay—the debate now seemed to focus on just two of the nine candidates.

A close examination of Columbus's descriptive writing—the second approach to the landfall problem—serves up more clues, but nothing to resolve the issue. Many words in the journal are open to different and sometimes contradictory interpretation. The phrase *camino de* can mean either "the way from" or "the way to." It is impossible to know the distinction Columbus meant in his use of the words *isla* (island), *isleo* (small island), and *isleta* (tiny island). Sometimes passages in the journal, as transcribed by Las Casas, contain erasures, illegible words, and presumably miscopied directions.

Columbus's first words about the landfall, as paraphrased by Las Casas, were of "a small island . . . which was called Guanahani in the language of the Indians." Next, he wrote that the island was quite big *(bien grande),* flat, and without mountains. It had a large lake or lagoon in the middle *(laguna en medio)* and many other waters *(muchas aguas)* elsewhere. The island was green, covered with trees, fruits, and other vegetation. So far, as investigators have pointed out, the description matches Cat Island, Conception Island, Watlings, and several others, including perhaps Samana. One of the most prominent features of Watlings is a large lake in the center.

At least one coast of the island, Columbus said, ran north-northeast, which is true of Watlings and others. In the words of Las Casas, the island had the shape of a bean pod, which has prompted interminable debate over the species of bean and whether Watlings or Grand Turk is the one that looks more like a bean. The island was encircled by a reef, a common Bahamian feature, and had a harbor inside the reef large enough to hold all the ships of Christendom. Columbus could be guilty of hyperbole. He also saw one piece of land "that is made like an island even though it is not"—a peninsula that with two days of work, he said, could be cut off as a separate island for a fortress.

Not much to go on, but the descriptions, taken together, seem to favor Watlings. One difficulty is the reference to the island's flatness. Watlings has more relief than many Bahamian islands, including a prominence that is all of 140 feet high and dignified with the name Mount Kerr. Such an island must have seemed flat, though, to a man like Columbus, who was more familiar with the rugged islands of the Azores and Canaries.

Another piece of evidence seeming to favor Watlings has come from archeologists. Columbus handed out to the Indians "many things of slight value": brass rings, hawk's bells, coins, and green and yellow glass beads. Digging on Watlings, at a site a few hundred feet in from the beach on Long Bay, where Morison locates Columbus's first steps ashore, archeologists have found several glass beads, a copper-alloy coin, and a bronze buckle. The coin was of the type minted in the 1470s. Charles A. Hoffman, an archeologist from Northern Arizona University who directed the excavations in the 1980s, stopped just short of saying the coin and beads proved that Columbus had been there. Caution is advised, because no one can establish whether the artifacts were left by Columbus or brought to the island through subsequent trade with other islanders who had been visited by Spaniards.

After the *National Geographic* study, Judge concluded that Samana conformed to the landfall island in shape, flatness, and its string of small lakes. The configuration of the reefs and harbor, he said, is even more like the place Columbus described. And there is a small peninsula that could be the island that was not an island. But Samana is now uninhabited, and Columbus had found an island heavily populated *(mucha gente).* Experts have contended that Samana is too small, remote, and waterless ever to have supported a settlement of people. When Hoffman moved over to Samana for some digging, however, he found pottery, hearths, and other artifacts at nine places. He concluded that Samana could have been inhabited at the time of the discovery.

On a flight over Samana in 1986, moving along the shore at sixty feet, the approximate height of *Santa María*'s mast, the historian Taviani shook his head many times. The island below did not measure up to Judge's descriptions, not to mention Columbus's. There was no large central lake, and the few ponds did not seem to be the "many waters" of Columbus's report—nothing like the interior lakes at Watlings. Where was the calm harbor capable of holding all the ships in Christendom? Also, Samana runs east-west, not north-northeast. As for the peninsula, Mauricio Obregón, an ardent defender of Morison and the Watlings claim, said: "It would take a bulldozer to separate its 'peninsula' from the main island."

If plots of the ocean crossing and descriptions of the island itself cannot resolve the issue, then the only recourse is to examine more thoroughly the admiral's travels from the landfall to three other islands on his way to Cuba. Columbus gave these islands the names of

Santa María de la Concepción, Fernandina, and Isabela. Since no islands in the area carry these names today, the problem is to figure out which islands correspond by position and description to the places visited. The Columbus journal is somewhat more informative about this issue than about the crossing course and the initial landfall, though there are still problems in interpreting his sailing directions and some references to shore features.

According to the Geographic Society's reconstruction of the track, Santa María de la Concepción is the place now called Crooked Island; Fernandina is the southern end of Long Island; Isabela is Fortune Island. Morison, who sailed the course in a ketch while researching his book, advocated a much different itinerary, and this is the one that, with some modification, continues to be favored by most experts. For them Santa María de la Concepción is Rum Cay; Fernandina, the northern end of Long Island; and Isabela, Crooked Island.

A review of all the intricate arguments pro and con would test the patience of most readers. Suffice it to say, neither of the proposed tracks is without problems. Rum Cay is less than half the size of the Santa María de la Concepción described by Columbus. Several legs of the course from Samana have Columbus virtually backtracking and failing to remark on several landmarks a mariner could hardly ignore.

William Keegan proposes that the key to the puzzle is Isabela, Columbus's last stopover in the Bahamas. A careful reading of the journal, he contends, produces a reasonably complete description of the island—more so than of any of the others. On the morning of October 19, Columbus wrote, the ships reached the island "at a north point where it forms an *isleo* [small island] and a reef of stone outside of it to the north and another between the *isleo* and the big island." This, Keegan says, strongly suggests that Isabela is the horseshoe-shaped cluster consisting of Crooked, Fortune, and Acklins islands. Off the northwestern cape of Crooked Island is a lone promontory known today as Bird Rock. And it is separated from the main island by a reef. Bird Rock could thus be the *isleo* that Columbus had in mind when he named this end of the island Cape of the Small Island. Other descriptions recorded as the ships sailed south along Isabela's western shore also correspond to Crooked Island and its immediate neighbor to the south, Fortune Island.

"All of which is to say that there is virtually complete congruency between Columbus's description of Isabela," Keegan writes, "and the cluster consisting of Crooked, Fortune, and Acklins islands. The *isleo*

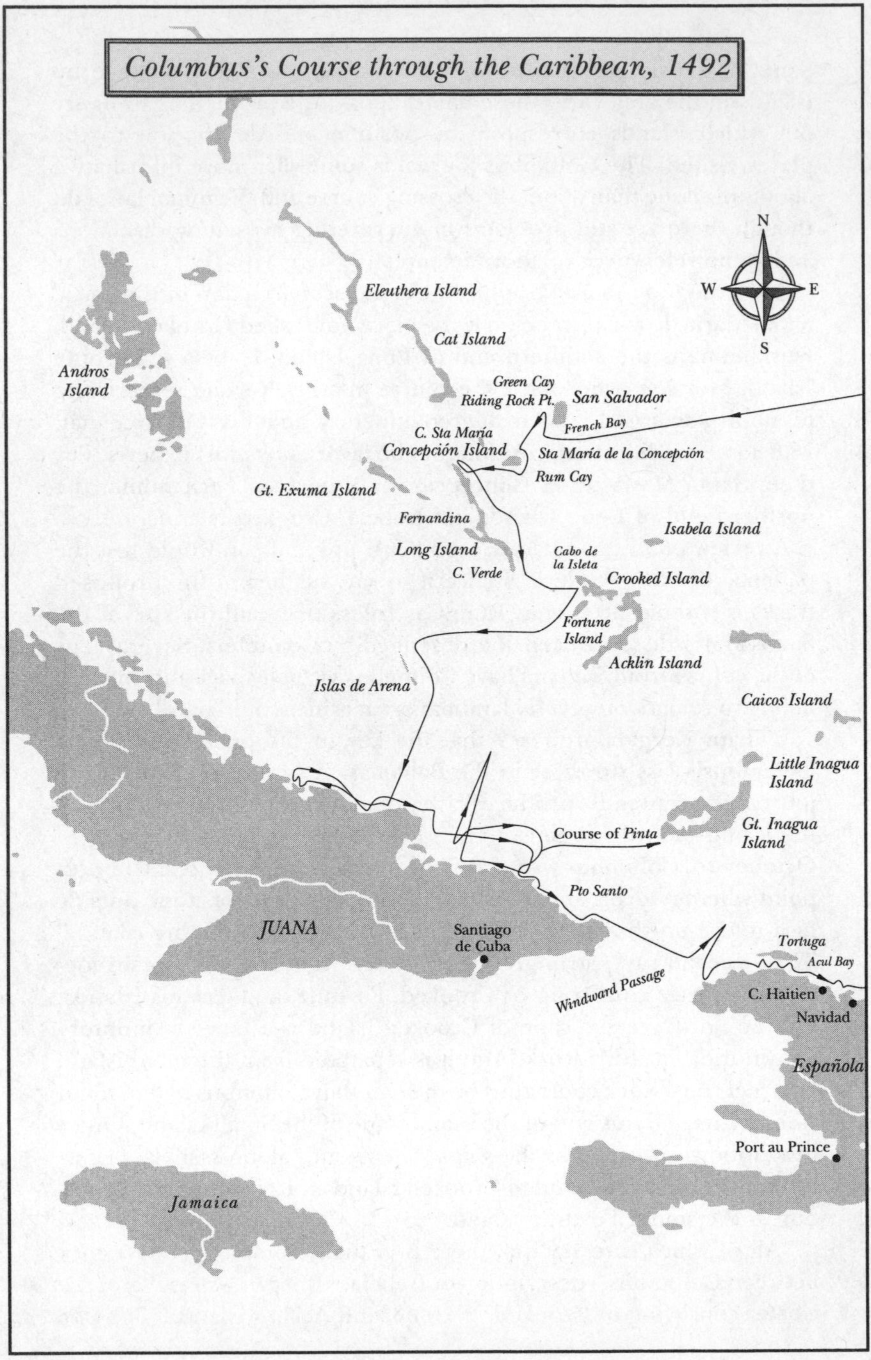

Columbus's Course through the Caribbean, 1492

N
W
E
S
Eleuthera Island
Cat Island
Andros Island
Green Cay
Riding Rock Pt.
San Salvador
French Bay
C. Sta María
Concepción Island
Sta María de la Concepción
Rum Cay
Gt. Exuma Island
Fernandina
Isabela Island
Long Island
Cabo de la Isleta
C. Verde
Crooked Island
Fortune Island
Acklin Island
Islas de Arena
Caicos Island
Little Inagua Island
Course of *Pinta*
Gt. Inagua Island
Pto Santo
JUANA
Santiago de Cuba
Tortuga
Acul Bay
Windward Passage
C. Haitien
Navidad
Española
Port au Prince
Jamaica

of the log . . . is therefore the benchmark by which the locations of San Salvador, Santa María de la Concepción, and Fernandina should be judged. In short, whatever route one proposes for Columbus's passage through the Bahamas, it must bring him within sight of Bird Rock on the morning of October 19."

The proposed track from Samana fails to do this. Such a route would have brought Columbus in sight of Bird Rock on October 15. If so, he made no mention of the prominent feature in the log, which Keegan says is "completely out of character for him." He also finds it implausible that Columbus's first and third landfalls after San Salvador, wherever it was, would be separated by only ten miles—first at Crooked Island, according to the Samana scenario, and then at Fortune. Either the native guides or Columbus, the shrewd navigator, would have recognized the relationship between the two places.

Instead, working backward from Isabela, Keegan traces a course that generally follows the one favored by Morison, the one leading back to Watling–San Salvador. Keegan reports archeological excavations confirming the presence of native villages at sites matching Columbus's descriptions.

The most serious objection to this route centers on the size of Rum Cay. It lies twenty-three miles to the southwest of the initial landfall island, which corresponds to the journal distance of seven leagues. But it is considerably smaller than the estimate, of five leagues by ten leagues, that Columbus gave for the island he named Santa María de la Concepción. This may be another instance of Columbus's tendency to overestimate the size of places. Or, more likely, in abstracting the journal, Las Casas or an earlier scribe confused the terms for "leagues" and "miles."

One other island still has a few persistent partisans: Grand Turk, capital of the Turks and Caicos Islands, a British possession at the extreme southern end of the Bahamas chain. Robert Power, a restaurant owner and respected amateur historian from California, has argued for years that this island, more than any other, fits the description given by Columbus. Grand Turk's North Creek could be the *laguna en medio muy grande.* Hawk's Nest anchorage could be the harbor large enough to hold all the ships in Christendom, and Eve's Hill could be the island that is not an island. The description of the island having the shape of a bean pod, Power says, "fits Grand Turk as comfortably as the Prince's slipper onto Cinderella's foot."

Critics had dismissed the argument for Grand Turk, mainly because no remains had ever been found of fifteenth-century human settlement there. It was thought that the island was too short of fresh water to support pre-Columbian settlement. In 1989, however, Keegan and Maurice Williams, also of the Florida museum, dug up some pottery shards suggesting that there could have been Indians living there at the time of Columbus's arrival. Although Keegan calls the excavations inconclusive and continues to support the San Salvador–Watlings candidacy, Power and leaders of Grand Turk grasped this straw and intensified their campaign for recognition of the island as the historic landfall.

Helen Wallis, former curator of maps at the British Museum, offered encouragement by noting evidence that on the crossing Columbus's ships were driven six degrees of latitude to the south by a westerly magnetic variation of the compass. Because there is no record that Columbus corrected his compass for such variations, Wallis says, his course would have brought him to a landfall in the area of Grand Turk. At the suggestion of Josiah Marvel, an independent scholar living in the Turks and Caicos, Power further contends that Columbus's compass, if made in Seville, would have been precalibrated for 5⅝ degrees easterly variation, which "would have caused the latitude of his landfall to be some 4½ degrees further south than he supposed"—or closer to Grand Turk than to Samana and San Salvador.

"What goes around comes around," Parker remarked in 1990, noting that Navarrete's casual placement of the landfall at Grand Turk had kicked off the endless debate. "Landfall has to be some place. Since every place that's been proposed has some problem, as far as the journal is concerned, no place is a perfect fit, and so it comes down to which has the fewest negatives and the most positives."

In October 1986, several dozen historians and other scholars gathered on the island of San Salvador to exchange research results about Columbus in general and about the landfall problem in particular. The venue may have prejudiced the proceedings. An official of the government of the Bahamas, welcoming the visitors, said: "I hope that most of you agree with me that we are gathered on the real Guanahani, and that your explorations here will put the lie to the elaborate notion from *National Geographic.*" The Bahamians, Judge remarked later, want it to be San Salvador because, with a stone monument already in place, an airstrip, and a few tourist facilities, this island has the potential to draw visitors that Samana Cay lacks. The visiting scholars behaved as considerate guests and, with few exceptions, lent their qualified support to San Salvador as the place where Columbus first landed.

In addition to the more familiar arguments, an early-sixteenth-century map and several historical accounts were introduced as evidence in support of San Salvador over Samana Cay. Obregón pulled out a copy of the map drawn by Juan de la Cosa in 1500 and pointed to the central Bahamas, declaring with relish: "One island is called Guanahani. The other is called Samana. They are not the same island." Though the La Cosa map is one of the best of the early illustrations of the discoveries, experts in cartography caution that all the charts of that period are riddled with inaccuracies. Accordingly, Judge dismisses the evidence, calling attention to the fact that Samana was the old name for Crooked Island. Indian guides sailing with Columbus had identified Crooked Island as a place they called Saometo. The name "Samana," as Jacques W. Redway, an American geographer, wrote in the late nineteenth century, "has been a sort of homeless waif, having several times been transferred" on early maps.

An account of the voyage of Juan Ponce de León from Puerto Rico to his discovery of Florida in 1513 was also cited in behalf of San Salvador. He stopped at an island called Guanahani. His pilot had apparently been with Columbus and must have pointed out to Ponce the importance of the place. The Guanahani mentioned in the account, scholars argued, was more likely to be San Salvador, the former Watlings, than Samana Cay, because one can sail, as Ponce did, in a straight line from San Salvador to Abaco Island without encountering any other of the Bahamian islands. If the route had been from Samana northwest to Abaco, they said, Ponce would have run into San Salvador.

Nearly all the evidence points to Guanahani—Columbus's San Salvador—being in the central Bahamas, which would rule out the candidacies of Egg Island in the north or Grand Turk and the Caicos in the south. That presumably leaves only San Salvador, or Samana. In what may be the only indisputable statement that can be made on the issue, Obregón concedes: "Nobody will ever say the last word on this."

The quest will doubtless continue, for the sake of historical completeness or perhaps merely to satisfy a desire to know that this water here or that sandy beach over there is where two worlds first converged. On a boat trip one afternoon, out in the harbor of San Salvador—supposedly large enough to hold all the ships in Christendom—and headed for the island that is not an island, James Kelley relaxed in the warm sun and gentle breeze. Gazing out on the blue water, he took in the many reasons to return and happily take up again and again the unresolved issue of the Columbus landfall. With a sigh and a smile, he said: "I hope we never find the answer."

10

The Encounter

At daybreak that October morning in 1492, off the island Columbus said was called Guanahani in the language of the inhabitants, the men of the three ships caught their first sight of naked people on shore. Columbus and his captains, with their most trusted functionaries, clambered into armed launches and headed for the sandy beach and green trees. There they exhibited the panoply of their European tribe, or at least all they could muster after more than a month aboard the cramped little ships. Las Casas, in his excerpts of the Columbus journal, tells that the admiral "brought out the royal banner and the captains two flags with the green cross, which the admiral carried on all the ships as a standard, with an F and a Y, and over each letter a crown, one on one side of the ✝ and the other on the other." A solemn Columbus, without so much as a thought that it was anything else but his to take, proclaimed possession of the island "for the king and for the queen his lords." Columbus and his officers then dropped to their knees in prayer.

Soon many people of the island gathered at the beach for a closer look at these strange bearded white men. They had never seen ships so large, or with billowing sails. They had been visited before by people coming in long dugout canoes from the other islands; people like themselves whose intent usually was trade but sometimes invasion. What they saw and heard now, however, was beyond their ken. If they were wary at first, curiosity nudged them forward, and the friendly gestures of the Europeans put them at ease. Columbus offered trinkets. In his journal he wrote: "In order that they would be friendly toward us—because I recognized that they were people who would be better freed [from error] and converted to our Holy Faith by love than by force—to some of them I gave red caps, and glass beads which they put on their chests, and many other things of small value, in which they took so much pleasure and became so much our friends that it was a marvel."

Columbus often made a point of the ulterior motive behind any expression of generosity, as if to gainsay any interpretation that his behavior could be based on careless sentiment. He appraised the island with the eye of a colonist and an exploiter. He sized up the people as converts and workers. But time and again, his descriptions of the people of Guanahani showed Columbus to be enthralled with their appearance, customs, and every movement. His journal entries for those first days in the islands revealed Columbus to be a surprisingly acute observer of people, a better anthropologist perhaps, alert to the unfamiliar, than he was a geographer, a role in which he too often sought in unfamiliar surroundings confirmation of his preconceptions. The paucity of his descriptions of the land and natural resources of the island probably reflected disappointment over what he saw. But he seemed truly astonished by the people living there, so different from Europeans or the subjects of the Great Khan he was seeking.

It could not escape Columbus that the people "go around as naked as their mothers bore them; and the women also." He remarked several times on the features of the people: their broad foreheads, straight legs, handsome bodies, and good faces. "All of them alike are of good-sized stature and carry themselves well," he reported, noting that their only physical defects were the "marks of wounds on their bodies." He observed that they had coarse hair "almost like the tail of a horse." They wore their hair down over their eyebrows and let it grow long down their backs. Their skin coloring, neither black nor white, reminded him of the Canarians. Some of them painted their faces or whole bodies in black or white or red.

Columbus sought to communicate with them by signs. He inquired how the people received the cut marks on their bodies and gathered that they came from fighting invaders. It was his understanding that the enemies came from the mainland to seize prisoners as slaves. "They should be good and intelligent servants," he concluded, "for I see that they say very quickly everything that is said to them; and I believe that they would become Christians very easily, for it seemed to me that they had no religion." Columbus the anthropologist had his priorities.

"They do not carry arms nor are they acquainted with them," Columbus continued in his journal entry for that first day. When he had shown the people some swords, "they took them by the edge and through ignorance cut themselves." They carried javelins that were tipped not with iron but "a fish tooth and . . . other things." Columbus frequently remarked on the harmlessness and docility of the people on this and the other islands he visited in the days ahead.

Later that first day, some of the people swam to the ships' launches with parrots, cotton thread in balls, javelins, and many other things to trade for more of the trifling glass beads and bells. "They took everything and gave of what they had very willingly," Columbus said. At dawn the next day, the people came out to the ships in their dugouts, which Columbus noted were each made from the trunk of a single tree and were so long that one held forty to forty-five men; the West Indian term for them was *canoa*—and so a new word entered European speech. "They row with a paddle like that of a baker and go marvelously," observed Columbus the impressed mariner. "And if it capsizes on them they then throw themselves in the water, and they right and empty it with calabashes that they carry." Again the people brought cotton, parrots, and javelins to trade, and the sight of them moved Columbus to repeat his praise of their handsome features.

Something else Columbus noticed with rising interest. He saw that some of the people had a little piece of gold hanging from a hole pierced in their noses. By signs he inquired about the source of the gold, and they led him to understand that it came from an island to the south where there was "a king who had large vessels of it and had very much gold." On such evidence it has been suggested that these people were not entirely naïve. Seeing that the white men were covetous of gold, and might not leave until they knew where to find it, the people said, in effect, for them to try the next island. And so Columbus did, leaving on the third day.

But Columbus had remained long enough to be touched by the people of Guanahani. They were gentle and friendly. They were poor, too, as he adduced, and generous. "It seemed to me that they were a people poor in everything," he wrote. "They gave everything for anything that was given to them."

The experience of the encounter seemed, if anything, to inspire even more wonder among the islanders. At least this was Columbus's impression—and there is no other impression on record. The people brought water and food to the Europeans. They would swim out to the ships and ask, as Columbus understood them, "if we had come from the heavens." Some of them, he reported, called in loud voices to the others: "Come see the men who came from the heavens. Bring them something to eat and drink." Some even threw themselves to the ground and raised their hands to the sky.

Columbus was pleased with this reception, and probably relieved. Only the appearance of the Great Khan, bearing gold and precious stones, could have been more to his liking. But he grew restless. Not for anthropology had he sailed across the ocean, and increasingly his journal entries reflected an interest less in the people as they were than in what they and their land could mean for Spain. He made an estimate of how many ships the harbor could shelter and where a fort might be built. He remarked again on the people's innocence of modern weaponry, and his thoughts ran to conquest. "Whenever Your Highnesses may command," he wrote, "all of them can be taken to Castile or held captive in this same island; because with 50 men all of them could be held in subjection and can be made to do whatever one might wish."

Sailing away from Guanahani, Columbus was accompanied by seven of the islanders "that I caused to be taken in order to carry them away to [Your Highnesses] and to learn our language and to return them." They were not volunteers.

This was the moment of discovery, as recorded by Columbus, communicated to us by Las Casas, and etched in our memories as schoolchildren. This was, from a historical perspective that has long prevailed, the discovery of America. To say without qualification that Columbus discovered America, however, is to accept the Eurocentric view and ignore reality. The Norse had reached its northern shores several centuries before. Perhaps the Polynesians and Chinese, the Phoenicians and Africans had made it to America, too. But their deeds left no imprint on America, and the American experience had no impact in their own societies; as we have seen, theirs were not true discoveries. The same cannot be said of the ancestors of the people Columbus first encountered and called Indians. They were the original discoverers of America.

Accordingly, John H. Parry's interpretation is the more cosmopolitan view of what happened in 1492. "Columbus did not discover a new world," he writes; "he established contact between two worlds, both already old." Columbus thus set in motion the forces that brought about the reunion of separate strands of the human race and the virtual reuniting of the continents.

Historians can take this more global view now because of recent advances in geophysics, archeology, and paleoanthropology.

Once the lands of the world were joined in one supercontinent, Pangaea. With its disintegration more than 200 million years ago, the continents began drifting their separate ways, first as two landmasses, Laurasia in the north and Gondwanaland in the south, and finally as the fragments that approximated the shapes of today's continents. The oceans widened between them, creating barriers to the spread of life except by land bridges between Europe and America, for a time, and America and Asia, up until about 14,000 years ago. The dinosaurs had managed to radiate freely across the deconstructing landmasses, but with their extinction some sixty-five million years ago, life isolated on the separate continents increasingly evolved in its own peculiar ways, especially in Australia and the Americas.

A clever descendant of the apes emerged on the plains of Africa some three million years ago, and its own descendants would know no bounds, continental or oceanic. Through the endless processes of extinction and survival, adaptation and evolution, the australopithecines developed into walking, tool-making, large-brained *Homo habilis* and then *Homo erectus.* Africa was no longer big enough for these human ancestors. By at least one million years ago, out of necessity and perhaps curiosity, *Homo erectus* set off on a slow migration that took them north. Crossing the connecting lands of the Middle East, these creatures fanned out in opposite directions, into Europe and across Asia.

What eventually happened to these separate strands of prehumanity is not clear. Either they evolved into *Homo sapiens,* modern humans, in place—in Asia, in Europe, and also back in Africa—or their cohorts who remained in Africa took the fateful evolutionary step alone (the African Eve hypothesis) and there followed a second migration into Europe and Asia, perhaps around 100,000 years ago. The *Homo sapiens* then supplanted the vestigial *Homo erectus* communities. Either scenario is, of course, more complicated and controversial than presented here; issues in early human studies, as with Columbus, invariably are. But there is no dispute over the consequence. Two branches of migrating humans found themselves at opposite ends of the Eurasian landmass.

The Cro-Magnon humans, Ice Age hunters whose artistry on the cave walls of France and Spain has dazzled archeologists and been hailed as the first flowering of human creativity some 30,000 years ago, were the ancestors of the Europeans who would leap the ocean barrier to the west. The equally intelligent and adaptive *Homo sapiens* who hunted the woolly mammoth and caribou in Siberia were ancestors of the people who found their way east to America. And the *Homo sapiens* who had never left Africa would soon after 1492 be unwilling migrants to the same new world.

How and especially when people from northeastern Asia first entered—discovered—America is one of the more intractable problems in archeology. The general assumption is that they came across in the last Ice Age, when much of Europe, Siberia, and northern North America were covered by massive sheets of ice. With so much water locked up in ice, sea levels plunged more than 300 feet, exposing the sea floor between Siberia and Alaska, where the Bering Sea is now, and creating a dry connecting plain at least 1,000 miles wide. This connecting plain is known as Beringia, or the Bering land bridge, and was the presumed site of the first American discoveries.

For a long time after 1492, Europeans had no knowledge of this, of course. Their theories about the people of America stemmed from the Bible and the classics. Perhaps these were descendants of the lost tribes of Israel, an idea that in the nineteenth century became a central part of the Book of Mormon. Another theory, proposed by Oviedo and adopted by others, was derived from the Greek legend of the lost continent of Atlantis. Perhaps this continent had once stretched from Iberia to America as a route of migrations. José de Acosta, a Jesuit missionary among the Indians of Mexico and Peru, came remarkably close to the truth a century and a half before the Bering Strait appeared on world maps. In 1589, he theorized that small groups of "savage hunters driven from their homelands by starvation or some other hardship" had come overland through Asia and then across "short stretches of navigation." (The perceptive Acosta also speculated that people might wish to open a canal in Panama to join the two oceans, though he doubted the project's feasibility and disapproved of anyone's "wanting to correct the work which God, so wisely and providentially, ordered in making the Universe.") Not until 1856 did the Bering migration scenario enter serious scientific discourse. Samuel Haven, librarian of the American Antiquarian Society, assessed the mounting evidence about the origins of North American Indians and concluded that "All their characteristic affinities are found in the early conditions of Asiatic races." It seemed safe to say that the first Americans had come across the Bering Strait.

They presumably were hunters, wrapped in animal skins and carrying spears, who were pursuing their prey across the tundra. Word got back of the new hunting grounds, and many others followed, in small groups and then in successive waves of migration. New interpretations of archeological and geological findings, however, have led some scientists to offer an alternative hypothesis that many, if not all, of the first Americans were not primarily big-game hunters but a maritime people. Evidence from fossilized pollen shows that the land bridge might have been too bitterly cold for the vegetation that would attract large animals. Artifacts uncovered in recent years have revealed that a relatively advanced seagoing people inhabited the coasts of Siberia and Alaska in prehistoric times. A few scholars have thus suggested that the migrants came along the more hospitable southern coast of Beringia, not across the interior tundra, or even crossed in skin boats. But most scientists continue to hold to the game-hunter hypothesis.

Archeologists are more sharply divided over when the migration occurred: whether it came as much as 50,000 years ago, or no more than 15,000 years ago. Geologists believe the land bridge disappeared about 14,000 years ago, when the massive glaciers melted and released a tremendous volume of water, raising sea levels and cutting off easy access to America. For much of this century, the earliest firmly documented evidence, finely worked stone spear-points first collected near Clovis, New Mexico, put the human presence in North America at 11,500 years ago. Clovis-like points were soon discovered elsewhere, indicating to archeologists that the technology—and humans—had spread to the southern tip of South America in only a few centuries.

But the Clovis hunters were almost certainly not the first Americans. Recent digs have produced traces of people in North America at least 4,500 years earlier, at the Meadowcroft Rockshelter in Pennsylvania, and in South America 1,500 years earlier, at Monte Verde in Chile. After much resistance, archeologists now believe these dates are firmly documented, and are beginning to suspect that even earlier ones will be established. Digging deeper at the Monte Verde site, Tom D. Dillehay, an anthropologist at the University of Kentucky, has found modified stones and charcoal dated at 33,000 years. In 1986, French and Brazilian archeologists reported an even more astonishing discovery. The leader of the expedition, Niède Guidon of the Institute of Advanced Social Science Studies in Paris, described rock shelters at the Pedra Furada site in Brazil that may have been occupied by humans at least 32,000 years ago; subsequent investigation, she said, established occupation at least 10,000 years earlier than that. The shelters also contained rock with red painted lines, revealing that, as Guidon said, Americans were expressing themselves in cave art about the same time as their European, Asian, African, and Australian relatives.

Although the Brazilian findings have yet to be accepted by most archeologists, the accumulating evidence has both challenged and confused thinking about the first Americans. If humans were in South America that early, where was the evidence that they had been in North America as early or earlier? They had to have been, if there is any truth to the Beringia hypothesis. Otherwise, archeologists might have no choice but to revive the generally discredited idea, espoused most recently by Thor Heyerdahl, the Norweigian explorer, that the first humans came from across the Pacific by boats, landing in South America and then moving north. But the prehistoric Polynesians, though accomplished navigators, apparently did not occupy any of the Pacific islands east of the Solomons until about 3,500 years ago. It is equally doubtful, according to skeptics of the transoceanic hypothesis, to conceive of people from Australia, occupied by humans for at least 50,000 years, reaching the Americas by way of Antarctica.

At this stage, scientists are left to assume that the remains of the very first people in North America, predating the Clovis hunters by thousands of years, have been obliterated by the glaciers or else have eluded the archeological spades. For other lines of research tend to support the Beringia hypothesis.

Studies of blood, language, and teeth suggest a direct link between the early Americans and Asians from North China and northeastern Siberia. Christy G. Turner II, an anthropologist at Arizona State University, has examined the teeth from skeletons of 9,000 pre-Columbian American Indians, Aleuts, and Eskimos. From this he concluded that the founding American people must have come from North China 20,000 years ago, probably in three waves of migrations of different but related people. Judging from the teeth, he said, the Aleuts and Eskimos must have descended from people who migrated directly from China along the southern rim of the land bridge. Indians of the American Northwest, a linguistic group known as Na-dene, probably sprang from people who traveled from the Siberian forest through the interior of the land bridge. The rest of the American

Indians probably descended from game hunters who moved across the northern edge of Beringia. Some linguists see evidence for a tripartite migration in the native-American languages. In a controversial analysis, Joseph H. Greenberg, a linguist at Stanford University, has concluded that the 1,500 or so native-American languages can be classified as belonging to one of three linguistic families: Eskimo-Aleut, Na-dene, and Amerind. Each group, he has postulated, represents a different wave of migration. Many other scholars, however, doubt that languages afford a reliable means of exploring the roots and timing of American migrations.

Beyond question, though, humans inhabited the Americas, from north to south, many thousands of years before Columbus. They were the ones who discovered the two continents and pioneered human life there.

If they came as hunters and gatherers, or fishermen, they eventually learned to domesticate American plants and sustain growing populations. Except for some possible commerce across the Bering Strait, they lived in isolation from the rest of the world. Yet, in Mexico, Central America, and the Andes, they developed civilizations that manifested considerable social, economic, and astronomical sophistication and left a legacy of soaring architecture. Their circumstances of isolation, with less human interaction and fewer ecological challenges, presumably accounted for the slower advancement of the most magnificent American cultures, compared with those in Europe and the Middle East. As William H. McNeill, professor emeritus of history at the University of Chicago, has said, the Aztec, Maya, and Inca civilizations had reached a level that resembled what the Old World civilizations had been like about in 1500 B.C., at the time of the Babylonian ascendancy and a full 3,000 years before Columbus crossed the ocean.

The archipelago where Columbus landed, today's Bahamas, was apparently among the last places in America to be settled permanently. The people he encountered on Guanahani stemmed from migrants who began moving into the Caribbean from the northeastern coast of South America shortly before the birth of Christ. As far as scholars can determine, mostly from ethnographic and archeological research in this century, nearly all of the islands of the Caribbean and Bahamas were colonized by people speaking the same Arawak language. These were the Tainos, a name meaning "good and noble people" that was bestowed on them posthumously by nineteenth-century scholars. Finding that the people lacked an overall name for themselves, Irving Rouse, an anthropologist at Yale University, recounts, the scholars adopted Taino from an adjective that the natives used to explain to the Spanish how they differed favorably from the Caribs to the south.

The classic Tainos of Hispaniola and eastern Cuba practiced manioc agriculture, harvested the shore waters, and apparently were wide-ranging traders. A more primitive group, the Guanajatabey, or Ciboney, may have lived in western Cuba in a pre-ceramic, non-agricultural society. William Keegan of the Florida Museum doubts that the Ciboney culture survived to the time of Columbus or ever existed, except in the Spanish accounts and the minds of ethnographers. To the south, in the Lesser Antilles, lived the Island Caribs, or Cariban, who also spoke a form of Arawak. The Spanish, hearing the Tainos tell of invaders from the south, attributed to the Caribs a bellicose behavior that ran to the practice of eating the flesh of their captives. Our word "cannibal" is thought to be a corruption of "Carib."

By some accounts, Tainos seeking refuge from marauding Caribs moved north into the Bahamas, beginning around the year 800. More than likely, they had visited the islands first to collect salt and dried conch and then, for whatever reasons, began to settle there. The population of the Bahamas grew steadily and by the arrival of Columbus may have numbered 20,000 to 40,000 Tainos, who are classified as Island Tainos or Lucayans.

Richard Rose, an anthropologist formerly with the Rochester Museum and Science Center, has for years conducted systematic excavations at the Pigeon Creek site on San Salvador, where the landfall is widely believed to have occurred. The site appears to be the largest Lucayan settlement ever found. Situated on a long dune ridge, it was occupied as early as 1100 and probably was still a community when Columbus appeared; so it could have been one of the villages of twelve to fifteen houses he reported seeing on Guanahani. From the excavated ruins Rose has found evidence for a chieftain's residence and a row of small houses built side by side along the crest of the ridge overlooking an estuary. In the hard-packed sand that constituted the floors of the houses, archeologists uncovered fish bones, fragments of charcoal, bird-bone needles, dart points of shell and bone, and pieces of pottery. Like other Tainos, the Lucayans lived on fish, conch, birds, corn, and cassava bread made from the bitter manioc root. They kept a "pepperpot" stew simmering on the fire for days, and also roasted meat by the method known today by the Arawak word *barbeque.*

A limestone sculpture found in a Pigeon Creek midden, Rose reports, "gives us a rare glimpse into Lucayan ritual and belief." Carved in the likeness of a parrot fish, it is probably the image of a zemi, which was the principal symbol of the Taino religion. Zemis were natural spirits or deities represented as idols of stone, wood, or clay and even painted on the body. Zemiism was seen as the personification of spiritual power achieved with the aid of supernatural forces represented as idols. It was an integral part of the Lucayan culture that Columbus overlooked when he visited and professed to find no sign of a religion.

The Lucayans were also experienced traders. Archeologists digging in the Bahamas have found numerous non-local artifacts, such as quartz-tempered pottery, stone axes, polished stone pestles, and quartz beads. X-ray analysis of a piece of jade from Pigeon Creek indicates that it came from as far away as either Guatemala or Nicaragua. No wonder the people of Guanahani so readily exchanged parrots and skeins of cotton for the Europeans' trinkets. Trading was what they did with visitors.

From archeological research, Rose concludes, the Lucayan culture was seen to be not as impoverished as Columbus judged it in his journal. "To the contrary," he affirms, "the Lucayans lived in a region of abundant food resources, enjoyed social and economic relationships with other peoples of the Caribbean, and had developed a level of technology that was particularly well adapted to a carbonate island ecology. It appears that the Lucayan lifestyle was enhanced by their participation in an economic interaction sphere that included many islands in the northern Caribbean."

These were the people whom fate decreed to be on the island intersected by three ships from Spain, bringing face to face branches of humanity unknown to each other.

As the history of war is said to be written by the victor, the history of exploration is almost always told by the explorer rather than those explored. How the Tainos reacted to these white strangers comes to us through a wholly European perspective. Columbus said they were friendly and generous and believed the Europeans were men come from heaven. But their first impressions and their thoughts on reflection will never be known, and so the history of this critical human encounter is forever incomplete. The Tainos, like most discovered people, could not put their feelings into writing. The only possible way for their story of the discovery to have entered history would be through folk art and oral accounts passed down through generations. But their story died with them, for the Lucayans and most Tainos became extinct in less than a generation.

Scholars have sought clues to the Taino view of the encounter by examining the meager record left later by other Indians. Wampum belts, smoking pipes, effigy combs, and other crafts sometimes bear depictions of the first Europeans seen by North American Indians of the seventeenth century.

In his 1988 book, *After Columbus: Essays in the Ethnohistory of Colonial North America,* James Axtell relates stories of the first impressions some French explorers made on Indians in the St. Lawrence valley. In 1633, a young Montagnais recalled his grandmother's saying that they thought the big French ship was a "moving island." The French must have been upset to learn what Indians thought of their cuisine. When they were offered a barrel of the ship's biscuits and some red wine, the Indians were appalled to see that these people "drank blood and ate wood." The Micmacs in the Gaspé peninsula mistook some French bread for "a piece of birch tinder." Others also remarked on the white-faced men with beards who drank blood "without repugnance" and carried thunder tubes and came in giant winged canoes. Some oral histories suggest that many Indians took the Europeans' ability to make guns and metal knives as evidence of a superior spiritual power.

How accurate are these handed-down mental images? "When people aren't literate, they tend to have tenacious memories," says Axtell, an ethnohistorian at William and Mary College. "Maybe it isn't always very accurate history or geography, but oral testimony is as good as gold in conveying the emotional resonance of these first encounters."

If discovered people, the Tainos or any others, could have left a record of the encounter, it might reveal that at first the event seemed of much less importance to them than it was to the discoverers. The people of Enewetok in the Marshall Islands, for instance, seem to have no stories in their oral tradition of any early European visitors. After all, the discovered people knew they were there all along and, after the brief incursion of a few strangers, were left in familiar surroundings with no intimation that their society was about to change forever or, in the case of the Tainos, crash. Those discovered, moreover, were not the ones challenging the unknown at great risk in search of something, prepared for the unexpected and eager to proclaim its discovery. Inevitably, then, the story of discovery is initially told from the discoverer's point of view.

It should not be surprising that the first characteristic of the Tainos to strike Columbus was their nakedness. Culture shock, not prurience, is the most likely explanation. Their lack of clothing was the most conspicuous cultural feature setting these people apart from Europeans, or the Asians he had hoped to find. From the moment of landfall, Tzvetan Todorov, a modern French writer and literary critic ("My main interest is less an historian's than a moralist's"), has suggested, the absence of apparel influenced Columbus's entire thinking about the Indians. To him clothes symbolized culture. These naked people must be deprived of culture. So, without any particular inquiry, Columbus allowed himself to generalize that these people were lacking in customs, rites, and religion.

His other immediate reaction betrayed him as an explorer who was not prepared to be surprised. By a stretch of genealogical reckoning, Columbus was closer to the truth in calling these people Indians than he or anyone else could have appreciated: these Indians were descendants of Asians. But Columbus knew nothing of this. He chose the name because he wanted to believe he had reached Asia. He had grown up in a world everyone believed to consist of three continents, and since he had crossed the ocean, he must have reached the fringes of Asia. He was an inspired mariner, but an orthodox thinker.

And he was a man with a purpose. Although his initial attention to anthropological detail was an expression of astonishment, he overcame it as he got down to the business he had come for: seeking gold, locating the Asian mainland and the Great Khan, and converting these lost souls to the European God. His interest in discovering the Americans diminished with each island encounter. His assessment of them as poor reflected his European conception of wealth, a common approach of explorers and those who follow to capitalize on explorations. Columbus was not inclined to give reunion a chance, even if he could have viewed his accomplishment in such a light.

The Lucayans, the naked people who came to the shore to meet

Columbus, were even less prepared by heritage for the encounter. They had lived on their little islands innocent of a world as large even as the constricted one known then to Europeans. All the foreigners they had ever traded with or fought were much like themselves. They also lacked the means and motivation to go off seeking more distant worlds. Of more immediate and ultimately terminal importance, their bodies, which Columbus described as erect and well formed, lacked the inherited resistance to most diseases that come from living in more crowded populations. Nor did they have the knowledge, such as it was in the fifteenth century, to treat those illnesses. Nothing in the very first encounters, all in all harmonious, could have been seen by the Tainos as an omen of their impending doom. Yet the kiss of the European, even his breath, would afflict them. Their zemis could not save them. They were the unwitting victims of the reunion they never understood, eradicated by European disease. In the somber if hyperbolic words of Las Casas, to sail to the Lucayan islands one needed only to follow the floating corpses of Indians that marked the way.

11

The Foreshadowing

The first extended contact between Europeans and these New World cultures occurred at a place Columbus named La Villa de la Navidad, honoring the birth of Jesus, who had preached the Golden Rule of doing unto others as you would have them do unto you. The experience at La Navidad did not bode well for the Spanish, and especially the "others," or for the future.

Columbus had sailed from Cuba across the Windward Passage. He was stubbornly looking elsewhere for what Cuba had not been: the Asian mainland. In a month of exploration, he had given Cuba every benefit of the doubt. After the unprepossessing islands of the Bahamas, the shores of Cuba seemed to stretch on and on, suggesting a substantial land that he wanted to believe was a peninsula of Cathay. The single-minded Columbus tended to see what he wished to see and, as became apparent in Cuba, to hear what he wished to hear. John V. Fleming, a medieval scholar at Princeton University and an expert on Columbian iconography and philology, has said: "Columbus worked within a closed semiotic system; the signals he put in determined the signals he could take out."

Communications between Columbus and the Indians must have been imperfect, the story of people with tails being a case in point. Columbus or his men probably asked the Indians if they had ever seen any monstrous people. What better confirmation of his arrival in the Indies than to catch sight of some of the monstrous races straight out of the pages of Sir John Mandeville? Writing in French in the middle of the fourteenth century, this unknown writer—Mandeville is a *nom de plume*—borrowed from ancient and medieval accounts in telling of travels to the marvelous East, where there were men with no heads but eyes on their shoulders, men with heads of dogs and feet of horses, and men with ears so long the flaps covered their entire bodies, making clothing unnecessary. When the Indians were asked if they had ever seen men with tails, as Mandeville had also reported, the Indians, probably thinking they were talking about monkeys, nodded in the affirmative. The story of an island inhabited only by women seems to be another example of miscommunication. Columbus may have asked about the islands Masculina and Feminea that Marco Polo said lay in the Indian Ocean. Either the Indians misunderstood the questions or had a similar myth, but they led Columbus to believe in an island of Amazon-like women called Martremonio or Matinino.

From his knowledge of Mandeville and Marco Polo, Columbus expected to encounter strange creatures. What he found instead were other humans who differed from Europeans but were less exotic than the black Africans he had seen on his Portuguese voyages and at the docks of Lisbon. Perhaps these poor, simple islanders could point him to the creatures who were part of the Asia of his expectations.

Time and again, Columbus interpreted native words for certain places as mispronunciations of places in Cathay as described and named by Marco Polo. Las Casas gives an explanation of how Columbus was thus deluded and misled. Cubanacan, an Arawak name for a region in the interior of Cuba where gold could be found, became for Columbus El Gran Can. He had himself believing that he was definitely within a march of the seat of the Great Khan, the emperor of Cathay.

With eager heart, Columbus dispatched emissaries to the Great Khan. Luis de Torres, the expedition's interpreter, headed the delegation and carried a Latin passport, a letter from Ferdinand and Isabella, and a royal gift. Traveling inland, they saw strange trees and fragrant flowers, came upon "dogs that did not bark," and finally reached a settlement of fifty huts. They were received with hospitality by naked people who would feel the visitors' hands and feet, Columbus wrote, "attempting to see if they were, like themselves, of flesh and bone." The curiosity of the Spanish visitors ran more to what the Indians might know of gold, spices, and an imperial city—which was nothing at all. The emissaries returned to Columbus with more disappointing news.

They did make one discovery that would have enduring social and economic implications. In the interior, as Columbus recorded in his journal, the emissaries saw "many people going back and forth between their villages, men and women with a firebrand of weeds in their hands to take in the fragrant smoke to which they are accustomed." The Tainos called these rolled cigars *tobacos.* They lighted them at one end and sucked on the other end or inserted them in a nostril to inhale the smoke. Thus Europeans discovered tobacco, which, as Mauricio Obregón has observed, was "as valuable as gold, and perhaps as harmful."

Away from Cuba and across the Windward Passage, Columbus sensed his prospects brightening. The "grandeur and beauty" of the large island he raised next so reminded him of Spain that he named it La Isla Española. Peter Martyr Latinized the name to Hispaniola, by which it is known today—an island that came to be shared by Spain and France and is now divided between the Dominican Republic and Haiti.

Cruising along the northern coast of what is now Haiti, going ashore here and there, Columbus was impressed by the fertile land and the populations denser than he had previously encountered. The people, also Arawak-speaking Tainos, seemed to have evolved a more diverse economy than anything on other islands, some form of organized religion, and in general a more sophisticated culture. Their villages were larger and governed by caciques, or chiefs, whose dignified bearing reinforced Columbus in his belief that these people were superior to the other Tainos. Of course, he was even more impressed by finding gold ornaments to be more plentiful on this island. Asked where the gold came from, the people told of a mountainous region in the interior known as Cybao. To Columbus this sounded enough like Cipangu to loft his expectations again. Likewise, when he heard of the notorious Caribs living on a nearby land called Caritaba, Columbus, as we have seen, took them to be soldiers of El Gran Can.

The capture of a "very young and pretty woman" enabled Columbus to make contact with the Taino leaders. He ordered her clothed and, as he said, "returned her to land very courteously." The woman showed her escorts where her village was, and her favorable report allayed the fears the people must have had of these white strangers. In a short while, Tainos in great numbers paddled canoes and swam out to the ships with gifts of food and scraps of gold. A young chief was received on board with much ceremony. On December 22, the Spaniards, through messengers, made contact with Guacanagarí, the first chief they would encounter whose dominion extended over many lesser chiefs and encompassed a wide region. The chief invited Columbus to visit him at his residence in a large town a few miles east of present-day Cap Haïtien. Arrangements were made for a meeting on Christmas Day.

At daybreak on December 24, Columbus weighed anchor in Acul Bay and in the light wind and contrary current made slow progress east. Only *Santa María* and *Niña* were together at this time, Martín Pinzón having gone off in *Pinta* on his own search for gold. The two ships passed the promontory that would be known as Cap Haïtien. They were headed for the only major accident of the voyage, which set in motion a train of events leading to the creation of the first European settlement in the New World—excepting presumably the short-lived Norse venture in Vinland.

Shortly before midnight on Christmas Eve, everyone aboard *Santa María* save the gromet, one ship's boy, was fast asleep. Columbus had retired after the change of watch at 11:00 p.m. He had had no rest for two days and a night, what with all the commotion over the visiting Tainos. A few minutes later, for the same reason, the officer of the watch also decided to get some sleep. Left alone at the tiller was the one boy, who could not have been wide awake himself. The new moon cast little light. The sea was calm. Suddenly the boy felt the rudder scrape and catch on the bottom. As Columbus wrote, it "pleased Our Lord" that the current had carried *Santa María* onto a shallow coral reef.

Seeing that his flagship was hopelessly stranded, Columbus sent men in a boat to inform Guacanagarí, whose town he knew to be only a league and a half away (approximately four miles). The chief proved to be a friend in their need. Upon hearing of the grounding, he is said to have cried and sent his people out in their long canoes to help unload the stricken ship.

Columbus decided that he had little choice—all the men could not possibly return to Spain on the two remaining ships—but to establish a garrison here among these friendly Tainos. If, as he believed, the accident was the work of God, it must be God's will that a fort should be built here. He was further persuaded by the stories he heard the chief tell about "gold in Cipangu, which they call Cybao, in such degree that they hold it in no regard."

Over the next few days, the men stripped timbers, boards, and nails from the ship and erected a tower and fort at the Taino town. Many of the men vied for the opportunity to stay behind, and thirty-nine or forty were selected, including a caulker, carpenter, tailor, gunner, and cooper. Diego de Arana, the cousin of Columbus's mistress, was put in charge. Torres, the interpreter, and Rodrigo de Escobedo, the secretary, also remained. The company was supplied with bread and wine for more than a year, the ship's launch, and seed for sowing. They were instructed to trade for gold and await a return voyage within the year.

"Everything has worked out opportunely for this beginning to be made," Columbus wrote. After christening the outpost La Navidad, because the wreck had occurred on Christmas Eve, he ordered a show of force to impress the chief with Spanish power. A bombard was fired, sending a barrage of shot into the remains of *Santa María.* Columbus said that he did this "so that the cacique would consider as friends the Christians that [I] was leaving and, by making him afraid, make him fear them." Equating friendship and fear must not have seemed contradictory to him. Finally, in early January, Columbus sailed off in the *Niña* and a few days later rejoined the *Pinta* off the coast to the east.

Why did Columbus decide, as recorded in his journal entry for January 8, to return to Spain "with the greatest speed possible"? Pinzón had told him of finding large amounts of gold, some of the pieces being "larger than beans." Columbus may have feared that Pinzón would make even more such discoveries and be able to return with boasts that he, not Columbus, had enriched the Spanish crown. There was bad blood between the two, and the sooner Columbus could get home, he reasoned, the sooner he could "leave such bad company." Strained relations with companions and lieutenants would cause even greater problems for Columbus on his future voyages.

The two ships made one final stop, at a bay 200 miles east of La Navidad. The Spaniards who went ashore came upon some Tainos wearing plumes of parrot feathers and carrying bows and arrows. After bartering two of the bows, the Tainos refused to give the Spaniards any more. They ran away. When they came back with cords, either to trade in the place of bows or to tie up the Spaniards, as was feared, the Spaniards attacked. They gave one Taino a slashing blow on the buttocks with a sword. They wounded another in the chest with a crossbow shot. The Tainos took flight.

This first known skirmish between these Europeans and the people of the New World occurred January 13, 1493. Columbus named the place the Golfo de las Flechas, the Gulf of Arrows. Robert Fuson has identified the site as Puerto Rincón, on the northeastern coast of the Dominican Republic. Others believe it was more likely at a bay known as Bahía de Samaná, nearby.

Columbus professed to be satisfied with the results of the encounter. This is his journal entry, as paraphrased by Las Casas: "He was pleased because now the Indians would fear the Christians, since without doubt the people there, he says, are evildoers and he believed they were people from Carib and that they would eat men."

Thus ended Columbus's first visit to the lands he had "discovered."

As promised, Columbus returned to La Navidad on his second voyage, anchoring off the coast on the night of November 27, 1493. The seamen lighted flares and fired cannon. They heard no response. Presently, a canoe approached one of the ships. The Indians at first assured Columbus that all was well at La Navidad, except for some sickness and a few deaths. Then the whole truth came out. The next morning, a landing party went ashore, walked inland, and came upon a scene of desolation. Both the European garrison and the surrounding Taino town had been burned to the ground. Later, Columbus inspected the ruins with the fleet physician, Diego Álvarez Chanca, who reported that they also visited a small village of huts and saw pieces of Spanish clothing and the *Santa María* anchor. They eventually came upon the bodies of seven or eight of the former shipmates buried near the fortress and three others in a field nearby.

The Spaniards finally got the brother of Guacanagarí and other people to give an account of what had happened. According to Las Casas, the Tainos said that the men left at La Navidad had been wiped out by warriors of a neighboring cacique who was called Caonabó. The men of the garrison had probably brought their fate on themselves. Who is to say what their lust for gold and women might have done to provoke the docile Tainos or turn the Spaniards against each other? It was said that soon after Columbus's departure the men had begun to quarrel and fight with knives and swords. They split into rival gangs, living apart with as many as five women each and striking out separately on raiding parties inland. In the land of Caonabó, where the gold mines were supposed to be, eleven of the marauding Spaniards met violent deaths. After many days, Caonabó appeared with his men and torched La Navidad. The six Spaniards who were still there fled to the sea and drowned. Guacanagarí was reported to have been seriously wounded trying to protect the Spaniards. Columbus seems to have accepted this account, owing perhaps to the chief's previous friendship and not wishing to alienate a potential ally.

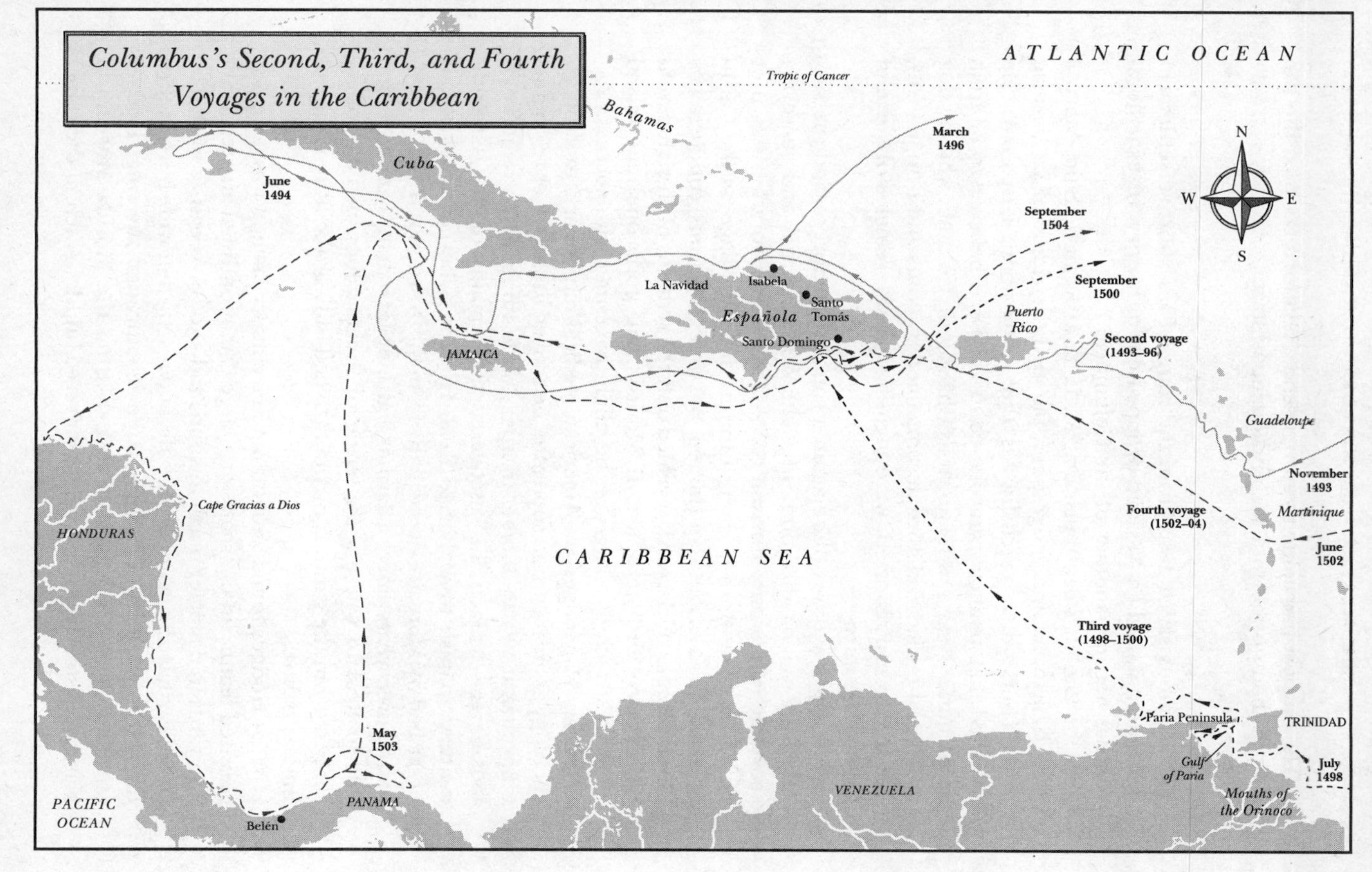

Columbus's Second, Third, and Fourth Voyages in the Caribbean
ATLANTIC OCEAN
Tropic of Cancer
Bahamas
Cuba
June 1494
March 1496
N
W
E
S
September 1504
September 1500
La Navidad
Isabela
Santo Tomás
Española
Santo Domingo
Puerto Rico
Second voyage (1493–96)
JAMAICA
Guadeloupe
November 1493
Martinique
Fourth voyage (1502–04)
June 1502
Cape Gracias a Dios
HONDURAS
CARIBBEAN SEA
Third voyage (1498–1500)
Paria Peninsula
TRINIDAD
Gulf of Paria
July 1498
Mouths of the Orinoco
VENEZUELA
May 1503
PANAMA
Belén
PACIFIC OCEAN

The outpost had come to an ugly end. Relations between the two cultures had got off to a sad and ominous start.

Columbus sailed away from the ruins of his abortive settlement attempt, and La Navidad dropped out of history. Its exact location has become another of the Columbian mysteries.

In the late eighteenth century, M. L. E. Moreau de Saint-Méry, a French historian and geographer, pursued the riddle of La Navidad in the course of research for his 1797 book about Hispaniola. He reported that an anchor uncovered in 1780 was believed to be from *Santa María.* Near a ruin known as Château de Colomb, workers dug up several buried skeletons accompanied by coins and iron utensils. These, Moreau reported, were identified as the remains of some of Columbus's men.

Not until 1939 was there again a concerted effort to find the site. Analyzing sailing directions in Columbus's journal and surveying shoreline conditions, Morison concluded that the location was at or near Limonade Bord de Mer, a forlorn fishing village on the Caribbean ten miles east of Cap Haïtien. But his excavations, conducted by Stanley Boggs of Harvard, revealed only the remains of an eighteenth-century French blockhouse. If Morison had gone one mile inland across a stretch of mangrove, he might have met with success.

William H. Hodges, an American medical missionary, took up archeology as an avocation soon after he arrived in the 1950s to operate a hospital at nearby Limbé. In 1974, while rambling through fields looking for artifacts, he discovered the remains of the sixteenth-century Spanish town Puerto Real. Hodges believed the skeletons described by Moreau were actually from this town, not from La Navidad. Three years later, a farmer led him less than a mile beyond Puerto Real to where a scattering of Indian relics, mainly pottery shards, lay in the gardens by the thatched huts of the little village of En Bas Saline.

What Hodges found and dug up in a cursory fashion was a slightly elevated feature in the shape of a large C that outlined an area about 390 yards in diameter north to south and 330 yards east to west. The raised earth is all but imperceptible, about sixty feet wide but less than three feet in elevation. Cutting trenches through the ring, Hodges and, later, professional archeologists from the Florida Museum of Natural History in Gainesville uncovered middens rich in the refuse of a Taino settlement. Among the shells were animal bones, stone and shell tools, and earthenware pots and bowls. The ceramics were identified with the Caribbean period that archeologists call the Carriere culture, that is to say, the time immediately prior to and during the early European discoveries.

Archeologists surmised that the earthwork ran around most of the edge of the main town. The feature has one distinct break to the east, where the town probably opened to the river and the people beached their canoes—and perhaps where Columbus and his men landed to call on Guacanagarí for help.

Kathleen A. Deagan, curator of anthropology at the Florida museum and director of the excavations in the 1980s, concluded that the evidence, though largely circumstantial, strongly supported Hodges's claim that this was the site of the Taino town where La Navidad was established. The location, for one thing, is right. En Bas Saline is situated less than a mile in from Limonade Bord de Mer, in the bounds of Morison's educated conjecture. Columbus had said the chief's town was well inland but was reachable by water. The excavation site is bordered in part by salt flats that geologists have determined were once channels of a brackish stream leading to the sea.

This had all the marks of having been a large Taino town, one presumably fit for a ruler of the stature of Guacanagarí, and the only one dating to the time of Columbus ever to be discovered for miles around. Much of the central area of the site is level and virtually free of artifacts; Columbus wrote of a well-swept plaza that could have held 2,000 men. Near the center also is a feature the archeologists believe could have been a well; the Tainos did not dig wells, but the men of La Navidad supposedly did, and Columbus, on his return, said that he examined the bottom of a well in search of gold his men might have stashed there.

Even more tantalizing clues were the piece of Venetian glass and fragments of Spanish ceramics found at the site. The people of this town could have had some dealings with Europeans, either the sailors of *Santa María* or others soon afterward. Or they could have obtained these goods indirectly, through trade with other Indians who had come in contact with Europeans.

The time as well as the location seemed right for this to be La Navidad. Radiocarbon dating determined that charcoal found among the artifacts was burned in the late fifteenth century.

But it is the well, or well-like feature, that has yielded the most important clue yet. Archeologists picked out of the sediments the jawbone of a rat and the tooth of a pig, animals introduced to America by Europeans. The rats were stowaways (was this one of the rats to flee the sinking *Santa María?*), and live pigs were often taken on voyages to provide fresh meat for the officers. In fact, Jonathon Ericson, a scientist at the University of California at Irvine, examined the mineral content of the pig's tooth and found that its combination of radioactive carbon, nitrogen, and strontium isotopes, indicative of the plants the pig had eaten when its teeth were forming, matched those of animals raised in southwestern Spain, the area where Columbus had embarked. "The fact that the En Bas Saline pig had its origin in Europe," Deagan said, "is a potentially strong argument for its association with La Navidad."

The search at En Bas Saline is another example of the small but growing role of archeology in the study of Columbus. Historians have learned just about all they can from available written documents of the time. Except for the rare discovery of a new archive or an insight gleaned from improved transcriptions and translations, they may have exhausted their sources of knowledge. Archeology's "words from the earth," to borrow a phrase used by Deagan, may now expand and enrich our understanding of this crucial time.

Even if it is never proved that this is La Navidad, further excavations promise to be a valuable extension of what is termed the "archeology of the inarticulate." The exploration should produce a revealing picture of the possessions, subsistence strategies, and social organization of the people without a written history who lived in the Caribbean on the eve of European contact, and therefore on the eve of their destruction. If it can be authenticated as the site of La Navidad, which seems probable, then we may steal a glimpse of the moment when Europeans first came into armed conflict with the people Columbus had discovered.

"The site," Deagan said, "is of particular political interest to many groups in the Americas as the location of the first conflict with Native Americans and the first resistance to European invasion of the New World—a conflict which in the short run at least, the Europeans lost."

For at La Navidad we see Columbus beginning to make a personal transition from discoverer to imperialist. Though hardly surprising, given the temptations and the times, this was, as it turned out, an unhappy metamorphosis, both for him and for all mankind.

Upon leaving the somber ruins, Columbus led his second expedition east along the northern coast of Hispaniola, looking for a more promising place to establish what he hoped would be a permanent colony. This was his new mission. He had returned from the first voyage with specific ideas about colonization. At his royal reception in Barcelona, he had presented to the king and queen a written plan. As many as 2,000 volunteer settlers would go and build three or four towns in the vicinity of the gold fields of Cybao. Governors of the crown would license and regulate the mining, processing, and shipping of the gold. The crown, the colony, the church, and, of course, Columbus would share this wealth. Churches would be built and priests installed for the conversion of the Indians to Christianity.

With the wholehearted endorsement of Ferdinand and Isabella, the first step in executing the plan was taken in the autumn of 1493 with the launching of Columbus's second expedition. A fleet of seventeen ships, carrying some 1,200 people, including priests, artisans, and farmers, and loaded with tools, seed, and farm animals, left the port of Cádiz. Columbus the discoverer proved that his first crossing was no fluke; he had no trouble returning and finding the new lands. It remained to be seen how well he would perform in his new role as colonizer, administrator, and agent of nascent European imperialism.

Columbus had put La Navidad behind him. Near the present city of Puerto Plata in the Dominican Republic he found a new site about seventy miles east of La Navidad and there established La Isabela, the first planned European town in the New World.

From written records, the Spaniards are known to have erected a small fort, a church, and several stone buildings on a plaza by the water. Digging there in the last decade, José M. Cruxent, a Venezuelan archeologist, has identified foundations of many of these structures, including the house where Columbus had lived. Most of the settlers lived in the 200 palm-thatch huts. Life was unbearably hard. Many of the Spaniards had arrived sick from the voyage, and their health only worsened from the heat, strenuous labor, and assorted fevers and illnesses. The place Columbus had chosen proved to be ill-suited for a colony. There was no real harbor, insufficient rainfall, and little vegetation.

But Columbus had reason to believe the gold mines of Cybao were not far away, and so he dispatched a reconnaissance expedition headed by Alonso de Ojeda. He was a small man of exceptional courage who, Las Casas recalled, "was always the first to draw blood wherever there was a war or a quarrel." Ojeda brought back news of inland streams bearing gold. "All of us made merry," said Michele de Cuneo, the Italian gentleman who had accompanied Columbus on the second voyage.

In February 1494, as food supplies dwindled, Columbus ordered twelve of the seventeen ships to return to Spain, bearing what little gold Ojeda's expedition had collected and an urgent request for more provisions. He also sent a long letter to be delivered to the king and queen by Antonio de Torres, captain of the returning fleet. It is the only document from the hand of Columbus during his second voyage. The colony, he wrote, needed food, clothing, more arms, and some expert miners. Concerned with the smoldering dissension, he asked permission to put the noblemen in the colony, the hidalgos, on the crown's payroll, so that he might have more control over them.

The letter, usually referred to as the Torres memorandum, also betrayed Columbus's thinking about how the colony might pay for its needs until they could strike it rich in Cybao. Columbus wrote: "There are being sent in these ships some Cannibals, men and women, boys and girls, which Your Highnesses can order placed in charge of persons from whom they may be able better to learn the language while being employed in forms of service, gradually ordering that greater care be given them than to other slaves." Knowing the queen's ambivalent feelings about slavery, Columbus couched his ideas in language suggesting this would be a favor to the natives. The people, he said, would lose "their inhuman custom of eating people and, learning the language of Castile, they will more readily receive baptism and secure the welfare of their souls." Historians who acknowledge the dark import of the Torres memorandum see this as a discreet feeler by Columbus seeking royal permission to institute a slave trade from the newly discovered lands.

Meanwhile, the situation at La Isabela deteriorated. Part of the problem was in the colony's composition and organization. Columbus lacked the absolute authority he had had on the first expedition. The crown had seen to that. Royal treasury officials kept an eye on finances and any gold to be found. Priests accompanying the expedition answered to Father Bernardo Boyl, an Aragonese and a close confidant of the king. The soldiers were commanded by an Aragonese knight named Pedro Margarit, who had established his reputation in the war against the Moors. Both Boyl and Margarit had been instructed by the crown to report on Columbus's activities and the true state of the new lands. In a study of Columbus as a colonizer, Stuart B. Schwartz, a historian at the University of Minnesota, writes: "All the elements for trouble were now present: the crown hoping to maintain control and recapture powers it had ceded too readily; the colonists hoping to get rich; and the stubborn Genoese still dreaming of a commercial outpost for slaves and gold, jealous of his rights and interests."

Grumbling led to dissension and then open rebellion. Bernal de Pisa, the comptroller, schemed to seize some of the remaining ships and try to get away with a load of gold. Columbus had him arrested, but this did not put an end to the troubles. He also had to crack down on malingering workers: no work, no rations. For the hidalgos, manual labor was considered degrading and beneath them. They resented the foreigner Columbus's ordering them about. From "this seed," Las Casas wrote, came the "fall" of Columbus as a leader and colonizer. The priest-historian had found much to admire in Columbus, and was not without sympathy in his appraisal of the man's plight. "The Admiral had to use violence, threats, and constraint to have the work done at all," Las Casas wrote.

This is getting ahead of the story. Las Casas was writing many years later, identifying the place and time—La Isabela in 1494—of a historic shift in Columbus's reputation. For the moment, Columbus had trouble enough. Matters had grown worse while he was away on expeditions into the interior and off looking for new islands.

In March 1494, Columbus led a party of 500 men inland on a march that in spirit and panoply, Morison writes, set a pattern followed by all later conquistadors. With banners flying and trumpets sounding, they crossed the plains and climbed the hills. It was there and then that Columbus learned that the coveted Cybao was definitely not Cipangu—one more disillusionment. But he decided to establish a fort there, which he named Santo Tomás. Las Casas believed Columbus chose the name in response to the doubting Thomases among his men, who wondered if there was any gold to be found.

Not long after his return to La Isabela, Columbus received word from Santo Tomás of native unrest. The cacique Caonabó was gathering forces for an attack on the fort. Columbus's reaction in subsequent weeks disputes accounts by historians protective of his reputation who often absolve him of blame and shift it to his headstrong captains. Some of his officers were given to rash acts. But there can be no denying Columbus's own hand in what the appalled Las Casas called the "injustice and wickedness" of Spanish behavior in Hispaniola.

Columbus responded by ordering Ojeda to lead a force of 400 soldiers to the fort and, as Las Casas wrote, "spread terror among the Indians in order to show them how strong and powerful the Christians were." When Ojeda heard that Indians had stolen some Spanish clothing, he must have felt he was only doing his duty in having the ears of one of the cacique's men cut off. This was not the first Indian blood drawn by Columbus's soldiers. But Ojeda's action spelled the end of friendly relations with neighboring Tainos in Hispaniola and foreshadowed more cruelty.

A cacique who trusted his relations with the Europeans to be amicable accompanied the clothes-stealing offenders when they were brought as prisoners before Columbus, seeking to win their release. Instead, Columbus sentenced the prisoners, and the cacique as well, to public decapitation. Even though Columbus revoked the sentence, Las Casas condemned the behavior as "the first injustice committed against the Indians under the guise of justice and the beginning of the shedding of blood which was to flow so copiously from then on all over this island."

With what may have been a sense of relief, Columbus left unhappy La Isabela in late April for another voyage of discovery. He reached Jamaica for the first time, but his primary goal was a return to Cuba. He had heard Indians speak of Magon, which to Columbus could be none other than Mangi, a province of Cathay described by Marco Polo. Clearly, he persisted in his belief in the proximity of the Asian mainland, but now his actions betrayed his growing desperation. On June 13, when he once more had to abandon the search in Cuba and head back to Hispaniola, Columbus forced all his crew to sign a declaration that they had indeed reached the mainland. He could not face his sovereigns again without news of Cathay.

Back at La Isabela, exhausted and ill, he found that things had really got out of hand. He had left his brother Diego in charge, and, if anything, Diego had even less talent for political leadership than Christopher. Las Casas considered Diego a "kindly young man" who was perhaps not worldly enough for dealings with the headstrong hidalgos. Relying on Diego was one of Columbus's many mistakes at La Isabela. History's consensus on Columbus is reflected in Winsor's judgment: "No man ever evinced less capacity for ruling a colony." Even an admirer like Paolo Taviani, the historian who is also a distinguished Italian senator, has said that Columbus was woefully lacking in two qualities of a successful politician. He had not the capacity to make firm decisions for the long run, and he surely lacked the indefinable ability to appoint the right man to the right job.

An Indian uprising spread through the island late in 1494. Pedro Margarit had exacerbated relations with his marauding through the hills, terrorizing the Indians and stealing food. In response, Morison writes, Columbus acted on "the principle that no Christian could do wrong." Instead of chastising and curbing Margarit, he rounded up hundreds of Indians and punished the victims. Unappeased and more restive than ever, Margarit seized three of the resupply ships that had recently arrived and with his confederates, including Boyl, sailed away to Spain. Their report to the court—an unsparing litany of accusations against Columbus that was exaggerated, no doubt, but not without foundation—made Ferdinand and Isabella wonder for the first time if they could depend on this man they had so recently received in festive triumph.

At about this time, Ojeda captured Caonabó, an act that brought swift retaliation from the combined forces of many Taino chieftains. Indian retaliation was met with Spanish revenge, leading to all-out war for many months. Ferdinand Columbus's account gives the Spanish view. The soldiers, he wrote, "pursuing and killing, wreaked such havoc that God was served in a short time. Our men won such a victory that many were killed and others were captured and defeated. . . ." Las Casas took a much different stance, a brave one not shared by most Europeans of the day. Citing Hernando's version with disapproval, he commented: "God was not served by such detestable injustice."

The story of La Isabela, of the first prolonged relations between Europeans and the Tainos, is not a pretty one. And two other acts fix Columbus's responsibility without question.

When Antonio de Torres returned from Spain, he brought a reply to Columbus's memorandum in which the king and queen urged him not to resort to slavery. But Columbus had little else to send back that he felt might justify continued royal support. Before Torres was to sail back to Spain once more, in February 1495, some 1,600 Tainos had been rounded up and brought as captives to La Isabela. Cuneo, who made the voyage himself, recorded that 500 of the "best" men and women were loaded onto the ships as slaves to be sold in Spain. The settlers of La Isabela could take any of the remaining Tainos as their own slaves. "And when everyone was thus provided there were left over about four hundred who were turned loose to go wherever they wished, among whom were many women with babes at the breast," Cuneo wrote. "They, in order the better to escape and fearing lest we might again seize them, abandoned their children indiscriminately and took flight, as persons in desperation." By the time the ships reached Spain, more than one-third of the Tainos had died and were thrown into the sea. "We landed all the slaves at Cádiz, half of them sick," Cuneo concluded his somber account. "They are not people suited to hard work, they suffer from the cold, and they do not have a long life."

Those Tainos who were not shipped as slaves found themselves subjugated and required to pay tribute each quarter to the Spanish at La Isabela. Columbus and his brother Bartholomew, who had joined him in running the colony, ordered each Taino fourteen years of age or older to pay a hawk's bell full of gold every three months. Those who lived away from the mines were to contribute twenty-five pounds of cotton. Such demands were unrealistic. The Tainos had no means of collecting such amounts of gold through mining; the only gold they could gather was the flakes and grains they sometimes came upon in streams. The tribute system, Las Casas judged, was "an unreasonable, very difficult, impossible, and intolerable burden and extortion."

The best that can be said in defense of Columbus is that he was now a desperate man. His power to rule La Isabela was waning. His visions of wealth for himself and the crown were fading. He feared that, short of some triumph or a load of gold, his influence back home would be irreparably diminished by critical reports from Margarit and others.

Columbus decided to return to Spain in 1496 to defend himself. He had discovered his first settlement, La Navidad, in ruins and established a new colony, La Isabela, but was leaving it in a state of terminal chaos. His last instructions to those left behind were to build a new town, which became Santo Domingo. By 1498, the failed La Isabela was abandoned and uninhabited. Today the site is occupied by forty families of fishermen, living in rude huts without running water or electricity, connected to the rest of the country only by an unpaved road.

Exploration brings out many of the human qualities held in highest esteem: active curiosity, courage, and the indomitable spirit that looks for challenge and perseveres in the face of anything and everything. Exploration seeks to transcend ignorance and physical limitations. The successes and failures of the most daring explorers fill us with awe as we realize how hard-won is our knowledge of the world.

But the corollary of exploration is imperialism. All too often this has been the motive for much of our questing, and certainly a major consequence. Explorers have not been content to find; they must seize as well. They—we—wish not only to know but also to possess. That which is discovered is there to be taken and used as the discoverer sees fit. The prize becomes tarnished, and the discoverer with it. The burden of the practices Columbus initiated or condoned weighs heavily on his reputation in history.

Greed and lust, those less attractive human traits, left La Navidad a somber ruin. At La Isabela the Spaniards turned on each other and the hapless Tainos. They exacted harsh tribute from the Indians and, when the Indians began to die off from strife, exhaustion, and disease, they were replaced with slaves from Africa.

The dig site at En Bas Saline offers a stark reminder of this legacy. No shard in the ground or pig's tooth tells this tale. The message is there today in the faces of the village's poor farmers. They are all black, descendants of African slaves. They sometimes work with the archeologists, hired for $15 each a week, which is somewhat more than the going wage in that part of impoverished Haiti. They help comb the ground for clues to what happened to the Spaniards who founded a fort on this land. Yet they themselves are struggling survivors of the consequences of that encounter. These people are there because the first contacts between Europeans and the native people of the New World were a human failure.

Half a century after Columbus's first voyage, Las Casas sadly lamented the practices of his countrymen: ". . . if we Christians had acted as we should."

12

A Question of Humanity

More than he could have realized, Michele de Cuneo expressed the prevailing attitude of white Europeans toward the people of these new lands. He was a gentleman having a jolly time among the savages. What he saw and did he reported with unvarying frankness, which makes him one of the most prized witnesses to this period in history. His descriptions of brutality toward the Indians were stunningly casual, reflecting no doubt the banality of such behavior and the absence among the brutalizers of embarrassment or contrition.

The second Columbus expedition had reached Santa Cruz (St. Croix in the Virgin Islands) in November 1493. Cuneo and his companions jumped into the flagship's boat and gave chase to a canoe bearing three or four Indian men with two women and "two Indian slaves." They believed the Indians to be Caribs of fierce reputation. "While we were approaching [the canoe] the Caribs began shooting at us with their bows in such manner that, had it not been for the shields, half of us would have been wounded," Cuneo said. "But I must tell you that to one of the seamen who had a shield in his hand came an arrow, which went through the shield and penetrated his chest three inches, so that he died in a few days. We captured the canoe with all the men, and one Carib was wounded by a spear in such a way that we thought he was dead, and cast him for dead in the sea, but instantly saw him swim." They were not through with him. "We caught him and with the grapple hauled him over the bulwarks of the ship, where we cut his head with an axe. The other Caribs, together with those slaves, we later sent to Spain."

No remorse was expressed. No excuse was offered, and presumably none was expected.

At the same time on Santa Cruz, Cuneo captured a beautiful Indian woman and had his way with her. With Columbus's blessing, Cuneo wrote, he took the woman into his cabin. "And she being naked as is their custom, I conceived the desire to take my pleasure," Cuneo said. "I wanted to put my desire into execution, but she was unwilling for me to do so, and treated me with her nails in such wise that I would have preferred never to have begun. But seeing this (in order to tell you the whole even to the end), I took a rope-end and thrashed her well, following which she produced such screaming and wailing as would cause you not to believe your ears. Finally we reached an agreement such that, I can tell you, she seemed to have been raised in a veritable school of harlots."

This earliest preserved account of sexual intercourse between Europeans and Indians symbolizes the rape, of the people and the land, that was only beginning. It also offers a sad insight into the guiding assumptions of these Europeans. "There never crossed the mind of Columbus, or his fellow discoverers and conquistadors, any other notion of relations between Spaniard and American Indian save that of master and slave," Morison writes by way of explaining his hero, though not condoning his behavior in this regard. They were the superior people, and these Indians were their inferiors, to be seized and used. Columbus seemed to feel it his right to distribute captured women to his men for their pleasure. It did not occur to his men, if Cuneo is any indication, to ask the women's consent. Finally, as the ultimate insult pointed out by Todorov, Cuneo's woman "who violently rejected sexual solicitation finds herself identified with the woman who makes this solicitation her profession."

The Spanish would engage in fervent debate over the justice and morality of their treatment of the Indians. Were these people truly human? If so, under what circumstances was it just to make war on and enslave other humans? Were the Indians born slaves, according to Aristotelian doctrine? Could they be Christianized? By persuasion, or force? While they argued these questions, more blood was shed indiscriminately. Others, to be sure, perpetrated atrocities on the Indians with no more remorse. But the opprobrium of history has fallen hardest on the Spanish. Their cruelty to the Indians was the first, establishing the woeful pattern, and was especially relentless. It was well documented by matter-of-fact chroniclers like Cuneo and, most tellingly, by the crusading Las Casas. In contrast to Cuneo, Las Casas rendered harsh judgment. "Note here," he wrote in a comment on Columbus's journal, "that the natural, simple and kind gentleness and humble conditions of the Indians, and want of arms or protection, gave the Spaniards the insolence to hold them of little account, and to impose on them the harshest tasks that they could, and to become glutted with oppression and destruction."

Ever since, Spain has had to bear the burden of what came to be known as the Black Legend, a burden of violence and destructive greed that should be distributed more widely.

Distressed by reports of unremitting hostilities, Ferdinand and Isabella sent a new governor to Española in 1502 with instructions not only to restore order and discipline in the Spanish colony itself but to see that "the Indians are well treated, that they may go safely throughout the land, and that no one may use force against them, or rob them, or do any other evil or harm to them." The man charged with this responsibility was Nicolás de Ovando, a high officer of a religious order founded to garrison Christian outposts in Spain against the Moorish infidels. He was small and seemingly mild-mannered, but with a reputation as a strict disciplinarian. Ovando arrived with a fleet of soldiers and settlers at Santo Domingo in April.

Among the passengers was a settler, Bartolomé de las Casas, who would testify to the utter failure of the Spaniards to comply with the crown's wishes. Las Casas, like the others, had arrived with no thought but to exploit the land and the Indians. His change of heart would come later, in 1514, at the age of forty. But he kept his eyes and ears open, and years later his accounts of unabated violence and subjugation would promote and document the Black Legend. His testimony was unsparing, as illustrated by incidents he described as occurring in the time of Ovando.

The Spaniards enjoyed friendly relations with Indians on Saona Island, near Santo Domingo, and frequently visited them to pick up a supply of cassava bread. On one visit, Las Casas said, the Indians were loading the ship "with great joy." Then the illusion of tranquillity was shattered.

"Just as Spanish civilians never take a step without girding their sword," Las Casas wrote, "so these always brought along dogs trained to tear Indians to pieces and of such ferocity that the Indians feared them more than the very devil. The Indians, then, were loading cassava onto a small boat that was to take it to the caravel, while their chief, staff in hand, walked to and fro in order to expedite matters and please the Christians."

One of the dogs, agitated by the waving of the chief's stick, pulled and strained at the leash. The Spaniard who held the dog could hardly restrain him. "What if we let him loose?" he supposedly said to another man. Las Casas described what followed: "Then for a laugh, he and his friend, both devils incarnate, told the dog to attack, thinking they could control him. But the dog charged like a mad horse and dragged the Spaniard behind him; he was unable to hold his grasp and let go of the leash. The dog jumped on the cacique and with his powerful jaws tore at the man's stomach, pulling out the intestines as the cacique staggered away. The Indians rushed to the unfortunate chief but he died shortly thereafter and, carrying him away for burial, they wailed and lamented their sorrow to the winds. The Spaniards returned to the caravel with their good dog and his master, then sailed to Santo Domingo, leaving such a good deed behind them."

As word of the vicious attack spread, other Indians swore revenge at the first opportunity. Eight Spaniards happened to come ashore at Saona to stretch their legs and rest. They had had nothing to do with killing the chief. But they were Europeans and, for all the Indians knew, could have belonged to the crew with the attack dog. All eight men were slain, the first victims of the vengeance. Innocent though these men may have been, Las Casas felt that the Indians were justified in their act. "The Indians had a most excellent reason to suppose that whoever came to their island from Castile came as an enemy," he reasoned, "and thus could rightfully resolve to kill him. But let God be the ultimate judge of this."

Ovando responded with a declaration of all-out war. Armed horsemen rode out, slashing Indians with swords and spearing them with lances. They surrounded villagers, Las Casas recalled, and "pitilessly slaughtered everyone like sheep in a corral." All the Indians taken alive were enslaved. The small island of Saona, once fertile, was razed and left barren. No more cassava bread; they had, in that familiar phrase, cut off their noses to spite their faces.

"It was a general rule among Spaniards to be cruel—not just cruel, but extraordinarily cruel—so that harsh and bitter treatment would prevent Indians from daring to think of themselves as human beings or having a minute to think at all," Las Casas declared. "So they would cut an Indian's hands and leave them dangling by a shred of skin and they would send him on saying, 'Go now, spread the news to your chief.' They would test their swords and their manly strength on captured Indians and place bets on the slicing off of heads or the cutting of bodies in half with one blow."

These were not isolated episodes. Bent on quelling a rebellion in the troublesome province of Xaragua, Ovando took 370 troops and met with the Indian leaders, notably Anacaona, the woman who had succeeded her dead brother as the ruler. Las Casas referred to her as Lady Anacaona or Queen Anacaona. As he told the story, Anacaona treated the Spaniards as royal guests, providing feasts, dances, and festive games. Ovando repaid the hospitality with a massacre.

Under the pretext of staging a jousting tournament, Ovando ordered some of his armed men and their horses to take positions outside the main house. Anacaona and her chiefs waited inside, as they were told. Ovando entered, as if to inform the Indians that the tournament was about to begin and lead them out for the show. He stood without speaking. He wore on his breast a gold medal of his religious order. When he knew the preparations to be complete, he raised his hand and touched the medal as the signal. The trap was sprung. Soldiers drew their swords and tied up the Indians. Anacaona alone was let outside. The house was set afire, and all inside, Las Casas reported, "were soon turned into burning embers."

Meanwhile, the horsemen outside rampaged through the town and, Las Casas said, "speared as many Indians as they could while those on foot ripped bellies open." Few were spared, as Las Casas testified: "great were the ravages and cruelties done to men, old people and innocent children, and great was the number of people killed. It happened that if a Spaniard, from pity or greed, snatched a child away to save him from slaughter by lifting him to his horse, someone would come from behind and pierce the child with a lance. Or again, if the boy was on foot, even though someone held him by the hand, another would slash his legs off with a sword. As for the Queen, they hanged her as a mark of honor."

Defenders of Spanish colonial policies have accused Las Casas of gross exaggerations. Fair-minded historians have questioned how much store to put in his accounts. In his *Historia,* Las Casas produced one of the most comprehensive accounts of the Indies in the sixteenth century. But in this and his more frankly polemical writings, the historian was acting also as an impassioned propagandist. He was seeking to shame Spain into treating the Indians as humans. The authentic history in his writing must be sifted from the propaganda.

Ferdinand Columbus, in his father's biography, ignored or glossed over Spanish terrorism. He would write that Indians who disobeyed Spanish orders were "punished," whereas Las Casas would likely be more graphic and report that they had had their hands cut off. Describing a battle in which unarmed Indians were slashed and killed and others were disemboweled by war dogs, Hernando would announce with satisfaction that the Spaniards "with God's aid soon gained a complete victory, killing many Indians and capturing others who were also killed." Suppression of the full truth cannot be more acceptable in history than exaggeration of a discomfiting truth.

Many succeeding histories, particularly those celebrating Columbus a century ago, followed Hernando's example in their stirring accounts of Spanish conquests. They came, they saw, and they did what had to be done, as they deemed it. Such blinkered versions are a subversion of history. Only in a footnote did the editor of a laudatory book on Columbus in 1892 acknowledge the dark side of the encounter between Europeans and the Indians: "He . . . stands convicted in the light of history as the prime author of that blood-drenched rule which exterminated millions of simple aborigines in the West Indian Archipelago." The enormity of this offense requires that the indictment not be dismissed in a footnote to fulsome encomiums. Other histories of the time, excepting Justin Winsor's in 1891, tended to absolve Columbus of blame, insofar as they aired the issue at all, and shift it to the Spanish nation. In their view, not even a Columbus could control Spanish lust and greed and, as Las Casas said himself, their proclivity to be "not just cruel, but extraordinarily cruel."

Las Casas was not the only one to bear witness to unspeakable cruelty against the Indians. Peter Martyr dutifully recorded numerous examples of Spanish atrocities, though not with the judgmental vehemence of a Las Casas. Still, Martyr's accounts were widely read in Europe years before those of Las Casas. Oviedo, who would become the official historian of the Indies, had a generally low opinion of the Indians, in the fashion of most colonists, but did not always turn a blind eye to Spanish excesses. Although Las Casas denounced Oviedo as "always condemning the Indians and excusing the Spaniards for the decimation they brought about in the Indies," Oviedo related horror stories of his own and asserted in his *Historia general* that the New World was a victim of the "conquistadors, who would more accurately be called depopulators or squanderers of the new lands." Spanish soldiers, he charged, were guilty of "various and innumerable cruel deaths." But in describing how the ships of Cortés were greased and caulked "with the fat of the enemy Indians that the Christians killed," Oviedo defended the practice with black humor; "it was commonplace for the Indians to dine off each other," he commented, and so why not use their fat for assuring victory? Even Antonio de Herrera, another establishment writer, did not ignore in his history the horrifying particulars of the Anacaona massacre.

By the middle of the sixteenth century, the Black Legend had gained a firm foothold. The English, French, and Dutch seized on the evidence of Spanish atrocities to fan the fires of national rivalries and religious hatreds. The Protestant North, growing more assertive by the year, coveted a share of the riches of the New World, which heretofore had flowed almost exclusively to Catholic Spain. To the Protestants, the Spanish colonial behavior was no more than could be expected from that brooding, medieval nation that had institutionalized injustice with the Inquisition. Most of all, the Protestants could not abide Spain's air of divinely endowed superiority as a culture imbued, in the words of J. H. Elliott, with "its own unique status and position in God's providential design."

Not that the other nations would become paragons of virtue. Sir Francis Drake and the other Elizabethan sea-dogs left their own trail of blood. Without scruple, John Hawkins inaugurated a brisk trade in slaves. No Spaniard, it is pointed out, ever stooped as low as Sir Jeffrey Amherst, a British commander in North America, who proposed sending blankets used by smallpox victims to the Indians involved in a rebellion in 1763. But "the Spaniards offered many more hostages to fortune than their rivals," according to Elliott, a modern British historian. In *The Old World and the New: 1492–1650,* Elliott writes: "Although the Black Legend possessed a long, if hardly respectable, European ancestry, the Spanish record in the Indies gave it a new and terrifying lustre. Even in the earliest histories of the conquest, like Peter Martyr's *Decades,* there was material enough for the indictment of the conquerors." Then, with the publication in 1552 of Las Casas's *Brief Account of the Destruction of the Indies,* and Girolamo Benzoni's gossipy *History of the New World,* published in Venice in 1565, Spain's enemies had all the ammunition they could want, and the Black Legend of Spanish atrocities was rooted in the European consciousness.

Non-Spanish historians perpetuated the legend through the generations. A century ago, the American historian John Fiske contrasted the medieval atmosphere of Spain unfavorably with England's encouragement of individualism and pluralism, unfettered by church control. "When we contrast the elastic buoyancy of spirit in Shakespeare's England with the gloom and heaviness that were creeping over Spain," Fiske writes in *The Discovery of America,* "we find nothing strange in the fact that the most populous and powerful nations of the New World speak English and not Spanish."

The Black Legend still pervades writing about the initial encounters between Europeans and the Indians. But only rarely now is Spain singled out for castigation. In more recent reassessments of the encounter, a generally useful corrective has been introduced and in some cases emphasized with a righteous force worthy of Las Casas: all white Europeans are now indicted for their role in setting in motion a history of greed, cruelty, slavery, and genocide. Another generation is viewing history through its own peculiar lenses.

The lenses have been ground to compensate for the myopia of past histories. Eurocentric history, once dominant, is being vigorously rejected and replaced in many instances with accounts interpreted more from the point of view of the victims, the Indians and the African slaves. One especially rousing but not uncommon sample of the new view is given by Hans Koning, a novelist and an essayist. Writing in *The New York Times* in 1990, Koning accuses Columbus of instigating "an extermination of native Americans" and of being "as mean, cruel and greedy in small matters as he was in vast ones." He concludes: "We must end the phony baloney about the white man bringing Christianity, and about Columbus the noble son of the humble weaver. Our false heroes and a false sense of the meaning of courage and manliness have too long burdened our national spirit."

A more scholarly amplification of this view was published in 1990 by Kirkpatrick Sale, a writer and environmental activist. The title of his book, *The Conquest of Paradise,* sums up its thesis. The first European adventurers, beginning with a ruthless Columbus, invaded and despoiled an idyllic land whose people were ethically superior to Europeans. The Black Legend meets the Noble Savage. Sale's history is symptomatic of a radical revisionism that is bent on demolishing the uncritical image of Columbus the hero.

The spirit of the Black Legend, it seems, has not been laid to rest.

Any history of Columbus must address the issue of slavery, another form of brutality that was a pervasive part of the European experience in the New World and yet was usually submerged to the vanishing point in earlier histories. On this issue, Columbus was neither ahead of the time nor behind. He had seen Africans seized and brought to Portugal and Spain as slaves (which the church condoned), and never thought of it as anything more than the normal state of affairs. Columbus's attitude was manifest that first day on Guanahani. The gentle Tainos, he observed in his journal, "should be good and intelligent servants."

Robert Fuson, a translator of the Columbus log, insists that this remark has been misinterpreted by those "who see Columbus as the founder of slavery in the New World." In fact, he writes, "Columbus offered this observation in explanation of an earlier comment he had made, theorizing that people from the mainland came to the islands to capture these Indians as slaves because they were so docile and obliging." Perhaps so, but it is a lame defense. There can be no misinterpretation of Columbus's later statements ("They are fit to be ordered about and made to work") and actions (his shipment in 1494 of the 550 Tainos to Spain for sale as slaves, fulfilling a promise he had made in his Letter to Santángel). Columbus looked upon slavery as an economic expedient, the more so as he began to despair of finding gold in sufficient quantity to satisfy the crown and support the colony. He proposed to make regular shipments of humans in exchange for cattle and provisions for the struggling outpost at La Isabela.

A century ago, before it was the fashion in history, Winsor said that this first shipment of Indian slaves "was a long step in the miserable degradation which Columbus put upon those poor creatures whose existence he had made known to the world."

The king and queen were ambivalent about slavery in the Indies and tried to discourage Columbus's traffic in humans. They felt it their duty to convert the Indians to Christianity; if the Indians became Christians, then they could not be enslaved. The sovereigns also considered the Indians to be their vassals, and thus protected against enslavement. Only those beyond the religious and political pale could be candidates for slavery. Accordingly, the Spanish developed a legal-religious policy that would salve their consciences and leave them free to round up people to use or sell as slaves. (A similar doctrine had been exploited in the enslavement of natives in the Canary Islands.) The principle was that anyone captured in a "just war" could be enslaved. When the Indians rebelled against the soldiers and settlers at La Isabela, the Spanish retaliated with force throughout the countryside. The Tainos shipped to Spain in 1494 were captives in a just war, which the Spanish defined as virtually any hostile act against them.

The Spanish thus had an inducement to wage war. When the Indians took revenge for the death of their chief by the war dog, Las Casas reported that the rebellion was greeted as "happy news because we now had a reason to get slaves." Another time he said that, like all Spaniards, Ovando "seized the slightest pretext to provoke war." Las Casas again: "All the Indians taken alive were enslaved since this was the principal goal of Spaniards here and everywhere in the Indies." After the massacre of Anacaona and her people, Las Casas was awarded a prisoner as his slave.

The people called Caribs were particularly fair game for enslavement. They were held to be beyond redemption because they were believed to be belligerent and in the habit of eating human flesh. From their reading of classical and medieval literature, Europeans were expecting to find distant lands inhabited by "monstrous races," including anthropophagi, or man-eaters. Nearly all enemies and aliens were so stigmatized at one time or another. Strabo the geographer wrote of Ireland: "I have nothing certain to tell, except that the inhabitants are more savage than the Britons, since they are man-eaters." Strabo admitted to having "no trustworthy witnesses." On Guanahani, Columbus learned from the Tainos of their dread of invaders who came hunting slaves and, as he understood, consumed the flesh of some unfortunate captives. One must be circumspect in accepting Columbus's version, given the unreliability of initial communications between whites and Indians and Columbus's tendency to hear that which accorded with his preconceptions. He never witnessed such practices, and did not encounter any of these people until later voyages. Nevertheless, in his report to the king and queen, Columbus announced that anthropophagy existed in these islands and identified the practitioners as the Canabilli, a warlike people who also were called Canibales, Canibas, or Caribas. Their very name became attached to their reputed practice—cannibalism.

Columbus had made believers out of those who accompanied him on the second voyage. Everywhere they went, they looked for and suspected they found Caribs. Of Dominica, sighted in November 1493, Guillermo Coma wrote: "These islands are inhabited by Canabilli, a wild, unconquered race which feeds on human flesh. . . . They wage unceasing wars against gentle and timid Indians to supply flesh; this is their booty and is what they hunt." Cuneo assumed the Indians they captured and killed or raped at Santa Cruz were also Caribs, in which case they presumably deserved what they got. On a visit to an abandoned village, Dr. Chanca said that "the neck of a man was found cooking in a pot." Peter Martyr reported on cannibals who captured children and gelded them "to make them fat as we do cock chickens and young hogs, and eat them when they are well fed." Where did he hear that story? How could Dr. Chanca be sure he had not seen an animal's neck? Were the Caribs, in fact, cannibals?

Indeed, anthropologists disagree as to whether cannibalism as a custom has been documented to exist or have existed in any society. In extreme circumstances, people have eaten human flesh in order to survive. But this is different from cannibal societies in which people purportedly eat other humans as a custom or an intrinsic part of religious rites, or simply as a gastronomic treat. In *The Man-Eating Myth,* published in 1979, William Arens, a social anthropologist at the State University of New York at Stony Brook, contends that there is no credible evidence that customary or gastronomic cannibalism has ever been practiced. Nearly all tales of such practices, he says, can be traced to accusations by neighboring enemies, reminiscences that one's ancestors (but never oneself) were cannibals, or travelers' accounts drawn from hearsay. They reflect a myth-making process whereby one people, out of prejudice or ignorance, create an image of others as being less than human. (In the case of people speaking of their ancestors' habit, it is a way of pointing up how far they have progressed.) Arens's book infuriated other anthropologists. Many of them agree with Thomas J. Riley of the University of Illinois, who said that "very few anthropologists question the existence of cannibalism." But Riley endorsed Arens's advice that the imputation of cannibalism to any social group should be made with the utmost care.

This applies even to the eponymous cannibals, the Caribs. Columbus, though, believed they were cannibals, and acted accordingly. In making his first shipment of Taino slaves, he wrote to the king and queen that in the future he would provide slaves from among these cannibals, "fierce but well-made fellows of good understanding, which men, wrested from their inhumanity, will be, we believe, the best slaves that ever were." Like many anthropologists and an increasing number of historians, William Keegan suspects that the "image of Carib cannibals chasing peaceful Arawaks from island to island finds its origins in Spanish efforts to justify their New World slave trade."

Real or imagined, cannibalism served Spanish purposes. "Early in the conquest Spaniards attempted to distinguish between the fierce and supposedly cannibalistic Caribs and other Indians," writes Lewis Hanke, an American historian. "If judged to be Caribs, the natives could be warred against unmercifully and justly enslaved. . . . [It] now appears that while some Caribs did eat human flesh, sixteenth-century slave raiders were inclined to apply the term 'Carib' rather loosely."

The crown, while officially discouraging slavery, responded to the colonists' need for labor to till the land and work the mines. Soon after the turn of the sixteenth century, the *encomienda* system was established to promote the conversion of Indian workers to Christianity, but became little more than institutionalized forced labor. The *encomenderos,* colonists who were assigned these laborers, had little regard for the health, welfare, or even conversion of the Indians in their charge. Conditions can be inferred from the language of the Laws of Burgos, promulgated in 1512 to protect the Indian laborers. The laws stipulated the food, clothes, and beds to be supplied them and also proclaimed that "no one may beat or whip or call an Indian dog or any other name unless it is his proper name." Abuses persisted until eventually native slavery was declared illegal in 1542, and eight years later so was the system of *encomienda* labor.

By this time, however, nearly all the labor in the Caribbean was supplied by black slaves shipped over from Africa. In 1510, in a step sometimes cited as the start of the systematic transatlantic traffic in black slaves, King Ferdinand ordered the shipment to the New World of 250 Africans, purchased in Lisbon. Demand grew as the Indians, weakened from disease and mistreatment, died off in alarming numbers. Oviedo would report in the years to come that every day saw the arrival in Santo Domingo of more black slaves, who were baptized within a day and herded off to the fields and mines. The sugar-cane plantations, he wrote, seemed "an effigy or image of Ethiopia itself."

Estimates cited by William D. Phillips, Jr., in his history of slavery indicate that, from the fifteenth century through 1650, more than 350,000 Africans arrived in chains at the ports of Spanish America, and some 250,000 were landed in Brazil. The slave trade to the French and British possessions was only beginning by 1650. In all, in the years preceding 1870, some nine million to ten million blacks were forced to migrate to America as slaves.

One of the early advocates of officially sanctioned black slavery in the New World was, of all people, Las Casas, and his many critics have used this in efforts to discredit him. Las Casas proposed in 1517 the licensing of an extensive trade in blacks, and Charles I* agreed. As

*Charles ruled Spain from 1516 to 1556 as Charles I. He was also the Holy Roman Emperor Charles V from 1519 to 1556.

Las Casas saw it, this was the only immediate alternative if his beloved Indians were to be spared destruction. It was years before he came to recognize that one form of slavery was just as evil as the other. In his *Historia,* Las Casas finally apologized and inserted a lengthy account on the injustice of African slave raids.

The encounter with strange people in a strange land, people of a race and color and culture never anticipated, posed a troubling moral dilemma for Christian Europe. Columbus, if he thought much about it, averted his mind. It was enough to Christianize the people and seize the wealth of the Indies for the power and glory of Spain and the church; in other words, ignore their own humanity and culture, force them to accept yours, and use them for your own purposes. Most settlers and conquistadors, their hands full subduing the land and people, were given more to action than contemplation. Even churchmen, the early record shows, were none too diligent at first in bringing the Indians under the protection of their God. But voices of conscience were raised, tentatively at first, then more insistently.

One of these voices was sounded with startling force as early as 1511. "I have come up on this pulpit, I who am a voice of Christ crying in the wilderness of this island," the Dominican Antonio de Montesinos began his sermon. "This voice says that you are in mortal sin, that you live and die in it, for the cruelty and tyranny you use in dealing with these innocent people. Tell me, by what right or justice do you keep these Indians in such cruel and horrible servitude? On what authority have you waged a detestable war against these people, who dwelt quietly and peacefully on their own land?" Montesinos raised other questions that the Spanish would confront many times in the years ahead: "Are these Indians not men? Do they not have rational souls? Are you not obliged to love them as you love yourselves?"

There was no rush to repent and mend sinful ways. Not even Las Casas, in the congregation that Sunday in Hispaniola, was moved to action. Perhaps the sermon did sow the seeds of his epiphany. The next year, he joined the Dominican order, and two years later freed his native serfs and committed himself to the defense of the downtrodden Indians. But the questions would not go away, and increasingly Spaniards up to the highest levels would agonize over their profound implications and begin a search for answers.

Surprisingly, in view of the Black Legend, the Spanish were the first colonial power to weigh these moral questions with such genuine concern. "Today it is becoming increasingly recognized," Hanke says, "that no other nation made so continuous or so passionate an attempt to discover what was the just treatment for the native peoples under its jurisdiction than the Spaniards." He attributes this in part to the nature of the Spanish people, "a people legalistic, passionate, given to extremes, and fervently Catholic." They had to determine the nature of Indians and their capacity—their humanity—before they could legitimately pursue either conquest or conversion.

Europeans had not yet developed true racial prejudices based on skin color. Their Bible taught that all people were descended from Adam and Eve, and so were created by God as one human race, though some, such as the descendants of Cain, had wandered off into a kind of limbo. Columbus had no thought but that the people who met him at Guanahani were human. But Europeans did divide the world into Christians and infidels. They looked down on certain peoples as barbarian, savage, primitive—inferior. Into this category nearly all colonists, from Columbus on, consigned the Indians. Pressed to clarify the church's position, Pope Paul III issued a bull in 1537 emphasizing that all people, without exception, "are capable of receiving the doctrines of the faith." So the Indians were fully human in the eyes of Christ and should be brought into the fold. The protests and preachings of Las Casas and others had borne some fruit. A more cynical interpretation, which is not without some foundation, has it that the Roman Catholic Church saw in the millions of Indians ready replacements for the multitude of defections to Protestantism.

Europeans reached back to Aristotle to justify another way of dividing the world's people. Aristotle, a philosopher much revered in the Renaissance, had contended that one part of mankind is set apart by nature to be slaves in the service of those born to be masters. As early as 1510, John Major, a Scottish professor in Paris, was the first to apply to the Indians the Aristotelian doctrine of natural slavery and argue that this justified the use of force against Indians to secure their services and convert them to Christianity. Three years later, this became official Spanish policy with the adoption of the Requirement. Conquistadors, before they could attack Indians, were required to read them their "rights." If the Indians acknowledged the Europeans' overlordship and allowed the faith to be preached to them, there were to be no hostilities. If they refused to comply, the Spaniards were justified in subjugating the Indians by whatever means necessary.

Las Casas led the protests against such practices and the doctrine of natural slavery that was their intellectual underpinning. His persistence and powers of persuasion finally moved Charles V to action—and provoked a climactic public debate that Hanke calls "the first full-length discussion in modern times of relations between peoples of different cultures."

In April 1550, Charles V took the unprecedented step of ordering the conquests in the New World to be suspended while a council of jurists and theologians considered how they should be conducted "in a Christian fashion." This set up the historic confrontation between Las Casas and Juan Ginés de Sepúlveda at Valladolid.

Sepúlveda, a respected scholar and translator of Aristotle, argued the case of the Spanish colonists and conquistadors by disputing the humanity of the Indians. The fourteen-member council, convened between mid-August and mid-September 1550, heard Sepúlveda apply the doctrine of natural slavery to the Indians. They are as inferior, he declared, "as children are to adults, as women are to men, . . . as cruel people are from mild people." These inferior people, he reasoned, "require, by their own nature and in their own interests, to be placed under the authority of civilized and virtuous princes or nations, so that they may learn, from the might, wisdom, and law of their conquerors, to practice better morals, worthier customs and a more civilized way of life." Thus, Sepúlveda concluded, the Spaniards were justified in carrying on war against the Indians in order to civilize and Christianize them.

In his defense of the Indians, Las Casas chose not to make a frontal attack on Aristotle, but instead read to the council an exhaustive treatise to the effect that the Indians were rational beings who compared favorably with the peoples of ancient times and even the Spaniards. Like most advocates, he emphasized and perhaps exaggerated their virtues. From his vast experience Las Casas argued that the Indians were religious, good parents, diligent workers, and, in the temples they built in Mexico and Yucatán, were accomplished in the arts. The Indians were not inferior beings, in the Aristotelian sense, but, in some respects, superior to Europeans.

The debate came to no clear-cut resolution. The council never reached a decision. Perhaps the councilors took their cue from Charles V, who may have sought a compromise. He would neither endorse the concept of natural slavery nor stay the hostilities against the Indians. In his excellent analysis of the confrontation, *Aristotle and the American*

Indians, Hanke observes that the king "could not accept the views of Las Casas without provoking a revolution in America," but regulations governing conquests became "steadily milder and more pro-Indian in tone." New laws governing colonial conduct were proclaimed in 1573, with exhortations to eschew unnecessary force and give due attention to the rules to be followed in waging a "just war."

Out of the deliberations at Valladolid also came one of the most eloquent declarations on human rights in that or any other century. Las Casas affirmed: "Thus mankind is one, and all men are alike in that which concerns their creation and all natural things, and no one is born enlightened. From this it follows that all of us must be guided and aided at first by those who were born before us. And the savage peoples of the earth may be compared to uncultivated soil that readily brings forth weeds and useless thorns, but has within itself such natural virtue that by labour and cultivation it may be made to yield sound and beneficial fruits."

Over the centuries, many of his countrymen branded Las Casas a disloyal Spaniard who almost single-handedly created the Black Legend. Hanke says that instead Spaniards "could, and should, flourish the undeniable fact that no European nation produced such a figure as Las Casas." And Spain permitted him to speak freely without once invoking the threat of the Inquisition.

It was too late for an uncounted multitude of native Americans. Their fate had already been sealed, and not always necessarily as a result of Spanish cruelty. They were victims of unwitting germ warfare.

Conventional history has offered a number of reasons why a relatively small force of Europeans was able to overwhelm the Americans, depopulating the land and opening it to transforming colonization. The favored explanation was that Europeans took advantage of their superior technology: steel against stone, firearms against bows and arrows, caravels against canoes. Without disputing the European power of arms, scholars in the past twenty-five years have come to realize that what ultimately tipped the balance was disease.

When Columbus and other explorers reached the New World, they unintentionally brought with them diseases new to the indigenous people: smallpox, measles, typhus, scarlet fever, tuberculosis, and the like. These were the contagious diseases of the European cities to which Europeans had developed considerable immunity. The Americans, separated from the Old World for ages, lacked an immune system adjusted by heredity and experience to these deadly microbes. These were "crowd" diseases, and the Americans lived in a sparsely settled habitat. Infectious diseases were virtually unknown to them. A Maya Indian was recorded as testifying to the good health of his people on the eve of the conquest: "There was then no sickness; they had no aching bones; they had then no smallpox; they had then no burning chest; they had then no abdominal pain; they had then no consumption; they had then no headache. At that time the course of humanity was orderly. The foreigners made it otherwise when they arrived here."

The Mayan's memory was perhaps afflicted with nostalgic exaggeration. Anthropologists are certain that the native Americans suffered some illnesses that are part of man's primate ancestry, such as dysentery, food poisoning, anemia, viral fevers, worms, insect-borne diseases, and arthritis. But this was nothing compared with what befell them almost immediately after the arrival of the Europeans.

A wave of epidemic and death swept through the Caribbean, everywhere the Europeans went and often spreading from one infected community to the next in advance of the explorers. The first major outbreak of smallpox hit Hispaniola in 1507, wiping out entire tribes. Within a generation, the Taino population was decimated, a people on the verge of extinction. Smallpox was Cortés's ally in conquering Mexico. Tomás Motolinia, a Franciscan who arrived there in 1524, observed: "As the Indians did not know the remedy for the disease and were very much in the habit of bathing frequently, whether well or ill, and continued to do so even when suffering from smallpox, they died in heaps, like bedbugs. Many others died of starvation, because, as they were all taken sick at once, they could not care for each other, nor was there anyone to give them bread or anything else."

Not only was there devastation of life, but of the spirit as well. The people felt helpless before these white Europeans. Their very presence doomed them in mysterious ways. Of the psychological effects, Henry F. Dobyns, an American ethnohistorian who was instrumental in the recognition of the probable impact of disease on the conquest, writes: "The effects were terrifying, and shook the confidence of the Indians in the power of their gods. Add to this their steel swords, their marvelous ships, and above all their horses—surely the gods of the Spaniards were stronger than their own gods."

No one can be sure of the American population in 1492—estimates, based on little hard evidence and many speculative assumptions, range from 33 million to 112 million, and are the subject of intense scholarly dispute—but it is now believed that diseases introduced by Europeans killed perhaps 50 to 90 percent of the population. The epidemic is assumed to have been so insidious that whole cultures would be wiped out before extensive contact with Europeans occurred. In 1539, the explorer Hernando de Soto described a complex native-American society in the southeastern part of North America. But when European settlers eventually arrived in the eighteenth century, the sophisticated people De Soto had encountered was gone, replaced by a smaller, simpler culture. Also, on their arrival in Peru in 1532, Francisco Pizarro's party was told by Incas that a disease had ravaged the people a few years earlier, killing thousands.

New studies of historical epidemiology represent a belated recognition of the biological consequences of the European entry into America. Alfred W. Crosby of the University of Texas at Austin has examined European expansionism in large part from the standpoint of what he calls "portmanteau biota"—weeds, animal vermin, and disease pathogens. In *Plagues and Peoples,* William H. McNeill in 1976 propounded a general theory of history that recognizes the fundamental importance of disease and epidemic episodes in determining events. A new approach to history can produce insights illuminating the past.

The Indians may have wreaked a measure of revenge on the Europeans. Although the origin of syphilis has long been a contentious subject, recent research finds that the disease most likely was introduced to Europe by the returning crews of Columbus. Syphilis leaves characteristic marks on bones. Brenda J. Baker and George J. Armelagos of the University of Massachusetts at Amherst found such traces in abundance in pre-Columbian New World specimens, but not in Old World skeletons until after 1492. The American form of the disease was apparently mild and not sexually transmitted, except when Columbus's men, lacking any immunity, had their way with Indian women. After their return, Spanish soldiers engaged in the siege of Naples under Charles VIII of France and left the city devastated by a plague thought to be syphilis. The venereal disease was variously called the "Neapolitan disease" or the "French disease." In fact, it was very probably the "American disease," but nothing to compare in severity with the European-borne epidemics that decimated the American populations.

Through arrogance, malice, and inadvertence, the first Europeans in the New World treated their discovery with fatal indifference. They confronted the question of the humanity of others, but in their actions, if not their political and philosophical outlook, inverted the question. For those separated long ago in prehistory from the rest of humanity, the Americans living apart on great rafts of land spun off from Pangaea, the surprise reunion was disastrous.

13

A Name for the New World

Exalted as Columbus has been in American history, it is passing strange that the New World does not bear his name. With any justice, one would think, the two continents in the part of the world Columbus happened on should be named something like Colombia—North and South Colombia. How could the honor go to someone else, and one who was not only a lesser navigator of disputed accomplishment but also a suspected self-promoter and prevaricator, Amerigo Vespucci? The man, if he is remembered at all, is so often vilified as a usurper of fame. But such a harsh judgment seems unfair. The circumstances whereby his name was applied to the New World point to its having been an innocent accident of history. Besides, an argument can be made that Amerigo Vespucci was not altogether undeserving of the honor.

Today the issue is usually raised only as a curiosity. Or it inspires nothing more than wry comment on history's vagaries in nomenclature, such as Victor Hugo's: "There are some men with bad luck. Christopher Columbus was unable to attach his name to his discovery. Guillotin was never able to detach his from his invention."

At an earlier time, emotions could run high on the naming of America. In 1697, when the stirrings of self-awareness were beginning to be expressed in the British colonies of North America, Samuel Sewall, a chief justice in Boston, wrote of the spiritual meaning of the New World as the New Jerusalem or New Heaven. He insisted that the New World should be named Columbina for "the magnanimous heroe Christopher Columbus, a Genuese, who was manifestly appointed of God to be the Finder out of these lands." At the time of the American Revolution, the poet Phillis Wheatley suggested that the name "America" be replaced with "Columbia" as a poetic designation for the aspirations of the new republic.

Of course, the name "America" is too entrenched and familiar to be changed; not that anyone now seriously proposes a change. "America"—the name has a ring to it and congruity with "Asia," "Africa," "Australia," "Antarctica," and even "Europe"—"Europa." And it is not as if Columbus is without honor. Few names in history are better known. Holidays and statues commemorate him. Maps bear his name in many forms: Colombia in South America, British Columbia in Canada, and the District of Columbia; towns and streets named Colón in nearly every Latin American country; Columbia River and Columbia University; fifty towns or cities named Columbus or Columbia in the United States alone, not to mention rivers and mountains, streets and squares, a broadcast network and a space shuttle. Columbus has not been ignored, by history or in cartography.

Even so, the controversy that raged for centuries around Vespucci and the naming of America has not entirely died out in academic circles. Morison, the Columbus partisan, found little to justify Vespucci's name's being given to the New World. In *The European Discovery of America: The Southern Voyages,* he issues a mocking toast: "So, here's to you Amerigo! Liar though you were, you made three long transatlantic voyages, wrote entertainingly about them, and played your cards so cleverly as to be elected to the exclusive club of the immortals."

Luck and perfidy, these are clouds that have long shadowed Vespucci's reputation. J. H. Parry, however, is more circumspect. "Vespucci's place in the story of discovery of the sea has always been difficult to assess," he writes, and concludes only that there is "plenty of room for differences of opinion."

Frederick J. Pohl, writing in 1966 in enthusiastic defense of Vespucci, charges that the "verbal intemperance" of Las Casas led to history's portrayal of Vespucci as "a sly thief who cunningly robbed Columbus of his rightful glory." In his *History of the Indies,* Las Casas said: "And it is well to give thought here to the injustice and offense that Amerigo Vespucci seems to have done the Admiral, or those who first printed his four voyages, attributing to himself, or alluding only to him, the discovery of this mainland."

These provocative words encapsulate the controversy. The central issues stem from the question of whether Columbus or Vespucci was the first to explore the mainland of South America and recognize it as a land of continental proportions. By extension, the argument is over whether Vespucci was the first to appreciate this mainland to be a "new world," and not an appendage of Asia, as Columbus had kept insisting. Finally, there is the matter of whether Vespucci exaggerated his reports, claiming more voyages than he actually undertook, and then had a hand in publicizing his exploits so effectively that his name was inscribed prominently on an influential map in 1507.

The Las Casas accusations have echoed through nearly all subsequent accounts. With the revival of scholarly interest in Columbus in the late eighteenth century and throughout the nineteenth, historians discounted Vespucci as an explorer, contending that many of his recorded exploits were sheer invention. In 1777, the historian William Robertson called Vespucci "a lucky imposter." Ralph Waldo Emerson expressed indignation that "broad America must wear the name of a thief." Disparaging Vespucci as "the pickle-dealer at Seville," Emerson charged that this man had "managed in this lying world to supplant Columbus and baptize half of the earth with his own dishonest name."

A less emotional and presumably more balanced look at Vespucci and the naming of America is now possible. Humboldt in 1837 uncovered evidence that he said "proved that Amerigo Vespucci had no part in the naming of the New Continent." Subsequent historical research also puts a more appealing face on Vespucci.

Vespucci, more than most participants in the early explorations, was a man of the Renaissance. Born in 1454 in Florence, he grew up in an upper-class family whose circle of friends included the artist Botticelli and the powerful Medicis, patrons of art, science, and philosophy who secured for Florence its central place in the Italian Renaissance. Domenico Ghirlandaio's painting in a Florence church preserves to this day likenesses of several members of the Vespucci family, including Amerigo as a handsome boy next to the Virgin. This was the kind of family background that Ferdinand, Columbus's illegitimate son and biographer, probably wished for himself.

Young Amerigo received a humanist education from a scholarly uncle and developed a voracious appetite for learning. While still in his twenties, he joined the banking and commercial firm of Lorenzo and Giovanni de' Medici. At the end of 1491, they sent him to Seville as the Medici representative dealing with Juanoto Berardi, the merchant banker who was one of Columbus's backers in 1492. Through Berardi, Vespucci very likely met Columbus on his return in 1493 and then handled many of the preparations for the second voyage. After

Berardi's death in 1495, Vespucci became one of Seville's leading outfitters of ships on his own and earned rare praise from Columbus as an honest ship chandler.

But Vespucci could no longer resist the lure of the new lands beyond the sea. His reading and his acquaintance with navigators had given him an expertise in cosmography, and soon he had to go and see for himself. This is where the controversy begins.

It is not certain, for example, whether Vespucci made four voyages or no more than two. The confusion arises because of the publication in Florence of pamphlets purporting to be written by Vespucci. The first tract, in 1504, *Mundus Novus (New World),* included letters he presumably wrote to his Medici patron, Lorenzo the Magnificent. The title itself is of considerable significance, for it planted in the minds of the reading public in Europe the idea that the discoveries represented a New World, and this idea came to be associated with Vespucci. Two voyages were mentioned in this account, each of which included extensive reconnaissance of the South American coast. A second tract, entitled *Four Voyages* and printed in 1505, contained the purported letter of Vespucci to Piero Soderini, an old schoolmate who had risen to chief magistrate of Florence. The so-called Letter to Soderini attributed four voyages to Vespucci. The first, in 1497, had him sailing with a Spanish expedition that reached the coast of South America a year before Columbus left on his third voyage, when Columbus sighted the waters of the Orinoco. On the 1497 expedition, Vespucci also was said to have coasted the continent of North America, along Central America, Mexico, and Florida, which, if true, would have made him the first European to do so. The second expedition described in the Letter to Soderini occurred in 1499 and had Vespucci exploring a stretch of the South American coast. The third, in 1501, was for the Portuguese and involved extensive explorations far down the coast of Brazil. And the fourth, in 1503, was another Portuguese voyage to the Brazilian coast.

The two pamphlets are now generally regarded as forgeries. Scholars had become suspicious because their publication had been ignored in Spain at the time by both friends and opponents of Columbus. The friends would surely have reacted angrily (the accusations by Las Casas were written years later, and he entertained the possibility that the blame should be placed not on Vespucci but on "those who first printed his four voyages"). The opponents would likely have used this as further evidence to discredit Columbus. No reference to any possible Vespuccian priority of discovery was made in the case of the Columbus heirs against the crown, even though the government was going out of its way to find excuses to limit or reduce the Columbus claims. It must, therefore, have been well known that Vespucci had no part in the published exaggerations.

Nor, it seems, did the publication cause the thin-skinned Columbus to alter his favorable opinion of Vespucci, of whom he never had any but kind words. In a letter in 1505 to his son Diego, Columbus said Vespucci "always showed a desire to please me and is a very respectable man." He may have been recalling the time when Berardi's bankrupt business was being liquidated. According to the historian Consuelo Varela, Vespucci apparently saw to it that an outstanding bill owed by the admiral to Berardi disappeared from the books. Vespucci's favors did not end there. After Columbus's death, Varela has written, it was Vespucci who came forward to aid the family by testifying to the authenticity of the admiral's signature on a document concerning a tract of land in Hispaniola.

Nearly all scholars agree with the judgment rendered in the 1920s by Alberto Magnaghi, an Italian authority on Vespucci. The printed letters, he concluded, were spurious, a case of skillful manipulations of the Florentine's actual writings. Authenticated letters written by Vespucci document his participation in two voyages of exploration; these were the second and third described in the Letter to Soderini.

On the first of these, the voyage of 1499–1500, he accompanied Alonso de Ojeda, the erstwhile Columbus captain. They reached the coast of South America in the vicinity of what is now French Guiana. When Ojeda remained to exploit pearl discoveries off Venezuela (the name is a Vespucci inspiration, because the villages built on piles in the coastal waters reminded him of Venice), Vespucci headed south with part of the fleet and sighted a muddy estuary that was presumably the mouth of the Amazon River. He finally turned back somewhere near Cape São Roque, on the Brazilian bulge. Vespucci had explored a small part of the Brazilian coast, he would learn, at approximately the same time as Pedro Álvares Cabral's historic landfall, word of which reached Lisbon in the summer of 1500. On returning to Spain, Vespucci spoke of lands he had explored as the Indies and proposed going back to search for a way around this peninsula to get to the Indian Ocean. Clearly, his thinking at that time accorded with Columbus's.

In May 1501, Vespucci embarked on his second voyage, this time with a Portuguese fleet commanded by Nuño Manuel. They sailed directly for the Brazilian coast near the equator and then made their way steadily south; how far south is not clear, but perhaps as far as the Río de la Plata or even down to Patagonia. The long coastline impressed Vespucci enough for him to write that "we came to a new land, which we perceived to be a continent." There it was, the glimmering of a new idea of fundamental importance in history. Whether Vespucci now suspected this was not the Indies but a continent separate from Asia is a matter of dispute. But he had seen enough to take back to Europe the news that would soon put a new continent on the map.

The Vespucci letters were entertaining as well as informative. His lively style some historians have labeled journalistic, meaning no compliment, and he did have an eye for the novel and colorful. Vespucci's description of what were to European minds exotic lands and people was detailed and explicit; he was unsparing in accounts of Indian warfare and cannibalism and unabashed in telling of their sexual mores.

The women, Vespucci tells his readers, were sexually attractive, even after childbirth, and more lascivious than the men. They were "graceful of body, very well proportioned, whose bodies reveal no defect or malformed member; and although they go completely naked, they are firm-fleshed." To satisfy their "inordinate lust," they enlarged the penises of their lovers by the application of insect venom. Vespucci left the reader to imagine that he was more than a detached observer. "They showed a great desire," he reports, "to have carnal knowledge of us Christians."

These people, Vespucci also records, did little work, cultivated no crops, and had no desire for riches apart from brightly colored feathers and necklaces of small stones. The people slept in nets, which came to be known in Europe as hammocks, after the Carib name for them. Vespucci told of people who thought nothing of urinating in public, often while in conversation, but took care to defecate out of view. He was sufficiently impressed with their cleanliness—they washed themselves frequently—for us to suspect that in this they may have been superior to Europeans of the day.

In a letter indisputably from Vespucci, the writing flair and choice of subject matter are revealed to be his own. The forgers of the pamphlets must have had plenty of authentic material to work from;

they may have enlarged on his geographic accomplishments, but not so much on his descriptions of people and places. This particular letter was a crisp account of people completely beyond the European experience. "They have no laws or faith, and live according to nature," he writes to Lorenzo the Magnificent. "They do not recognize the immortality of the soul, they have among them no private property, because everything is common; they have no boundaries of kingdoms and provinces, and no king! They obey nobody, each is lord unto himself."

On the subject of matrimony, Vespucci reports: "Their marriages are not with one woman but with as many as they like, and without much ceremony, and we have known someone who had ten women; they are jealous of them, and if it happens that one of these women is unfaithful, he punishes her and beats her and puts her away."

Vespucci came away without romantic illusions about these people living in nature. "They are a warlike people, and among them is much cruelty," he writes. They made slaves of their captives and, if they were women, slept with them. They cut up the enemy dead and ate them. Vespucci saw in their huts cured human flesh hanging like hams. One of the men told him of eating the flesh of more than 200 bodies.

What "astonished" Vespucci was the apparent absence of any reason for the warfare, he writes, "since they have no property or lords or kings or desire for plunder, or lust to rule, which seems to me to be the cause of wars and of disorder." This can be seen as a commentary on Europeans as much as on the perplexing native people of Brazil.

Vivid and entertaining, these Vespucci letters were a publishing sensation in Europe in the first decade of the sixteenth century. The Soderini Letter was soon translated from Italian into Latin, French, and German. The Columbus Letter to Santángel at the end of his first voyage had been widely published, but that was years ago, and his vague and cautious descriptions no longer satisfied readers intrigued by the new lands. Only a few fragmentary accounts of the second Columbus voyage were published. And the third voyage, from 1498 through 1500, was doubly disastrous to Columbus's reputation.

Departing from Seville in May 1498, Columbus steered a more southerly course and on July 31 reached an island off the northeastern coast of South America. The three high mountains he sighted inspired him to give the island the name Trinidad, for the Holy Trinity. A few days later, Columbus saw a coastline to the south and encountered the broad delta of the Orinoco River, probably at a place known today as Punta Bombeador. From the enormous volume of fresh water issuing from the river into the Gulf of Paria, he began to suspect that he had reached a mainland of considerable size. In his journal, as related by Las Casas, he expressed puzzlement "that he could not see a land which was large enough to contain the sources of such large rivers, unless, he says, it was a continent." Las Casas affirmed these to be the very words of Columbus. On August 5, he or some of his men set foot on the coast of Venezuela in what was probably the first landing of Europeans in South America.

But Columbus did not pursue these investigations. He seemed more eager to attend to his previous discoveries. He turned and sailed for Santo Domingo, where he found the colony in a profound state of crisis. His brothers, Bartholomew and Diego, had failed to maintain even a semblance of order. Some of the colonists had mutinied, and the mistreated Indians were retaliating with unceasing warfare on the colony. Finally, the crown had to send in Francisco de Bobadilla, who was empowered to take whatever action was deemed necessary to restore order. It was then that Columbus was arrested by Bobadilla's lieutenants, stripped of his titles, and sent back in irons to Spain in October 1500.

It was an ignominious end to Columbus's authority and to his fame in his lifetime. The crown eventually restored some of his titles, but never again was he allowed to serve as viceroy. He was given permission to make one final voyage, beginning at Seville in April 1502, but was specifically barred from returning to Santo Domingo. He explored the coast of Central America and attempted to establish a settlement in Panama, which had to be abandoned in the face of native opposition.

Historians cite the last voyage as one of his many "missed opportunities." With luck and more persistence, Columbus might have stumbled on the Maya civilization or the Pacific Ocean. As it was, he barely made it back to Spain. He was marooned a year on Jamaica, where he wrote Ferdinand and Isabella to beg for support to conquer the land of Veragua, as the coast of Panama was called, and there seize the mines of Solomon. He alone, so he claimed, knew the direction to these legendary mines on the island known as Ophir whence every three years Solomon's ships had fetched gold. The king and queen, their patience with Columbus sorely tried, did not deign to reply to the incoherent letter. Eventually, Columbus was rescued and arrived back in Spain in November 1504, never to sail again.

With Columbus in eclipse, the crown had increasingly looked to others to continue exploration and exploitation of the new lands, and Europeans turned to Vespucci's writings for the excitement of participating vicariously in the new age. The first discovery of the South American mainland, by Columbus on his third voyage, remained largely unknown to contemporaries. Columbus's letter describing the Orinoco River and his deduction that it flowed from a large continent was unknown to the public; the crown never released it for publication, and it remained unpublished until the nineteenth century. Peter Martyr had dutifully written to his Italian friends about some aspects of the third voyage and the growing apprehension that a new world had been discovered. But the first authorized edition of these letters was not published until 1511. Although pirated versions came out in 1504 and again in 1507 and 1508, by then the perception of a new world across the ocean was widely associated with another explorer, Amerigo Vespucci.

In those days, a small group of scholarly clerics lived in obscurity at the ancient village of St.-Dié on the slopes of the Vosges Mountains in Lorraine. Their isolation belied a deep interest on their part in the geography of the world at large, especially the recent news of discovery. Nor could it prevent them from influencing world thinking, for St.-Dié had a printing press. The canon, Vautrin Lud, had installed the little press in the house of his nephew Nicholas Lud for the dissemination of the works of these scholars. In a letter to the bishop, Vautrin Lud boasted: "You will soon see, God willing, the most important publications from our plates."

It happened that in 1507 their patron, René II, the duke of Lorraine, received a copy of the Soderini Letter, supposedly written by Vespucci, and also a map depicting the regions Vespucci had visited and the many other places explored by the Spanish and the Portuguese. René II turned the material over to his scholars, and presently the name of America entered history.

When the Soderini Letter came into their hands, the scholars put aside their work on a new edition of Ptolemy's geography and in April of that year produced a small volume called *Cosmographiae Introductio.*

The 103-page book contained a summary of principles of geography and cartography, in the manner of Ptolemy, and also the report of the four voyages of Vespucci and other knowledge that "was unknown to Ptolemy and has been recently discovered." The scholars, breaking with traditional practice, recognized that it was no longer sufficient to publish the second-century Ptolemy as the received word and the sum of all geographical knowledge.

These men produced, as they said, "a little work not only poetic but geographical in its character." Two of them, Jean Basin de Sandaucourt and Matthias Ringmann, were poets and may have conceived of the name America. The young Ringmann, in particular, had a fondness for words and geographical names. The romantic Ringmann may well have dreamed up the name, but the man given the most credit for the book, the one who prepared the accompanying map of the newly discovered lands, was Martin Waldseemüller, an illustrator and cartographer from southern Germany. In one of several similar passages, Waldseemüller delivered the book's most sensational proposal:

> Today these parts of the world [Europe, Asia, Africa] have been more fully explored, and a fourth part has been discovered by Americus Vespucius, as we shall see later. Since Europa and Asia have received the names of women, I see no reason why we should not call this other part "Amerige," that is to say, the land of Americus, or America after the sagacious discoverer Americus. We are exactly informed concerning its situation and the customs of its people by the four navigations of Americus.

Waldseemüller's large map, called "A Map of the World According to the Traditions of Ptolemy and the Voyages of Americus Vespucius," was decorated with two portraits: Ptolemy facing east, and Vespucci facing west. Columbus was not ignored. On a section of the map showing the Caribbean, the cartographer wrote: "These islands were discovered by Columbus, an admiral of Genoa, at the command of the King of Spain." To the south, though, he drew with remarkable accuracy the outlines of the South American continent (someone had definitely sailed much of that coast) and affixed to it, in the region of Brazil, the name America. No such name was applied to the North American continent, whose shape and extent were still poorly known. On the large map, the two continents were separated by a strait, but on an inset map, the two were joined at the Isthmus of Panama. With more prescience than he could have known, in those years before Balboa or Magellan, Waldseemüller's map showed a wide ocean between the New World and Asia.

The book and the map were immediate successes. To meet demand, the press at St.-Dié turned out more than 1,000 copies over the next year—a best-seller in those days. Other editions of the Vespucci letters enjoyed a popularity surpassing any writings of Columbus. And so the name America stuck. The 1507 Waldseemüller map has been called "the baptismal certificate of the New World." Other cartographers applied the name to a globe in 1509 and on several subsequent maps. Years later, having second thoughts, Waldseemüller removed the name from some editions, but after his death in 1518, printers restored the name America. Then, in 1538, the great cartographer Gerardus Mercator published a map of the world that extended the name to both continents. Thenceforth it was North America and South America.

The historian Daniel J. Boorstin has offered two ways of looking upon the naming of America, each rich in irony. In a lecture to the National Geographic Society in 1987, he remarked that the Waldseemüller book was an early demonstration of the "irreversible powers of the press." In *The Discoverers,* Boorstin accepted the results with equanimity. "It was appropriate," he writes, "that the name America should be affixed on the New World in a manner casual and accidental, since the European encounter with this new world had been so unintentional."

The influence of the 1507 publication was swift and widespread because it reflected and reinforced the emerging awareness among learned people of Europe of the true nature of the discoveries made since 1492. They were not sure what these lands were, but no longer did they put much credence in what Columbus said about their being the Indies. Metaphorically at first, then more literally, they began to speak of a new world.

The term "new world" was used by Cardinal Ascanius Sforza after the first Columbus voyage. But the prolific letter-writer Peter Martyr seems to have been the one to introduce the phrase into the parlance of the day. In a letter describing reports of Columbus's establishment of the colony at La Isabela on the second voyage, he wrote: "And there on the feast of the Three Kings (for when treating of this country one must speak of a new world, so distant is it and so devoid of civilization and religion) the Holy Sacrifice was celebrated by thirteen priests." Used here, the phrase was merely an expression of the exotic, without geographic significance. But Martyr was clearly taken with the metaphor, and the news he picked up in court circles must have emboldened him in its use. All the evidence suggested that these lands, wherever they fit on the globe, were far different from anything described by Marco Polo. A few months later, in a letter written in October 1494 revealing his intention to compile a book on the subject, Peter Martyr told his correspondent: "Day by day more and more marvelous things are reported from the new world [*ab orbe novo*], through that Colonus the Ligurian. . . ." At this time, Martyr also employed a term with more geographic meaning. "Hear what things have lately been discovered at the antipodes in the 'Western Hemisphere' [*ab occidente hemispherii antipodum*]." There must have been discussions as early as 1494 to the effect that Columbus had actually found a new habitable world at the Antipodes to balance the habitable world of the ancients. If this should vindicate the Greeks, who appreciated the symmetry of the concept, it challenged the medieval Christian thinkers who denied the possibility of Antipodes inhabited by "the race of Adam."

By 1500, some Europeans were using the term "new world" regularly and apparently meaning it in the sense of a new habitable part of the globe. Columbus's interpretations were thus received with increasing skepticism. No matter what Columbus had believed and forced his crew to swear to, on his map of 1500 Juan de la Cosa drew Cuba not as part of the Chinese mainland but as an island. La Cosa's map, however, though it traces a mainland from the northern regions sighted by English expeditions down to Brazil as a continuous littoral, had the land firmly attached to Asia as a tremendous peninsula.

A more questioning approach to Columbus's claims was also taken by Peter Martyr. In 1501, he recalled that Columbus had named the coast of Cuba "Alpha and Omega, because he thought that there our East ended when the sun set in that island, and our West began when the sun rose." Several times Martyr cautiously inserted phrases like "he thought" or "he expected" when reporting the geographic ideas of Columbus.

It was in 1498, in the Gulf of Paria and facing the Orinoco delta, that Columbus came close to a recognition of what he had really discovered. "I believe this is a very great continent, until today unknown," he wrote in his journal. The keen observer had studied the waters of the mighty river and reached the brilliant deduction that they could only issue from a land of great breadth. But the observer's medieval mind betrayed him. He persisted in believing the land to be an extension of the Asian continent.

In the same entry in his journal, after declaring this to be "a very great continent," Columbus cited as supporting evidence stories Caribs had told him of a mainland to the south, but he seemed to set more store by early Christian concepts of cosmography. There must be more land, he noted, because the Book of Esdras held that "the six parts of the world are of dry land, and one of water." Columbus's mind then drifted into denunciations of "enemies" and "doubters" who, according to his self-pitying way of thinking, had plagued his every effort to bring greatness and power to Spain. Pleading for understanding and appreciation, he wrote at the same time: "Your Highnesses have also gained these immense territories, which amount to Another World, in which Christendom will take great joy, and our Holy Faith will in time wax mightily. I say this in all honor, and because I wish Your Highnesses to be the greatest rulers in the world, I mean rulers of all."

For the first time, Columbus had used the term "another world" *(que son otro mundo)*—that is, a new continent, unknown to the ancients or Marco Polo. Even so, his mind could not accept this to be another landmass independent of the Orbis Terrarum, the known world of three joined continents. He believed this to be part of Asia. He also believed he was on to something still more wondrous.

The more Columbus brooded over what he had seen, the more he was convinced that he had indeed been close to the terrestrial paradise. As he wanted to believe he had reached Asia, the admiral also wanted so much to believe he had arrived at the threshold to the Biblical Eden.

The Garden of Eden is the first geographical site mentioned in the Bible, and as Delno C. West, an authority on medieval history, has pointed out, its existence and location were often debated by medieval writers from Thomas Aquinas to Dante. St. Augustine, whose works Columbus often quoted, concluded that Eden existed somewhere in the east a few degrees from the equator. Aquinas said it was "shut off from the habitable world by mountains or seas or some torrid region which can not be crossed." Dante placed paradise on the other side of the world, in the vast ocean exactly opposite Jerusalem on an island with the highest mountain on earth. Pierre d'Ailly located it on the edge of Asia. Before 1492, Columbus had made notations in his copy of d'Ailly's *Imago Mundi* next to the text reading: "Beyond the Tropic of Capricorn is found the finest habitable region because there it is found the worthiest and most noblest part of the world, namely the Earthly Paradise."

Finding the terrestrial paradise had been on Columbus's mind for years, and here he was, as he believed, within a few miles of it. He revealed his thinking in a letter to the crown written from Española.

"I have always read that the world comprising the land and the water is spherical, and the recorded experiences of Ptolemy and all others have proved this by the eclipses of the moon and other observations made from east to west, as well as by the elevation of the pole from north to south," Columbus wrote. Reasonable enough, so far. Then he reported his observations of irregularities in the position of the North Star. Since he also had been so near the equator and had observed the river flowing from a large land, Columbus sought a unifying explanation for these phenomena. He tried too hard. Morison has to concede: "He was not one to put two and two together and make four; rather, in the Admiral's way of reasoning, two and two make ten."

So it was that Columbus affirmed that the earth had "the form of a pear." Spacecraft orbiting earth have revealed as much, but hardly to the degree or in the manner imagined by Columbus. He believed the world to be round except at the stalk, which he described as a "prominence like a woman's nipple." This prominence, he affirmed, is the highest place on earth and nearest to heaven, and it is situated below the equator at the eastern extremity of the sea, which he believed to be the "countries and island of the East come to an end." The observed irregularities in the position of the North Star, he concluded, meant that as he sailed close to the equator he was rising in elevation (there is a slight bulge there) because of the proximity of the stalk of the pear-shaped earth.

Medieval Christian cartographers had made a practice of placing paradise at some vague site at the nether end of Asia, and Columbus felt sure he had identified the site. He was convinced this prominence in the pear-shaped earth "is the spot of the Earthly Paradise whither no one can go but by God's permission." For him it was a doubly momentous discovery. It not only confirmed his belief that he had reached the bounds of Asia, where Eden was to be found, but it also seemed to confirm the words of church fathers that he had read with passionate belief. The waters of the Orinoco, he said, must flow from the fountain in paradise. "There are great indications of this being the Terrestrial Paradise," he went on to state, "for its site coincides with the opinion of holy and wise theologians, and, moreover, the older evidences agree with the supposition, for I have never either read or heard of fresh water coming in so large a quantity in close conjunction with the water of the sea."

The crown must not have been impressed by Columbus's discovery of paradise, for this letter was apparently never discussed or published. If anything, it probably caused them to lose any remaining faith they had in him as a discoverer. Peter Martyr reported Columbus's claim in one of his letters but gave it little credence. Closing his comments on the subject, he wrote: "Let us now therefore return to the history from which we have too much digressed." Las Casas, writing later, found the ideas "neither absurd nor unreasonable," though he said that he did not believe it personally. Ferdinand Columbus must have been embarrassed, for he omitted any reference to this in his father's biography.

Columbus seemed to recognize that there would be doubters. "If this river does not come from the Earthly Paradise, then it must come from an immense land in the south, about which we as yet know nothing," he wrote in the letter to the crown. He had considered this alternative, but rejected it; he much preferred finding the way to paradise than finding a new continent that did not square with his geographic preconceptions based on the Ptolemaic-Christian cosmography of one single landmass comprising Europe, Asia, and Africa. "But I am quite convinced in my own mind," he asserted, "that the Earthly Paradise is where I have said."

An obsession with paradise was not new for Columbus. Returning from his first voyage, he declared: "The Earthly Paradise is at the end of the Orient, because it is a most temperate place." He was reasoning not from anything he had observed but from his reading of Pierre d'Ailly. Nor was this a singular case of letting his beliefs and the authority of early writers influence his interpretations. Despite the lack of evidence on that first voyage or any subsequent one, he insisted he had reached the Indies. On the third voyage, the Indians brought him pearls, and he pondered their origin but fell back on an explanation given by Pliny. As reported by Las Casas, Columbus wrote in his journal: "Close to the sea there were countless oysters adhering to the branches of the trees that go into the sea, with their mouths open to receive the dew which falls from the leaves, until the drop falls, out of which pearls will be formed, as Pliny says."

In *The Conquest of America,* Tzvetan Todorov observes: "There is nothing of the modern empiricist about Columbus: the decisive argument is an argument of authority, not experience. He knows in advance what he will find; the concrete experience is there to illustrate a truth already possessed, not to be interrogated according to preestablished rules in order to seek the truth." Only in matters of navigation did Columbus think and act on observed reality. As Todorov concludes: "Two characters exist (for us) in Columbus, and whenever the navigator's profession is no longer at stake, the finalist strategy prevails in his system of interpretation: the latter no longer consists in seeking the truth but in finding confirmations of a truth known in advance (or, as we say, in wishful thinking)."

Since the 1497 Vespucci voyage described in the Letter to Soderini has been discredited as a fiction, Columbus must have been the first European to sight the South American mainland. But, seeing the waters of the Orinoco in 1498, he shaded his eyes to anything but fantasy. It was there and then that he lost his chance to have a continent named for him.

Columbus had shown the way across the Ocean Sea and found new lands, but the clarity of vision that led him to these transcendental discoveries deserted him in his stubborn and increasingly muddled insistence that these were outlying islands of the Indies. Also, his western route to the Indies, if that was what he had discovered, had lost much of its importance with the triumphant return of Vasco da Gama to Lisbon in 1499 after a voyage around the Cape of Good Hope to what was indisputably India. His powers of persuasion failed him in the face of mounting evidence that it was not Cipangu or Cathay he had discovered, but some confounded barrier to the coveted Indies. Only in Spain were the new lands still called the Indies for years to come, even after the Spanish themselves recognized America for what it was: a new world.

The recognition there and elsewhere can be attributed in large part to Vespucci, whose writings caught the European imagination. He was an open-minded observer whose sound geographical judgment led Europeans to an understanding of what had been discovered. No one at the time seems to have seriously disputed the appropriateness of naming these lands for Vespucci.

Vespucci assessed the new lands from a more modern perspective than Columbus ever did. "If there is an earthly Paradise in this world," Vespucci once wrote, "then it cannot be far from these southern lands." That "if" reveals a man emerging from medieval thinking. Describing the variety of animal life in South America, he was moved to the brink of heresy by doubting that they could all have found room in Noah's Ark. He rarely invoked the Scriptures or church authorities. He was a man of the Renaissance, a Florentine, and more likely, in expressing the beauty and wonder of the sights, to be reminded of the paradise of Dante and Poliziano.

With Columbus's waning repute and Martyr's letters still not widely read, it was left to Vespucci to shape thinking with his stories and the clear geographical insights in two publications, one of which, it will be recalled, was titled *Mundus Novus—New World.* "It is lawful," he wrote in this book, "to call [the new countries] a new world, because none of those countries were known to our ancestors, and to all who hear about them they will be entirely new. For the opinion of the ancients was that the greater part of the world beyond the equinoctial line to the south was not land, but only sea, which they called the Atlantic; and if they affirmed that any continent was there, they gave many reasons for denying that it was inhabited. But this their opinion is false and entirely opposed to the truth. My last voyage has proved it, for I have found a continent in that southern part; more populous and more full of animals than our Europe or Asia or Africa, and even more temperate and pleasant than any other region known to us."

Here, in words conveying conviction and mounting excitement, was the identification of the lands as a New World. In *The Invention of America,* Edmundo O'Gorman credits Vespucci with understanding that the lands he had explored were a different geographic entity from the Orbis Terrarum, because he expressly distinguishes them from the three parts that make up that familiar world-view. But Vespucci's contribution to thinking went further. For Vespucci, O'Gorman observes, "the true novelty lay in the fact that the newly-explored southern lands not only were habitable but were in fact inhabited. That is why they appear to him not only as something 'new' in the sense of hitherto unknown, but also as a new 'world.' " Previously, the "world" was neither more nor less than the Orbis Terrarum.

Columbus may have suspected as much, and used the expression "another world," but he could not accept what he had seen, for to accept it carried the implication that he had been sorely mistaken in his estimate of the breadth of the Orbis Terrarum and his assumption that he would find Asia across the Western Sea almost exactly where he had arrived. Vespucci's voyage and observations, as O'Gorman points out, were the decisive turning point in the real discovery of America. His voyage, the Mexican historian writes, "became the empirical determinant that opened up the possibility of explaining the new-found lands in a way that contradicted the accepted picture of the world."

Furthermore, Vespucci provided evidence for the conception that the new lands were not only a separate geographic unity, but also constituted an imposing barrier running north and south across the ocean between Europe and Asia. Much of the early exploration of America would concentrate on breaching that barrier, rather than examining the new territory for its own sake.

Vespucci did not fully realize the significance of all this, or else shied away from expressly proclaiming a new geography. Instead, the recognition of the independence of the new lands, separate from the Orbis Terrarum, was first enunciated and illustrated by those scholarly clerics of St.-Dié. With their 1507 book, *Cosmographiae Introductio,* and the world map by Waldseemüller, the lands were identified as the "fourth part" of the world, distinct from the other three continents, and in recognition of this independence were given a proper name—America.

America, as O'Gorman writes, "did not suddenly emerge full-blown as the result of the chance discovery by Columbus of a small island on October 12, 1492." The "invention" of America, he continues, came "from a complex, living process of exploration and interpretation which ended by endowing the newly-found lands with a proper and peculiar meaning of their own, the meaning of being the 'fourth part' of the world."

Vespucci, it may be fair to say, *discovered* what it was that Columbus had *found,* and Waldseemüller interpreted, publicized, and immortalized this recognition as an achievement of surpassing magnitude. It earned Vespucci the respect of contemporaries. Spain elevated the Florentine to the new position of "pilot-major" and gave him responsibility for training and licensing mariners who went to explore the New World—America. He died in 1512 from malaria he had contracted in the land that would bear his name. Even if the naming of America was an accident of history, Amerigo Vespucci can be said to deserve the honor.

14

God's Messenger

In the last half of 1500, while imprisoned in Santo Domingo or during his voyage back to Spain in chains, Columbus wrote a long letter intended for the king and queen. How different it was from the missive he sent in 1493 proclaiming discovery. How different Columbus seemed—or was this a manifestation of the essential Columbus? He addressed the letter to Doña Juana de Torres, the sister of Antonio de Torres, a faithful captain on his second expedition. Since she was a confidante of Isabella, he was sure his message would reach the court. He was an infirm and dispirited man who felt himself to be misunderstood and unappreciated, and this was a cry from his soul.

"Of the new heaven and the new earth which the Lord made, and of which St. John writes in the Apocalypse, as the Lord told of it through the mouth of Isaiah, He made me the messenger, and He showed me the way," Columbus wrote. "None would believe me, but to my Lady the Queen He gave the gift of understanding, and of great courage, and made her the heiress of all, as His dear and best loved daughter."

As God's messenger, he reminded the court, he had secured for Spain "another world," a domain greater in area than Europe and Africa and including "more than one thousand seven hundred islands." And his reward, he lamented, was "insult and ingratitude." Was there no justice? "Not even if I had stolen the Indies, or had given them to the Moors, would I have been treated so dishonorably!" he wrote. "In this undertaking I have lost my youth, as well as my due honors."

Ferdinand and Isabella received the pathetic Columbus on December 17 and sought to reassure him of their sympathy and gratitude. Oviedo gave the following description of the meeting:

> The Admiral went to kiss the hands of the King and Queen, and, weeping, gave his excuses as best he could. And when they

> had listened to him, they comforted him with great gentleness and spoke such words as composed him to some degree. And since his services had been so great, though somewhat erratic, the princely gratitude of Their Royal Highnesses could not allow the Admiral to be wrongfully used, and accordingly they gave immediate instruction that all the revenues and privileges which had been taken from him at the time of his arrest be now restored to him. But they gave no promise that he would be reinstated as Governor.

The contrast between this royal reception and the one following the first voyage could not be sharper. The king and queen now were under no illusions about Columbus. He had been a failure as viceroy, and they had strong doubts about the validity of his claims to have reached the Indies. With the monarchs putting their faith in a new generation of explorers and colonial administrators, Columbus's influence had diminished further. They were in no hurry to fulfill the promise of restoring revenues and privileges to the troubled and troubling explorer.

To historians, Columbus's behavior in this interlude has been perplexing, not to say disconcerting and rather embarrassing. They have never quite known what to make of his self-proclaimed calling as God's messenger.

No doubt Columbus was a pious man—demonstrably so. His journals and letters are replete with expressions of faith in God, invocations of the names of Christ, Mary, and the saints, and affirmations of a missionary fervor to spread the Gospel throughout the world. His affinity with the Franciscans is well established. He was a careful student of the Bible and the writings of church authorities, and regularly cited them in interpreting his actions and discoveries. But even if his piety might exceed conventional standards of the day, it did not necessarily follow that this was the lever that hoisted him to the pinnacle of history: spirituality was only one side of the man, in the prevailing estimate of history.

It may be, on closer examination, that spirituality, which fed his apocalyptic view of history, lay at the heart of the man and was the dominant force in his life and actions.

A remarkable document, prepared after his third voyage but long ignored by historians, reveals the depth and passion of Columbus's belief that he was God's messenger. This work can be read as compelling evidence that his spirituality was the force motivating his vision and sustaining him through years of ridicule, hardship, and achievement. At the very least, it outlined a framework for interpreting the discoveries of Columbus, as he wished the world and his monarchs to understand them.

While he awaited his audience with the king and queen in late 1500, Columbus lived at the monastery of Las Cuevas across the Guadalquivir River from Seville. There, in collaboration with Gaspar Gorricio, a Carthusian monk, he began collecting materials for an extensive notebook of Biblical scriptures and the words of a wide range of ancient and medieval authors. A basic draft of the notebook was completed a year later. All the entries were composed in Latin (except for some verse in Spanish) and exhibit traces of eight different hands at work. The handwriting is mostly that of Gorricio and Ferdinand Columbus and, in a few instances, Columbus himself. Correspondence between Columbus and Gorricio has convinced scholars that in content and concept, if not always in the actual writing, the manuscript was the work of Columbus.

Columbus described the document as a notebook or handbook "of sources, statements, opinions and prophecies on the subject of the recovery of God's Holy City and Mount Zion, and on the discovery and evangelization of the islands of the Indies and of all other peoples and nations." The work revealed a man who believed he had a special relationship with God and was acting as the agent of God's scheme for history. Nothing had altered Columbus's conviction that he was a divinely called man of destiny, and in the manuscript he marshaled evidence from the prophecies of the Bible to show that his recent discoveries were only the prelude to the realization of a greater destiny. He seemed to see his role as not unlike John the Baptist's vis-à-vis Christ. He had prepared the way for the king and queen of Spain to recover the Holy Land to Christendom and thereby set the stage for the grandiose climax of Christian history, the salvation of all the world's peoples and their gathering at Zion on the eve of the end of time.

Columbus never finished the manuscript and apparently never submitted any of it to the monarchs. The rough draft that has survived, with some pages missing, is the one Gorricio, after making only minor additions, had returned to Columbus in March 1502. At the time, Columbus was leaving Seville to begin his fourth voyage. Later, his son Hernando found the manuscript among Columbus's papers and used it in writing his biography. Las Casas also was familiar with it. But few other historians since have bothered to explore this source of insight into Columbus and his mission.

The manuscript is now known as *Libro de las profecías,* the *Book of Prophecies,* and it resides in the Biblioteca Colombina at Seville. The first full translation of it into English has just been completed by Delno C. West, a professor of medieval history at Northern Arizona University in Flagstaff. The document was not published in its entirety in any language until 1894, and this limited edition was seldom examined by scholars. In his own research, West came upon a copy in the Firestone Library at Princeton University in which the pages were uncut and obviously unread.

Historians have ignored the *Book of Prophecies,* West charges, because they are "curiously reluctant to admit that the first American hero was influenced by prophetic ideas." If the book indeed reflected Columbus's thinking before 1492, it undermined the popular model of Columbus as a man of the modern age who applied reason in conceiving his bold venture. It exposed him as one hopelessly mired in the medieval world, obsessed with eschatology and driven by a supposed call from God to carry out a mission of apocalyptic dimensions. That his actions ushered in the modern age, it would seem, was as much an accident as was his discovery of America.

For a long time, most historians who had read the document dismissed it as the product of his troubled and possibly senile mind. Since it was written after the disastrous third voyage, such an interpretation makes some sense; his letter to Doña Juana exposed a mind verging on paranoia. Henry Harrisse called the treatise a "deplorable lucubration," and Justin Winsor attributed it to Columbus's "mental hallucinations" in his later years. Filson Young believed Columbus's mind had sunk into "an entirely dark and sordid stupor." West notes that a few writers, attempting to prove that Columbus was a converted Jew, considered the manuscript to be a kind of *auto da fé;* his less-than-sincere intention was to convince the sovereigns and the world of his orthodox Christian beliefs. On the other hand, some biographers considered these ideas to be typical of the thinking of pious fifteenth-century Christians and thus of no particular value in defining Columbus. Some recent learned articles purporting to dissect his mind never even mention the *Book of Prophecies.* Morison, in only one brief reference to the book, decided this was merely a tactic to appeal to Isabella's mysticism and "convince her that he was the chosen man of destiny to conquer an Other World and bring home treasure wherewith to recover the Holy Sepulchre."

That may have been one immediate aim, but it is no excuse for dismissing the *Book of Prophecies* as being of only minor interest. West and a few other scholars have belatedly examined the document with the thoroughness it deserves. They believe it opens a window onto the motives and consuming passion of Columbus.

Columbus opened the *Book of Prophecies* with a letter to the king and queen. He described how God had favored him with "the spirit of intelligence," by which scholars, analyzing the context and use of words, believe he meant the special gift of understanding granted by God. This charismatic gift was in line with Franciscan thinking, with which Columbus identified, and is thought by today's fundamentalist Christians to be bestowed on a select few of God's agents. He also wrote that neither reason nor mathematics nor maps of the world had enabled him to fulfill the Enterprise of the Indies. Instead, he firmly believed it had been God's will:

> With a hand that could be felt, the Lord opened my mind to the fact that it would be possible to sail from here to the Indies, and he opened my will to desire to accomplish the project. This was the fire that burned within me when I came to visit Your Highnesses. All who found out about my project denounced it with laughter and ridiculed me. All the sciences . . . were of no use to me. Quotations of learned opinions were no help. Only Your Majesties had faith and perseverance. Who can doubt that this fire was not merely mine, but also of the Holy Spirit who encouraged me with a radiance of marvelous illumination from his sacred Holy Scriptures, by a most clear and powerful testimony from the forty-four books of the Old Testament, from the four Gospels, from the twenty-three Epistles of the blessed Apostles—urging me to press forward? Continually, without a moment's hesitation, the Scriptures urge me to press forward with great haste.

Some of this is a rehearsal of familiar Columbus expressions: the ridicule and rejection never to be forgotten, and his undying gratitude to the king and queen. But Columbus was also claiming, more explicitly than before, divine origins for his vision of sailing west to the Indies and suggesting that this was a critical element at the time of his negotiations with the monarchs. The *Book of Prophecies* calls for a serious reassessment of the decisive factors, spiritual as well as rational, motivating the enterprise that led to the discovery of America.

Continuing his letter, Columbus affirmed that his voyages of discovery were part of a larger plan. "The Lord purposed that there should be something clearly miraculous in this matter of the voyage to the Indies," he wrote, "so as to encourage me and others in the other matter of the Household of God." The other matter was a proposed crusade to recover the Holy Sepulcher in Jerusalem. It was clearly central to Columbus's thinking at this time in his life, if not earlier. Since the voyages to the Indies "turned out just as our redeemer Jesus Christ had said, and as he had spoken earlier by the mouth of his holy prophets," he wrote, "this is the way we really should believe that the other matter will turn out."

Ever mindful of past rejections, Columbus acknowledged that critics might think him "someone speaking presumptuously out of ignorance." In his defense, he called attention to the words from Matthew (11:25): "O Lord . . . because thou hast hid these things from the wise and prudent and hast revealed them to little ones." God's messenger left no room for doubt that he had been so favored.

His aim in compiling the book was, therefore, to persuade the king and queen that his discoveries had been the fulfillment, up to a point, of all the prophets had foretold and to encourage them to expect the other prophecies, of even greater import, to come to pass in the near future. Columbus outlined a new agenda. First, Christianity must be spread on a global scale, beginning with the lands he had discovered; for Isaiah had foretold the salvation of all people. Second, the riches of these new lands should be dedicated to the recapture of Jerusalem in preparation for the fulfillment of other prophecies in which the Bible foretells "great events for the world." Again he called attention to Isaiah, who was, he pointed out, the preferred prophet of St. Jerome and St. Augustine. Had not Isaiah foreseen the gathering of the faithful on Mount Zion for the culmination of history?

Much of the rest of the *Book of Prophecies* is a compilation of religious writings supporting Columbus's interpretation of his discovery as a critical part of God's scheme for history. Pauline Moffitt Watts, a historian at Sarah Lawrence College, who also has made a close study of the manuscript, has identified two themes running through his selections, particularly those from the Psalms. The first is his obsession with the recovery of Mount Zion, symbol of the Holy Land. A typical example is from Psalm 2:6–8:

I indeed have anointed my King
On Zion, my holy hill.
Let me tell of the decree of the Lord:
He said to me, "you are my son;
Today I have begotten you.
Ask of me and I will make the
nations your inheritance,
and the ends of the earth your possession."

Another example is Psalm 22:27–28:

All the ends of the earth will remember
and turn unto the Lord;
And the clans of the nations will worship
before him
For the kingdom belongs to the Lord;
And he rules over the nations.

A second recurring theme is Columbus's preoccupation with the final conversion of all people to Christianity. He based his conviction on the scripture in which Christ speaks of himself as the Good Shepherd. In John 10:16, Christ says: "And other sheep I have, which are not of this fold: them also I must bring, and they shall hear my voice; and there shall be one fold, and one shepherd." A passage from Augustine not only supported this prophecy, but cast it in words that must have had a special appeal to Columbus. Augustine wrote: "God will prevail, it is said, against them and He will wipe out all the gods of the peoples of the earth, and they will adore Him, each one from its own place, all the peoples of the islands. And indeed not only the peoples of the islands, but all peoples . . ." As Columbus saw it—and he said as much in his prefatory letter—his discoveries of the many islands of the Indies had surely set in motion the worldwide conversion that must precede the gathering at Zion.

Watts also found in the document selections by which Columbus was establishing his own predestined place in the realization of these prophecies. From a popular devotional work attributed to Augustine, Columbus quoted: "Before you formed me in the belly, you knew me, and before I left the womb, whatever pleased you was preordained for me. And those things that concerned me were written in your book, in the secret of your counsel." Another entry was taken from Seneca's tragedy *Medea,* which Columbus had meditated on many times in the years he sought support for his enterprise. "The years will come, in the succession of the ages," Seneca wrote, "when the Ocean will loose the bonds by which we have been confined, when an immense land shall lie revealed, and Tethys shall disclose new worlds, and Thule will no longer be the most remote of countries."

Now that he had accomplished Seneca's prophecy, Columbus felt it was time for the king and queen to assume their own preordained roles. His call to action was introduced by quoting a passage from Jeremiah 25 in which a warning is issued to listen to the message of His servant to spread God's message throughout the world. "God has been sending his messages to you [the king]," Jeremiah warned. "I have faithfully passed them to you, but you have not listened." God's message is that one last chance will be offered for salvation of all nations when the king stands before the Holy Temple in Jerusalem and, as a kind of emperor-messiah, announces God's word to all the world.

Then Columbus cited a letter brought to the Spanish monarchs in 1492 by Genoese ambassadors, on the occasion of the victory over the Moors and the expulsion of Jews from their kingdom. The ambassadors called on Ferdinand and Isabella to lead a new crusade to seize the Holy Land from the infidel: "Not undeservedly or without reason, I call earnestly to your attention, most noble sovereigns, some very important things that are to be observed, since indeed we did read that Joachim the Abbot of Southern Italy has foretold that he is to come from Spain who is to recover again the fortunes of Zion."

Joachim of Fiore, who lived in the twelfth century, was the most important late-medieval apocalyptic writer. His ideas—or what were passed on as his ideas—had enjoyed a revival in the last decades of the fifteenth century, often among the Franciscans. Joachim attempted to discern the patterns of history and to prophesy the events of the apocalypse.

Marjorie Reeves, a historian at Oxford University, has observed that Joachim's writings "opened up the prospect of new human agencies called to participate in the last decisive works of God in history" and this gave "enhanced stature to actors in history." This surely appealed to Columbus. Aspects of Columbus's view of history can be traced back to Joachim, Watts concludes, and some of the lost pages of the *Book of Prophecies* presumably contained many more Joachite materials that must have lent further support for Columbus's own ideas. Although Columbus attributed to Joachim the prediction that Jerusalem would be retaken by someone from Spain, scholars have determined that the source was more probably Arnold of Villanova, physician to the king of Aragon in the late thirteenth century. He was the Spanish conduit for Joachite thinking that flourished in the time of Columbus.

Whatever the provenance of the idea, Columbus was imploring Ferdinand and Isabella to seize the moment and fulfill their roles as actors in the divine plan. There was no time to waste in launching the crusade, for the eschatological clock was ticking. "I believe," Columbus wrote, "that there is evidence that our Lord is hastening these things."

Columbus included in the manuscript a chronology of the world from the Creation, according to the calculation by King Alfonso, "which is considered to be the most exact." From Adam to the "Advent of our Lord Jesus Christ," there had been 5,343 years, making the new total for the year 1501 (the year the manuscript was compiled) to be 6,844 years. "Only one hundred and fifty years," Columbus pointed out, "are lacking for the completion of the seven thousand years which would be the end of the world according to the learned opinions that I have cited above."

The significance of the *Book of Prophecies* depends on the answers to several questions. Were these the thoughts of a broken and disappointed man seeking greater recognition for his accomplishments, embellishing them in his own pious way, and wishing desperately to recoup his fame with one final heroic venture? All the elements for such an emotional state lay in his personality; he was devout and could be self-righteous, proud and self-aggrandizing, and most certainly indomitable. Were these the ruminations of a man dwelling on his own mortal limits and projecting on this not only the end of his life but of the entire world? Or was this an outpouring of the real Columbus, as he had been in conceiving and executing his voyages of discovery?

For the last century and a half, Watts writes, "scholars have almost without exception elaborated the image of Columbus as the bold and innovative explorer who, armed with 'rational' or 'scientific' geography, battled the ignorance and superstition of influential ecclesiastics at the Aragonese court until he finally won royal support for his 'Enterprise of the Indies.' " The writings of Humboldt in the 1830s were influential in establishing this image. Following the lead of Hernando's biography, Humboldt cited two principal sources of Columbus's geographic knowledge and the impetus for his voyages. Columbus had carefully read and annotated his copy of Pierre d'Ailly's *Imago Mundi,* a compendium of knowledge about the world; among other things, d'Ailly argued that the Western Sea was not very wide. And Columbus is supposed to have received two letters written by Paolo Toscanelli, the Florentine physician, reassuring him that the ocean could be crossed and thus the Indies could be reached more quickly by heading west. Even if this correspondence might never have taken place, as has already been discussed, Toscanelli's geographic concepts were widely known in Lisbon and were no doubt familiar to Columbus. In his presentations to the Portuguese and Spanish courts, he drew on this geographic knowledge and projected an image in accord with that fostered by Humboldt and subsequent historians.

But there was the other Columbus, a second image, which must be given its due weight in any analysis of the man. John Leddy Phelan, an American scholar, is credited as the first modern writer to emphasize the other Columbus. In *The Millennial Kingdom of the Franciscans in the New World,* published in 1956, Phelan noted the importance of apocalypticism, specifically Joachimism, in understanding Columbus's mentality.

This second self-image, Watts observes, is epitomized in the signature that Columbus adopted, beginning in 1493. Nearly all of his letters and documents thereafter were signed Christoferens, a Latinization of his given name that means "Christ-bearer." Columbus had long seen in his first name his own destiny. Just as the legendary St. Christopher presumably got his name because he carried Christ over deep waters at great peril, Columbus, his son reported, "crossed over with his company that the Indian nations might become dwellers in the triumphant Church of Heaven." He thus saw himself as the Christ-bearer of the new age.

The complete signature, topped with a pyramid of letters arranged in an unvarying pattern, has mystified scholars for years. Could this be the encrypted key to Columbus's state of mind? Without question he considered it one of his most prized creations.

In 1498, Columbus instructed all of his heirs to continue to "sign with my signature which I now employ which is an X with an S over it and an M with a Roman A over it and over then an S and then a Greek Y with an S over it, preserving the relation of the lines and points." At the top, thus, is the letter S between two dots. On the palindromic second row are the letters S A S, also preceded, separated, and ended with dots. The third row has the letters X M and a Greek Y, without dots. Below that is the final signature, Xpo Ferens, a Greco-Latin form of his given name.

To this day no one can decipher the meaning Columbus had in mind, but it almost certainly bears on his religious outlook. The simplest explanations hold that the letters stand for seven words. It has been suggested that the first four letters represent "Servus Sum Altissimi Salvatoris," for "Servant I Am of the Most High Savior." The three letters of the third line could be an invocation to Christ Jesus and Mary, or to Christ, Mary, and Joseph. Another proposed solution is that the seven letters are the initials for "Spiritus Sanctus Altissimi Salvator Xristus Maria Yesus."

John V. Fleming, a medievalist at Princeton University, believes he has cracked the Columbian code, finding it to be an "acrostic of considerable complexity committed to a more or less learned and hermetic mystical theology." Columbus, he concludes, was borrowing from two medieval traditions in formal signatures, that of the church worthies, like St. Francis, who devised intricate crucigrams, and that

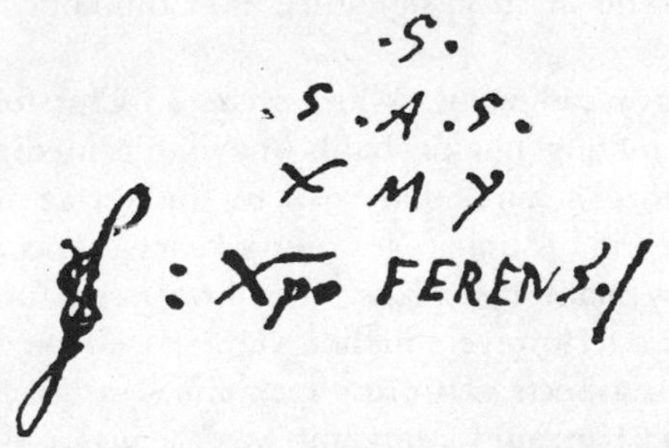

The legal signature of Christopher Columbus

of the mariners who often included in their craft-marks the symbols of anchors, masts, fishhooks, and so forth. For his signature, Fleming says, Columbus seems to have combined religious and nautical symbolism. The unifying idea is the medieval association of the Virgin Mary with Stella Maris, the indispensable navigational star also known as Polaris, or the North Star. The first cross bar stands for StellA MariS. The vertical "mast" stands for "Stella Ave Maris," after the vesper hymn *"Ave, stella maris."* By design, the structure represents both a Christian cross and a ship's mast. The line X M Y may have one meaning, *"Jesus cum Maris sit nobis in via"* (an invocation with which Columbus opened much of his writing), with the Y representing the fork in the road and the symbolism for his having chosen the hard way to destiny's fulfillment. Fleming suggests a double meaning. The X and Y at either end of the bottom line could also stand for "Christophorus," his name and destiny, and "Jacobus," for "Saint James," whose feast day and Christopher's are the same and who is, not incidentally, the patron saint of Spain, Santiago—Sant Yago.

Fleming's cryptographic skills have uncovered other clues in the signature to Columbus's "religious imagination." But, for understanding Columbus the mystical discoverer, Fleming draws insight from his associations with Mary, Christopher, and Santiago. He writes: "In Columbus's heavenly city, the Virgin Mary stands ever firm between her two Christ-bearing guards, Christophorus on the one hand, San Yago the Moorslayer on the other. And in the larger meaning of these two saints, both celebrated by the Roman church on a single day, which was of course Columbus's name-day, we may see adumbrated much of the glory, and much of the tragedy, of the European encounter with the New World."

In more than his mystical signature did Columbus reveal his spiritual side.

In Humboldt's judgment, Watts writes, "Christoferens" represents "a discomfiting but probably inevitable medieval residue in the great explorer's mind that rose to the surface as his rational powers declined in his unhappy waning years." This is the interpretation given by many historians who have been dismissive of the *Book of Prophecies.* However, in her view, based on a study of the book and other aspects of Columbus's life, his spiritual dimension was no latter-day manifestation but was "a major stimulus for his voyages." His apocalypticism, Watts concludes, "must be recognized as inseparable from his geography and cosmology if a balanced picture of the historical significance of his Enterprise of the Indies is to be achieved."

West takes a similar position:

> Explorers do not go forth and probe about. They search for definite objects which they believe to exist based on the geographic information they have. Such information can be empirical or nonempirical: Columbus had what we would call a "spiritual map" in his mind as well as a physical map when he undertook each of his four voyages. The "spiritual map" included those imagined areas of the world mentioned in the Scriptures either lost after antiquity, and/or predicted to be found in the "last days" of the history of the world.

But when did Columbus form his spiritual map? If this was indeed decisive in mounting his venture, it must be established that he was thinking along such lines before 1492. West reports finding samples of his writing in 1481 that anticipated the *Book of Prophecies.*

Columbus made a practice of writing extensive notes in the margins and blank pages of books he was studying. One of these books was a copy of *Historia Rerum Ubique Gestarum,* written by Aeneas Sylvius Piccolomini (Pope Pius II) and printed in 1477. Four postilles, or marginal notes, found there indicate to West that, when he was only thirty years old, Columbus's "use of the Bible and his plan for a voyage of discovery are already discernible." (It was in this same book, on an end leaf, that Columbus reproduced in his own hand the letter from Toscanelli to Fernão Martins at the court of the king of Portugal.)

The first of these postilles, West has found, included quotations from the Bible that deal with three subjects prominent in the *Book of Prophecies.* From Isaiah he extracted a passage about the remotest ends of the earth, the islands of the sea, waiting to be taught the name of the Lord and to learn to glorify him. From II Chronicles he quoted a reference to the ships of Solomon that made journeys every three years to bring back tremendous wealth. And from Psalms he took a verse about God's arranging for his "saving work" to take place "in the middle of the earth," or the promised land.

Other postilles included a discussion of Hebrew prophets in Augustine's City of God; of Flavius Josephus, the Jewish historian, on the subject of Solomon's navigators going to "the Gold Country, which is in India"; and, finally, of a chronology of earth since the Creation—which includes a reference to 1481 as the date of Columbus's entry in the book. Taken together, West concludes, the four postilles "form an exact and complete outline of the plan that was executed in 1501–1502 in the compilation of the *Libro de las profecías.*" Thus, the postilles and the *Book of Prophecies,* he says, "serve as bookends around his mind and his discovery."

Also, in the years before 1492, Columbus gleaned more than a knowledge of geography from his readings of d'Ailly. His library included, in addition to *Imago Mundi,* a number of other small works, known to scholars as "opuscula," compiled by the French cardinal. D'Ailly's opuscula, written in 1414, considered the interrelationships between history, theology, astronomy, and prophecy. Judging from notations in these pages, Watts contends, Columbus must have read the opuscula around 1488, and certainly prior to 1492. He marked certain passages by drawing a hand with the index finger pointed to the text. Many of these recorded apocalyptic concepts were common in medieval times, and several passages from these works of d'Ailly would find their way into the *Book of Prophecies.* "If the testimony in Columbus's marginalia and his letters is taken into account," Watts writes, "these opuscula of d'Ailly played at least as important a role in motivating him to make his voyages of discovery as did his reading of *Imago mundi* and his alleged correspondence with Toscanelli."

Some historians remain unconvinced that the *Book of Prophecies* reveals the source of Columbus's self-assurance in promoting his plan. Writing in the journal *History* in 1988, John Larner of the University of Glasgow observes:

> Columbus, no doubt, always had a sense of destiny as do hundreds of people in every century who, unlike him, have no destiny. Yet this is something different from the belief that one is the Messiah of the Last Days. I find it difficult to think of him as holding such a momentous belief before 1492, before he had achieved something momentous. Columbus' earliest references to Jerusalem, in 1492 and 1498, could be, perhaps, conventional; the mystical delusions appear for the first time in 1500 and seem to resurface thenceforth sporadically and only at times of acute personal distress. . . . However important they are in any general assessment of Columbus' character

it is perhaps too much to make them the mainspring of his enterprise.

A defensible conclusion, however, is that Columbus saw himself as God's messenger years before 1492. His self-image as Christoferens may have consumed him in his later years, but all along it had been a force within him as he elaborated his plan and prevailed upon the Spanish monarchs to take a chance on him.

It may never be possible to fix with any certainty the priorities in his earlier thinking. As a mariner, he heard the talk of distant islands in the Western Sea and knew of the idea that there lay the direct sea route to Asia. The dream was born. He seems deliberately to have obscured the knowledge and motives underlying his pursuit of the dream. However, he may have felt from the beginning that it was God's will, and so required no elucidation in ordinary human terms. This would not be out of character for him. But, to obtain the necessary financial and political backing, he realized that he must persuade the cosmographers and other advisers to the royal courts he petitioned; he had to do what must be done. He thus built a case for the feasibility and worthiness of the enterprise in terms the experts would appreciate, employing the knowledge and theories he had gleaned from d'Ailly and Toscanelli and other authorities.

In this, "modern" Columbus met with little success, but there is suggestive evidence, as West has pointed out, that the arguments of the "medieval" Columbus, Christoferens, may have finally tipped the balance for Ferdinand and Isabella.

Columbus has provided several clues suggesting the importance of the evangelical and apocalyptic motives in securing support for the enterprise. This was the "fire," as he put it in the *Book of Prophecies,* that burned within him as he approached the Spanish court. He was even more explicit in writing the prologue to the journal he kept on the first voyage:

> This present year of 1492, after Your Highnesses had brought to an end the war of the Moors who ruled in Europe and had concluded the war in the great city of Granada . . . in that same month, because of the report that I had given Your Highnesses about the lands of India and about a prince who is called "Grand Khan" [and concerning] how, many times, he and his predeces-

sors had sent to Rome to ask for men learned in our Holy Faith in order that they might instruct him in it and how the Holy Father has never provided them; and thus so many peoples were lost, falling into idolatry and accepting false and harmful religions; and Your Highnesses, as Catholic Christians and Princes, lovers and promoters of the Holy Christian Faith, and enemies of the false doctrine of Mahomet and of all idolatries and heresies, you thought of sending me, Cristóbal Colón, to the said regions of India to see the said princes and the peoples of the lands, and the characteristics of the lands and of everything, and to see how their conversion to our Holy Faith might be undertaken.

Columbus apparently had a more specific Christian objective in mind, too, and this could explain his obsession with gold. On December 26, 1492, he recorded in his journal his desire to obtain gold "in such quantity that the sovereigns, before three years [are over], will undertake and prepare to go conquer the Holy Sepulcher." For, he added, "I urged Your Highnesses to spend all the profits of this my enterprise on the conquest of Jerusalem, and Your Highnesses laughed and said that it would please them and that even without this profit they had that desire."

In his will, written in 1498 and adorned with the mystical signature, Columbus again reminded the court of this commitment to a new crusade. "At the moment when I undertook to discover the Indies," he wrote, "it was with the intention of petitioning the king and the queen, our Sovereigns, that they might resolve to expend the potential revenues occurring to them from the Indies for the conquest of Jerusalem. Indeed, it is the thing which I have asked of them."

Historians generally have concluded that this will contained the first unambiguous manifestation of Columbus's belief in his divine calling. "There is no excuse but the plea of insanity," Winsor wrote a century ago, discussing the will. But he recognized that the admiral's decline may have begun with the success of his first voyage, which "turned his head" and led to a "sad self-aggrandizement, when he felt himself no longer an instrument of intuition to probe the secrets of the earth, but a possessor of miraculous inspiration."

Columbus was not alone in his dream of a new crusade. Ever since Constantinople fell to the Turks in 1453, church leaders had sought to revive the crusading spirit. All the barbarians, from the Norse and

Germans to the Slavs and Tartars, had found their way to Christianity, but now Islam had rent Christendom by seizing its eastern capital. Two years later, Pope Nicholas V empowered the king of Portugal to "invade, search out, capture, vanquish, and subdue all Saracens and pagans whatsoever, and other enemies of Christ wheresoever placed." The Portuguese took these instructions to sanction their raids on Muslims in North Africa and to legitimize slaving operations among the blacks along the West African coast. A crusading zeal was alive in Portugal when Columbus was there and conceiving his enterprise. Portugal, Taviani writes, was "the birthplace of the obsession that accompanied him in his transatlantic project—the notion of using the fruits of his enterprise for the liberation of the Holy Places."

Repeated papal appeals to mount a crusade in the old tradition summoned no support. It is doubtful that the king and queen of Spain shared Columbus's supposed early enthusiasm for a crusade. They took seriously their title of Most Christian Monarchs and their concomitant duty to spread Christianity, but they showed little inclination to lead a military expedition to conquer Jerusalem. In *The Invasion of America,* a study of the conquest of American Indians, Francis Jennings writes: "If religious mission figured as a motive of either Columbus or his royal sponsors, it does not appear in their agreements. . . . The articles of April 17, 1492, speak of 'merchandise' and 'goods' and 'merchants' and 'traffic' and 'business' and tenths and eighths to be apportioned. Nor was there mention of missionary obligation as a condition of Columbus's titles and powers. . . . His function was to find wealth; salvation would be offered in exchange later when it could be debited to the account."

Of course, if Columbus had returned with more of the promised gold than he actually did, they might have been more inclined to entertain the idea. But their subsequent diplomatic maneuvers and colonizing efforts suggested that the priorities of Ferdinand and Isabella, as leaders of an emerging nation-state, were political and economic. Their encouragement of efforts to Christianize the newly discovered people did not mean they were prepared also to take on the Turks any time soon. Insofar as crusading continued as a factor in American exploration, it was as a legal and philosophical precedent. The Crusades had established the doctrine that war conducted in the interest of the holy church was automatically just.

Regardless of what the king and queen might have had in mind, Columbus seems to have thought the prospect of mounting a crusade was decisive in his negotiations with the court, for it was apparently an integral part of his own vision.

In a cautionary and insightful analysis, Fleming seeks to fit the mystical Columbus in the context of the times and the mariner's relationship with Ferdinand and Isabella:

> We must neither blame Columbus for having thoughts with which we ourselves may be uncomfortable nor attempt to "rescue" him by supplying him with thoughts wholly inappropriate to the cultural formatting of his mind. He was a lover of gold, for he associated gold with the virtuous wealth, magnificence, and power of the earthly lords whom he served. No less sincere, once he had encountered the reprobate nations of his new-found islands, was his Franciscan love of souls, the special cure of the heavenly Lord whom he served. Ferdinand Colón, in the proemium of his biography, unequivocally identifies the evangelization of the New World as the principal fruit of his father's life-work. This also is the principal motive claimed by the Reyes Catolicos themselves, and granted them by the secular-minded Oviedo, who writes that they sought the salvation of souls "more than treasures and new estates." Indeed missionary zeal was the wavelength on which Columbus and his royal patrons spoke to each other no less than to themselves of their shared election in the divine scheme of things.

New attention to the spiritual side of Columbus does not necessarily bring this complex man into clarifying focus. The image of the spiritual Columbus does not replace the more traditional image of the modern and innovative explorer; instead, the two must be superimposed to produce a stereoscopic picture of the man, revealing the depths and heights of the mental terrain through which he traveled in finding America.

Columbus, for example, was not averse to wealth for himself and his heirs, as his contract with the monarchs and other writings amply document. By pledging to use the gold to finance a crusade, he might have been trying to assuage guilt feelings over his mercenary obsession. Exploitation in the name of religion is not without precedent. Even so, a genuine religious fervor cannot be discounted as a motivating force, in the beginning, and a justifying principle, in his declining years. Columbus also was a man driven by ambition, as his life in Lisbon suggests. But was it the ambition of someone lusting only for fame and fortune or of a man of the Renaissance seeking to expand knowledge and the human experience? Or the ambition of God's messenger? In all likelihood, his ambition—his vision—was rooted in the medieval Christian cast of his mind, but was set in motion by an imagination fueled by the waxing power he sensed in Iberian harbors and the beckoning of uncharted islands and faraway Asia he felt from reading books and listening to returning mariners. There was room in his mind for the more mundane, remunerative ambitions, and for the Holy Spirit.

Although the spiritual influence comes into unblinking focus in the *Book of Prophecies,* the image Columbus had of himself as a chosen messenger of God and man of destiny is reflected throughout his earlier writings and before 1492. In looking for the palaces of Cathay, Delno West concludes, Columbus actually was seeking Jerusalem. "He had in mind from the beginning a vision of the other side of the world," West writes in his study of the *Book of Prophecies.* "Much has been written about what he thought was there and what other people thought was there. To Columbus, the important question was not what was there, but what would it mean to Christendom, especially Spain, to have access to and passage through those unknown parts of the globe."

This fixation on preparing the way for the recapture of Jerusalem, Tzvetan Todorov observes, made of Columbus "a kind of Quixote a few centuries behind his times." The last of the major Crusades came to an end in the thirteenth century, and no kings and princes since had seriously proposed riding off in shining armor to the Holy City. "It happens that the notion is preposterous in his era," Todorov writes of Columbus's probable thinking, "and since he is penniless as well, no one is willing to listen to him. How can a man without resources who wishes to found a crusade realize his dream in the fifteenth century? All he need do is discover America in order to obtain his funds. Or rather, merely sail to China by the 'direct' western route, since Marco Polo and other medieval writers have confirmed the fact that gold is 'born' there in abundance."

Other scholars, notably Jacob Wassermann, writing in 1929, have drawn parallels between Columbus and Don Quixote. Taviani cites with approval the endorsement of Wassermann's insight written by Gino Doria a few years later. "Whatever strict scholarly opinion may think," Doria observes, "in the Genoese Navigator those dark anti-scientific forces were powerfully at work: his always ardent faith, his conviction of divine will which he had to obey, the purely religious aim in which the results of his voyage were to be converted."

If Columbus's vision derived more from spiritual and mystical sources than from rational thought, this does not diminish his achievement. As Doria says, it may, in fact, explain Columbus more than anything else.

Without his self-awareness as a man of destiny, without the force of his unwavering belief, whether it derived from medieval or nascent modern sources, Columbus might have been unable to sustain the single-minded persistence it took to win support for the enterprise, or he could have turned faint of heart in the course of seeing it through. In the preface to the *Book of Prophecies,* Columbus gave the king and queen his views on the power of faith in a belief: "Saint Peter stepped out upon the water, and to the extent that his faith remained firm, he walked upon it. Whoever finds so much faith as a grain of mustard seed will be obeyed by the mountains. Knock and it must be opened unto you. No one should be afraid to undertake any project in the name of our Savior, if it is a just cause and if he has the pure intention of his holy service."

In the end, however, the belief that had so inspired and energized him clouded Columbus's vision. The man who, for whatever intuitive, rational, or spiritual reasons, had the foresight and courage to cross the ocean and discover a new world could not find his way out of the medieval world his actions would do so much to consign to the past.

Part Three

15

In Death No Peace

Columbus in death is a haunting re-enactment of Columbus in life. Ashes to ashes, obscurity to obscurity, mystery upon mystery. For the bones of the restless man there would be no peaceful repose, any more than for his reputation over the last five centuries.

The admiral of the Ocean Sea died on May 20, 1506, in Valladolid, Spain. He was probably no more than fifty-five years old, but much older in body and in tormented mind.

His fourth and final voyage had been an unmitigated disaster. Sailing from Cádiz in May 1502, accompanied by his brother Bartholomew and thirteen-year-old son, Ferdinand, Columbus made for Santo Domingo, though he had been expressly ordered not to go near the colony he had founded but could not rule with competence. When he arrived off Hispaniola, the winds and dark clouds told him a hurricane was brewing. His request to come ashore was denied by Nicolás de Ovando, the governor. "What man ever born," Columbus wrote, "not excepting Job, would not have died of despair when in such weather, seeking safety for my son, brother, shipmates and myself, we were forbidden the land and the harbors that I, by God's will and sweating blood, had won for Spain?" The authorities even ignored his warning of the impending storm. A fleet of ships set out for Spain, as planned, and the next day the raging winds sank nearly all of them, drowned 500 seamen, and dumped a load of gold bullion in the sea. One of the victims was Francisco de Bobadilla, the man who had sent Columbus back in chains at the end of his third voyage.

Columbus went on to cruise the coast of Central America, from Honduras south to Panama, looking for Solomon's gold and, as Hernando said, searching for a strait leading to the Asian mainland. His desperation only made more acute his disappointment, which was as unbearable as the pain he suffered throughout the voyage. Malaria tormented him with febrile deliriums. His eyes bled, leaving him blind for long periods. Arthritis stiffened his joints, immobilizing him.

In June 1503, reduced to two decrepit caravels, Columbus put in at St. Ann's Bay on the northern coast of Jamaica and realized their hulls were irreparable. He was marooned. He dispatched the brave Diego Méndez and some Indians to make the 105-mile crossing by canoe to Hispaniola to get help. Columbus entrusted Méndez with a letter to the monarchs that betrays the depths of the suffering admiral's despair.

The letter, known in history as Lettera Rarissima, includes an exaggerated report of finding gold mines in Central America that were "the best news that ever was carried to Spain," and rambling thoughts on cosmography. The letter's conclusion reflected Columbus's bitterness and resentment in his final years:

> I came to serve [Your Highnesses] at the age of twenty-eight, and now I have no hair upon me that is not white, and my body is infirm and exhausted. All that was left to me and to my brothers has been taken away and sold, even to the cloak that I wore, to my great dishonor. It is believed that this was not done by your royal command. The restitution of my honor and losses, and the punishment of those who have inflicted them, of those who plundered me of my pearls, and who have disparaged my admiral's privileges, will redound to the honor of your royal dignity. . . . I implore Your Highnesses' pardon. I am ruined as I have said. Hitherto I have wept for others; now have pity upon me, Heaven, and weep for me, earth! . . . I came to Your Highnesses with honest purpose and sincere zeal, and I do not lie. I humbly beg Your Highnesses that, if it please God to remove me hence, you will aid me to go to Rome and on other pilgrimages. May the Holy Trinity guard and increase Your lives and high estate.

On the second attempt, Diego Méndez succeeded in reaching Hispaniola and secured a ship to rescue the crew on Jamaica. Columbus, his brother and son, and several of his men finally made it back to Spain in early November 1504—twelve years and a month after the landfall at Guanahani. His letter had preceded him, but to no visible effect. The queen was dying. She was the one person he felt would hear his appeals with sympathy and understanding. But his request for an invitation to visit her bedside was ignored. Isabella died on November 26, 1504, at the age of fifty-three, and with her expired any hope Columbus might have had of regaining the titles and more of the wealth that was owed him, under the contract of Santa Fé, signed in 1492.

Infirm though he was, Columbus had lost none of the obstinacy that had carried him so far. Through his son Diego, who was a bodyguard in the royal court, the admiral made entreaties for the restoration of the hereditary title of "viceroy of the Indies." He also pursued his pecuniary claims—"my tenth, my eighth, my third." Columbus was by no means a poor man, popular legends notwithstanding, but he wanted to be richer, as he believed was his due.

The "tenth" he demanded was his share of the money gained in commerce with the newly discovered lands, as provided for in the Santa Fé contract. When Columbus finally arranged an audience with King Ferdinand in the middle of 1505, he was promised that a royal arbitrator would investigate these claims. The arbitrator, an archbishop, established that Columbus's share should be not one-tenth of gross revenues, but of the net amount that the crown collected, which came to one-fifth of the revenues. Columbus had to settle for what amounted to one-tenth of that royal fifth. The "eighth" that Columbus claimed had to do with his share of profits from ships sailing to the Indies in which he had a direct investment. This had also been promised him in 1492, but the royal arbitrator concluded that it was a private matter among the investors. The "third" was a claim Columbus asserted when he learned that the grand admiral of Castile, whose title was supposedly equal to Columbus's "admiral of the Ocean Sea," enjoyed the privilege of collecting one-third of the income from taxes on ships plying the waters under his jurisdiction. The king could hardly extend the privilege to Columbus and thus provide him with access to wealth almost as great as the crown's. Nor would he agree to giving the Columbuses hereditary titles to all the Indies. They would have to settle for a lesser title—the "duke of Veragua," it was eventually decided—and the hereditary rank of "admiral of the Ocean Sea."

But the importunate Columbus persisted. He must have been a querulous old bore in those last days. He had moved to Valladolid, following the court and pressing his claims to the end. He wrote once more to the king that, with the full income due him, in seven years' time he would have the means to realize his new dream, a crusade to reclaim Jerusalem.

It was there, in a modest house on a street that now bears the name Calle de Cristóbal Colón, that Columbus died, in bed. He was neither destitute nor alone. His two sons were with him, and two faithful companions from his last voyage, including the intrepid Diego Méndez. He had dictated a will the day before, naming his son Diego executor and providing for the care of Beatriz Enríquez de Arana, the mother of Ferdinand. She "weighs heavily on my conscience," Columbus said, adding cryptically: "The reason for this I am not permitted to write here."

His death went unheralded. There was no public ceremony of mourning. Not until twenty-seven days later did the official registry of births and deaths in Valladolid make a brief reference to the effect that "the said Admiral is dead." Peter Martyr, the inveterate correspondent, wrote at least five long letters about goings-on at the court in Valladolid at that time, never mentioning the death of Columbus. Only ten years later did Martyr publish a letter referring to "Columbus, already having departed out of this life."

Hernando said that his father died from afflictions caused by "the gout and by grief at seeing himself fallen from his high estate, as well as by other ills." The statement is vague enough to encourage any number of investigators to engage in speculative forays into one more aspect of Columbus, the final event in his life: what did Columbus die of?

Some of these investigations have produced diagnoses of diabetes or syphilis, either of which could eventually have caused death. On his later voyages, he was known to suffer agonizing bouts of fever and inflamed eyes, and it has been reported by his son and others that he was increasingly afflicted with gout, which was what most arthritis of the feet was called in the sixteenth century. By his fourth voyage, the arthritis had spread to his spine. Crippled and bleeding in the eyes, he was a pathetic figure of a man.

Gerald Weissmann, a rheumatologist and professor of medicine at New York University School of Medicine, has come up with a diagnosis that he believes fits most of the admiral's symptoms. For the last ten years of his life, Weissmann concludes, Columbus was probably plagued with an illness called Reiter's syndrome. In identifying this debilitating, crippling condition, Weissmann writes: "I find it likely that Columbus became ill because his genes lost a game of molecular roulette to a bacillus common in the tropics: *Shigella flexneri.*"

Military doctors in World War I, beginning with the eponymous Professor Hans Reiter in Germany, described the symptoms associated with Reiter's syndrome. Febrile diarrhea was followed by inflammation in the joints, eyes, and urinary tract. In 1962, nearly half the crew of an American naval fleet visiting a Mediterranean port came down with acute dysentery that in some cases developed into Reiter's syndrome. Subsequent studies, Weissmann recalls, showed that Reiter's syndrome is "the result of a unique genetic predisposition to an environmental insult." In one study, more than 80 percent of those patients with shigella dysentery that progressed to Reiter's syndrome displayed the peculiar genetic markers that seem to predispose people to the affliction. Its occurrence is most common among men living in groups, as in the military or at sea.

Weissman prepared a "case history" of a retired admiral, aged fifty-five, who became ill with an endemic intestinal disease on a voyage to the tropics. When he presented it to fellow rheumatologists, he says, "they almost uniformly put Reiter's syndrome at the top of their list of possible diagnoses." If this was indeed the source of Columbus's infirmities, Weissmann speculates that he might have died of aortic insufficiency, one of the rare complications of Reiter's syndrome, or of unrelated causes.

One is left not knowing for certain the cause of Columbus's death. It is enough, though, to realize that he suffered excruciating pain in his last years, and yet he persevered, obsessed and indomitable to the end.

The funeral procession attracted little attention. The body of Columbus was carried through the narrow streets of Valladolid to a Franciscan monastery near the center of the city. He was laid to rest in a crypt beneath the abbey. But his bones would know no rest, and no one can be sure where they lie today. This last Columbian mystery is almost a caricature of all the others and can be seen as a metaphor of the rootless, restless man who emerged from obscurity, made a transforming discovery, and then quite likely became lost in paranoia and fantasy.

All or part of Columbus's remains could be in Seville, Santo Domingo, Havana, or Genoa. Each city has laid a claim, and the boasts of Seville and Santo Domingo ring with authority, especially in their tourist literature. But the record, as in nearly everything concerning Columbus, is far from clear.

The sources of confusion began three years after his death. His son Diego had the body transferred then from the monastery in Valladolid to the Las Cuevas monastery in Seville. Diego was buried there, too, in 1526. More than a decade later, in accordance with Diego's wishes, his widow obtained royal permission to move the bodies of both Columbus and Diego to the cathedral in Santo Domingo. Officials of the cathedral resisted, apparently not wishing to turn the place into a private family chapel. For a time, therefore, the Columbus remains had to be kept in a temporary underground chamber. After repeated orders from Charles V, the cathedral relented and the bodies were interred on the left side of the high altar.

The Columbus remains supposedly rested there for more than two centuries. But in 1783 a lead box containing human bones was found in a vault on the right side of the altar. It was said to be similar to the coffin found "years earlier" on the left side. Had the remains been moved about? Whose bones were where?

In 1795, when Spain was forced to cede all of Hispaniola to France, the Spanish disinterred what they thought to be the body of Christopher Columbus and carried it to Spanish-held Havana, safe from the despised French republicans. The coffin that was taken was the one that had been on the right side of the altar at Santo Domingo. Its new resting place was in a wall of the high altar of the Havana cathedral.

When Cuba won its independence a century later, the coffin was moved again, this time to Spain for interment in the great cathedral of Seville. As a goodwill gesture, the Spanish sent some of the ashes to Genoa, where they are kept locked in a vault in City Hall. On the other hand, a Cuban historian insists that the bones never left Havana, and it can even be argued that they never left Santo Domingo.

Workmen repairing the cathedral at Santo Domingo in 1877 came upon a lead coffin on the left side of the altar that bore an inscription identifying its contents as the remains of Columbus's grandson, Luis. Next to it was a metal box containing bones and ashes; an inscription inside the lid identified the remains as those of "the illustrious and famous gentleman Don Cristóbal Colón."

Many historians suspect that the wrong box was transferred to Havana in 1795. The box that went to Havana and then to Seville more than likely contained the bones of Diego, the son. Officials of the Dominican Republic want to believe this, for the Columbus tomb in Santo Domingo is a major tourist attraction. The consensus of Spanish historians understandably favors the tomb in Seville. Seeking to settle the matter scientifically, an orthopedic surgeon from Yale University, Charles Goff, opened the tomb in Santo Domingo in 1960. He found that the bones therein appeared to belong to two different bodies—perhaps those of Christopher and his son Diego. But they are not the complete skeleton of either. It is possible that in the move to Havana the remains got mixed up, and so some of Columbus lies in Santo Domingo and some in Seville.

If this is beginning to sound like a variation on the British comedy *The Wrong Box,* a possible resolution to the mystery may be in sight. Jonathon E. Ericson of the University of California at Irvine has proposed a scientific test to determine where the real Columbus bones are today. It is one more of history's ironies: an Ericson seeking to resolve a Columbus mystery.

A few years ago, Ericson persuaded the authorities in Santo Domingo to let him examine the remains in the cathedral and take a piece of tooth back to his laboratory for study. The analysis would be the same kind that he had performed on the pig's tooth found in Haiti, the prime evidence pointing to the location of Columbus's La Navidad. Because strontium is an element whose isotopes occur in different amounts in food grown and eaten in different parts of the world, the strontium ratios in teeth can determine the locality where one grew up and developed adult teeth. The teeth of one who grew up in Genoa would have detectably different strontium ratios from those of one who came from southern Spain. Ericson had done his homework. Preparing for the test, Ericson had collected soil and plant samples in Genoa and Seville, as well as teeth from Genoese who were contemporaries of Columbus. The strontium signatures from Seville and Genoa were, indeed, distinctive. Thus, Ericson believed he could tell whether the bones were those of Christopher Columbus or his son Diego.

Just as Ericson was ready to conduct the test in 1985, he received word from the Dominican Republic that he was not welcome. He is circumspect in discussing the matter. But others who have followed the developments suspect that Dominican officials wanted to avoid a scientific showdown. Should the tests prove the bones to be those of Columbus, fine, but the results could be inconclusive or, worse, could rule out the possibility that Santo Domingo was the explorer's final resting place. Santo Domingo apparently had not wanted to take that risk.

A fitting conclusion to this last Columbus mystery would be to discover that in death the explorer found himself both in Europe and in the New World.

In the familiar story fostered by most historians, Columbus died believing he had reached the Indies, not a new world. But did he actually hold this belief to the very end?

On the first two voyages, Columbus certainly encouraged the belief that the islands he found were off the Asian mainland and that Cuba, as he forced his crew to attest to, was an extension of the mainland. On the third voyage, he finally sighted a continent, South America, but seemed to be too absorbed in the prospects of paradise to weigh seriously the evidence that he had discovered a new world that was possibly far to the east of Asia. But on the final voyage, according to Hernando and Diego Méndez, Columbus's objective in Central America was to find a strait leading to the Asian mainland. A cooper who accompanied Columbus on the third and fourth expeditions testified: "From Santo Domingo we went in search of a Strait, leading, according to what Christopher Columbus said, to the place where spice was found." Are we to conclude that in looking for the strait Columbus was acknowledging that he had not reached Asia, but either a new land altogether or previously undiscovered islands and peninsulas of the Great Khan's Asia? Perhaps. However, most historians can find no clear evidence that Columbus had by now changed his mind and recognized that this was a new world.

At Indian villages on the eastern coast of Central America, Columbus learned for the first time that this was an isthmus between two seas. On the western coast of this isthmus, he was led to believe, there was a province called Ciguare, where people wore rich garments and had warships with cannon. From that shore he thought it was a ten days' sail to the River Ganges. Moreover, in his Lettera Rarissima to the king and queen, Columbus again reported arguments suggesting that he was exploring the longitude of eastern China. He apparently assumed that he was sailing along the Malay Peninsula, the Golden Chersonese of legend.

But could Columbus have been so unmindful of the growing opinion to the contrary? Could he have been so blind to the reality that these people and lands, wherever he went, bore no resemblance to the Asia described by Marco Polo?

The skeptical Henry Vignaud doubts that Columbus continued to the end to believe that he had reached the Indies. Henry Harrisse cites a story by Michele de Cuneo of how Columbus prevented one of his companions on the second voyage from returning to Spain, fearing that he might inform the crown of the truth, as Columbus himself recognized, that Cuba was an island, not part of the mainland. The historian John Boyd Thacher expresses a similar opinion: "He knew that between the country of the Great Khan and the shores of Europe lay great continental lands and that he—Christopher Columbus—and none other was their discoverer."

Endorsing this minority view in *The Conquest of Paradise,* Kirkpatrick Sale writes: "My suspicion is that most historians have not bothered to look beyond the First Voyage and have been taken in by the falsifications put forth in the initial Journal and the Santángel Letter—put there, we presume, to induce the Sovereigns to sponsor a second trip for their new admiral; they may also have been misled by the interpretations of Hernando and Las Casas, which ignore this discovery of a continent in order to keep intact their notion that their hero was all along aiming for Asia and really thought he had reached it."

Several intriguing points are raised to support the argument that Columbus realized he had not made it to the Indies. Sale cites a passage in the *Book of Privileges,* a document Columbus dictated in about 1502 to spell out his achievements and claims of reward for himself and his heirs. For the first time Columbus used the phrase "Indias Occidentales"—West Indies—and added: "the said West Indies which were unknown to all the world." As Sale points out, this indicated that Columbus was aware that Vasco da Gama had recently reached some other Indies, the known Indies at the other side of the Orbis Terrarum, and that the lands he had found must be half a world away, in the Western Hemisphere. If so, Columbus had come to this understanding before his final voyage. Thus, when he described the Ganges as being ten days away by sea from Ciguare, Columbus can be seen as realizing that he was far from the Indies of his dreams. If he had not changed his mind by then, Columbus stood alone. Contemporary cartographers soon began producing maps showing Central America as a peninsula stretching north of a continent that was presumably not part of Asia.

His famous Lettera Rarissima can also be read in a way suggesting that Columbus had come to realize he was dealing with a new continent and not the Indies. In the document he never once mentions his search for the ocean passage to the Asian mainland, which Hernando said was the main objective of the fourth voyage. But Edmundo O'Gorman, the Mexican historian, offers an explanation. Columbus, failing to find the sea passage, abandoned previous conjecture regarding the existence of a southern mainland separate from the Orbis Terrarum and now believed he was cruising along the shores of a continuous Asian peninsula. Beyond, as the Indians had told him, lay the Indian Ocean and the rest of the mainland. In short, he remained certain that he had reached the Indies. O'Gorman concludes: "No one, nothing, to the day of his death ever made him relinquish this cherished conviction."

Once again, we must face the facts—or the woeful lack of them—and accept our ignorance on another important issue concerning Columbus. We cannot be sure whether Columbus did or did not realize he had not reached the Indies. All the evidence shows that he did not appreciate the full geographic dimensions of his discovery. And he never gave explicit expression to any recognition that he had found something other than Asia. It would certainly be in character for the stubborn Columbus to cling to the end to his belief in an Asian discovery. "Columbus had forgotten nothing and learned little," observes the historian Carl Sauer, paraphrasing the famous judgment of the Bourbons of France. "His image of the world experienced little rearrangement."

We can conclude that he died unsatisfied. Ambition and restlessness, the psychological engines that drove him to greatness, churned fitfully in his feeble body. He may have suspected that what he denied was the undeniable truth: he had failed to reach the Indies. If so, the weight of disappointment burdened his already troubled mind. He felt a failure. He had not fulfilled his self-proclaimed destiny. No one appreciated his sacrifice for Spain and for God. Time—if only there was time to pursue an even grander vision. Then he might find fulfillment and peace.

We know only that toward the end his mind had dwelled on monetary grievances and receding visions of Jerusalem. In his notebooks, F. Scott Fitzgerald wrote a line that might well have applied to Columbus: "Show me a hero and I will write you a tragedy." But there was nothing more Columbus could do about his fate. He passed into the hands of his revered Maker—and history.

16

His Place in History

Walt Whitman imagined Columbus on his deathbed, in the throes of self-doubt, seeming to anticipate the vicissitudes that lay ahead in his passage through history:

> *What do I know of life? what of myself?*
> *I know not even my own work, past or present;*
> *Dim, ever-shifting guesses of it spread before me,*
> *Of newer, better worlds, their mighty parturition*
> *Mocking, perplexing me.*

The man who wrote the Letter to Santángel, proclaiming discovery and assuring that he would not be forgotten, probably had no such thoughts. He could not foresee posterity's own "ever-shifting guesses" concerning his deeds and himself any more than he could assimilate in his inflexible mind what he had done and seen. But it was his fate to be the more or less accidental agent of a transcendental discovery and, as a result, to be tossed into the tempestuous sea of history, drifting half-forgotten at first, then being swept by swift currents to a towering crest of honor and legend, and now thrashing in a riptide of conflicting views of his life and his responsibility for almost everything that has happened since.

Columbus's reputation in history has followed a curious course. His obsession, obstinacy, and navigational skill had carried Europe across the ocean. "The Admiral was the first to open the gates of that ocean which had been closed for so many thousands of years before," Las Casas wrote in the middle of the sixteenth century. "He it was who gave the light by which all others might see how to discover."

Yet, in the century after 1492, Columbus was anything but the stellar figure in history that he was to become. Vespucci, by being a more perceptive interpreter of the New World and a more engaging writer, had already robbed Columbus of prominence on the map. His star also tended to be eclipsed by conquering explorers like Cortés and Pizarro, who cut a more glamorous swath (Bernal Díaz, chronicler of the conquest of Mexico by Cortés, contributed with passages evoking the romances of chivalry) and by other mariners, like Da Gama, who actually reached the Indies, and Magellan, whose expedition of circumnavigation was the first to confirm by experience the world's sphericity—and also left no doubt about the magnitude of Columbus's error in thinking he had reached Asia. His immediate reputation was diminished by his failures as a colonial administrator and the protracted lawsuit in which doubts were cast on the singularity of his plan for sailing west to the Indies. Humphrey Gilbert, the navigator who in 1583 established the first British colony in North America, at St. John's, Newfoundland, wrote: "Christopher Columbus of famous memory was not only derided and generally mocked, even here in England, but afterward became a laughing-stock of the Spaniards themselves."

Many books of general history in the first decades of the sixteenth century either scarcely mentioned Columbus or ignored him altogether. J. H. Elliott, the British historian, finds that writers of that time "showed little interest in his personality and career, and some of them could not even get his Christian name right." Responsibility for the neglect has been attributed in part to Peter Martyr. His letters made much of the years of discovery but gave only passing notice to Columbus himself (though acknowledging his fortitude and courage), and, with the poverty of available documentation about the man, there were few alternative sources of information; Oviedo, Las Casas, and his son Hernando had yet to publish their histories. Another explanation has been offered by Henry Harrisse. "The fact is," he writes, "that Columbus was very far from being in his lifetime the important personage he now is; and his writings, which then commanded neither respect nor attention, were probably thrown into the waste-basket as soon as received."

In his history published in 1552, Francisco López de Gomara devoted more attention to the exploits of Cortés and Pizarro, who obtained more gold and glory for Spain and had the good fortune to conquer not an assortment of islands but splendid empires like the Aztecs of Mexico and Incas of Peru. Still, Gomara reflected an awareness then growing among Europeans as to the significance of what Columbus had done. In a ringing assessment that would be repeated time and again, Gomara wrote: "The greatest event since the creation of the world (excluding the incarnation and death of Him who created it) is the discovery of the Indies."

On the strength of this realization, Columbus emerged from the shadows, reincarnated not so much as a man and historical figure as he was as a myth and symbol. He came to epitomize the explorer and discoverer, the man of vision and audacity, the hero who overcame opposition and adversity to change history. By the end of the sixteenth century, English explorers and writers acknowledged the primacy and inspiration of Columbus. "Had they not Columbus to stirre them up," Richard Hakluyt wrote in 1598. He was celebrated in poetry and plays, especially by the Italians. Even Spain was coming around. In a popular play, *El Nuevo Mundo descubierto por Cristóbal Colón,* Lope de Vega in 1614 portrayed Columbus as a dreamer up against the stolid forces of entrenched tradition, a man of singular purpose who triumphed, the embodiment of that spirit driving humans to explore and discover.

Nowhere were people more receptive to this image of Columbus than in the British colonies of North America, beginning in the late seventeenth century. No one in Boston, New York, Philadelphia, or Williamsburg is recorded to have celebrated Columbus in 1692. But five years later, in a book by Samuel Sewall, the Boston chief justice, it was clear that these colonists were thinking of themselves as a people distinct from the English. By virtue of their isolation and common experience in a new land, they were becoming Americans. And they looked to define themselves on their own terms and through their own symbols. Sewall wrote of the "New Earth," meaning the New World, and the "New Heaven," which was his way of expressing the spiritual meaning of the New World, or a kind of Promised Land. In bold letters, Sewall proclaimed: "LIFT UP YOUR HEADS, O YE GATES (OF COLUMBINA) AND BE YE LIFT UP, YE EVERLASTING DOORS, AND THE KING OF GLORY SHALL COME IN."

Sewall, as we have seen, was one of the first Americans to suggest that their land should rightfully be named for Columbus, "the magnanimous heroe . . . who was manifestly appointed by God to be the Finder out of these lands." The Columbus who thought of himself as God's messenger would have been pleased at this turn in his posthumous reputation. But Sewall was also indulging in a practice that would become rampant. He was enlisting Columbus—the symbolic Columbus—for his own immediate purposes. As the Columbus scholar Delno West notes, Sewall wrote the book in spirited defense of the colonies, which were being described by theologians at Oxford and Cambridge as the Biblical "infernal region," or, in plain English, "hell."

The association between Columbus and America took root in the imagination, though, and prospered in the eighteenth century. People had even more reason to think of themselves in distinctive American terms. Benjamin Franklin boasted in the 1750s that there were about a million Britons in North America, although a mere 80,000 had immigrated; the population was increasingly American-born, with less and less reason to identify with the "mother country." "Although a natural symbol for Puritan themes of a new world, new beginnings, paradise in a new land," West and August Kling write, Columbus "became transformed and secularized into a symbol of unity, national pride, progress and liberty." Columbus the man was transmuted into the national icon, Columbia.

The Boston poet Phillis Wheatley, in 1775, was the first to use in print the name "Columbia" as a poetic representation of the aspirations of Americans. Indeed, in the Revolutionary War, Americans elevated Columbus to a heroic position second only to Washington. The troops sang a popular patriotic song, "Columbia, Columbia, to Glory Arise," written by Timothy Dwight, a chaplain of the Connecticut brigade who, at Yale, had been a member of a literary and revolutionary group known as the Columbians. Dwight later wrote an epic poem, *Conquest of Canaan,* in which he identified Columbus as "a new Moses" who "through trackless seas, an unknown flight explores, and hails a new canaan's promised shores." Others adopted the Columbian theme. Philip Freneau published a book-length poem, *The Pictures of Columbus, the Genoese.* Joel Barlow's *The Vision of Columbus,* appearing in 1787, has an aged Columbus lamenting his fate until he is visited by an angel who transports him to the New World to see what his discovery had brought to pass. There he could glimpse the "Fruits of his cares and children of his toil." The angel reassures Columbus:

Let thy delighted soul no more complain
Of dangers braved and griefs endured in vain,
Of courts insidious, envy's poison'd stings,

The loss of empire and the frown of kings;
While these bright scenes thy glowing thoughts compose,
To spurn the vengeance of insulting foes,
And all the joys, descending ages gain,
Repay thy labours and remove thy pain.

The young republic's celebration of Columbus reached a crescendo in October 1792, the 300th anniversary of the landfall at Guanahani. By then, King's College in New York had been renamed Columbia, and the national capital being planned was given the name of the District of Columbia, perhaps to appease those who demanded that the entire country be designated Columbia. Some of the leading lights of New York City had recently organized the Tammany Society or Columbian Order, a name derived from a benevolent Delaware chief and, of course, Columbus. The name would later be disgraced by association with the corrupt political machine of Tammany Hall, but the original society's intentions were high-minded. Its first Sagamore, or leader, was John Pintard, who wrote to a friend that the society's purpose was to collect "everything relating to the natural or political history of America."

On October 12, 1792, the members gathered at Tammany Hall (also called the Wigwam) on Broad Street for a lavish dinner, an oration, and numerous toasts: "May peace and liberty ever pervade the United Columbian States"; "The memory of the renowned Columbus—may our latest posterity inherit the goodly land which his intrepidity explored, and his sagacity discovered"; "May the deliverers of America never experience that ingratitude from their country which Columbus experienced from his king." They also sang a song composed for the occasion:

Ye sons of freedom, hail the day,
That brought a second world to view;
To great Columbus' mem'ry pay
The praise and honor justly due.

Days later, Bostonians staged their own festivities with a dinner of the Massachusetts Historical Society. In his lengthy oration, the Reverend Jeremy Belknap hailed the "active and enterprising genius" of Columbus that "opened an important page in the history of man." He extolled America as a promised land and asylum from the tyranny of the Old World. Alluding to the Black Legend, he condemned the "avaricious Spaniards" and their cruelty that led to the "destruction of the native inhabitants of the West-India islands." In no way did he implicate Columbus. Though proclaiming Americans "as one great family sent into the world to make various experiments for happiness," Belknap did not presume that all was perfect. His words must have discomfited many in the audience: "I blush to own, that, by the Constitution of this Commonwealth, the Jew, the Mahometan, the Gentoo, and the Disciple of Confucius, are excluded from our public counsels, be they ever so good citizens; whilst men, who for convenience, call themselves Christians, though deeply tinged with infidelity, and destitute of moral principles, may freely be admitted." But, in the revered spirit of Columbus, Belknap took hope that "improvement is evidently pervading this country."

It is not hard to understand the appeal of Columbus as a totem for the new republic and the former subjects of George III. Columbus had found the way of escape from Old World tyranny. He was the solitary individual who challenged the unknown sea, as triumphant Americans contemplated the dangers and promise of their own wilderness frontier. He had been opposed by kings, and (in his mind and according to the accounts of his son, which were the primary source of the Columbus legend in those days) was ultimately betrayed by royal perfidy. But as a consequence of his vision and audacity, there was now a land free from kings, a vast continent for new beginnings. In Columbus the new nation without its own history and mythology found a hero from the distant past, one seemingly free of any taint from association with the European colonial powers. The Columbus symbolism gave Americans an instant mythology and a unique place in history, and their adoption of Columbus magnified his own place in history.

In *The Whig Interpretation of History* Herbert Butterfield, a British scholar of this century, properly deplores "the tendency of many historians . . . to produce a story which is the ratification if not the glorification of the present." But the responsibility here does not lie primarily with historians. They cannot control the popularizers of history, myth-makers, or propagandists, and in post-Revolutionary America the few historians who studied Columbus were probably not disposed to try. Even if they had been, there was little information available on which to assess the real Columbus and distinguish the man from the myth. With the discovery and publication of new Columbus documents by Martín Fernández de Navarrete in 1825, this was less of an excuse, and yet the material only provided more ammunition to those who would embellish the symbolic Columbus through the nineteenth century.

Washington Irving mined the new documents to create a hero in the romantic mold favored in the century's literature. Not unaware of the trap of hero-worship into which some writers fall, he criticized anyone "who paints a great man merely in great and heroic traits," observing that "he may produce a fine picture" but "will never present a faithful portrait." Then he proceeded to do just that. Irving's Columbus was "a man of great and inventive genius" and his "ambition was lofty and noble, inspiring him with high thoughts, and an anxiety to distinguish himself by great achievements." Perhaps. But an effusive Irving got carried away. He said that Columbus's "conduct was characterized by the grandeur of his views and the magnanimity of his spirit. . . . Instead of ravaging the newly found countries . . . he sought to colonize and cultivate them, to civilize the natives." Irving acknowledged that Columbus may have had some faults, such as his part in enslaving and killing people, but offered the palliating explanation that these were "errors of the times."

William H. Prescott, a leading American historian of the conquest period, said of Columbus that "the finger of the historian will find it difficult to point to a single blemish in his moral character" and affirmed that this character "was in perfect harmony with the grandeur of his plans, and with results more stupendous than those which heaven has permitted any other mortal to achieve." Even the scholarly Humboldt sought to mitigate the man's flaws and emphasize the best in Columbus, praising, for example, his untrained but keen observations of nature and the force of his idea that transformed history.

Daniel Boorstin observes that people "once felt themselves made by their heroes" and cites James Russell Lowell: "The idol is the measure of the worshipper." Accordingly, writers and orators of the nineteenth century ascribed to Columbus all the human virtues that were most prized in that time of geographic and industrial expansion, heady optimism, and an unquestioning belief in progress as the dynamic of history.

A typical expression of this was given by Alphonse Lamartine, a French writer and politician. In his *Life of Columbus,* he writes:

> All the characteristics of a truly great man are united in Columbus. Genius, labor, patience, obscurity of origin, overcome by energy of will; mild but persisting firmness, resignation toward heaven, struggle against the world; long conception of the idea in solitude, heroic execution of it in action; intrepidity and coolness in storms, fearlessness of death in civil strife; confidence in the destiny—not of an individual but of the human race . . . We know of none more perfect. He contains several impersonations within himself. He was worthy to represent the ancient world before that unknown continent on which he was the first to set foot, and carry to these men of a new race all the virtues, without any of the vices, of the elder hemisphere. So great was his influence on the destiny of the earth, that none more than he ever deserved the name of Civilizer.

In the United States, this image of Columbus accorded with the popular rags-to-riches, log–cabin–to–the–White House scenario of human advancement. This was the ideal Columbus schoolchildren learned about in their McGuffey readers. The orator Edward Everett reminded his audience in 1853 that Columbus had once been forced to beg for bread at the monastery doors of Spain. "We find encouragement in every page of our country's history," Everett declared. "Nowhere do we meet with examples more numerous and more brilliant of men who have risen above poverty and obscurity and every disadvantage to usefulness and honorable name. One whole vast continent was added to the geography of the world by the persevering efforts of a humble Genoese mariner, the great Columbus; who, by the steady pursuit of the enlightened conception he had formed of the figure of the earth, before any navigator had acted upon the belief that it was round, discovered the American continent."

The mythologizing of Columbus took a new tack with the influx of millions of immigrants after the American Civil War. He was made to assume the role of ethnic hero. In a response to adverse Protestant attitudes and to affirm their own Americanism, Irish Catholic immigrants organized the Knights of Columbus in New Haven, Connecticut, in 1882. The fraternity's literature described Columbus as "a prophet and a seer, an instrument of Divine Providence, a mystic of the highest order," and an inspiration to each knight to become "a better Catholic and a better citizen." The knights grew in number and influence, promoting academic studies in American history, lobbying for the Columbus memorial erected in front of Union Station in Washington, and seeking the canonization of their hero.

At the time, a campaign initiated by Count Antoine Roselly de Lorgues, a French writer, was gaining support for elevating Columbus to sainthood in the Roman Catholic Church on the grounds that he had brought the "Christian faith to half the world." The movement was especially strong in Italy and the United States. But, despite encouragement from Pope Pius IX, the proponents got nowhere with the Vatican. No one questioned that he had been a devout Catholic and the pathfinder in bringing Christianity to new lands. His rejection was based largely on his relationship with Beatriz de Arana, the mistress who bore him a son out of wedlock, and the lack of proof that he had performed a miracle, as defined by the church. Writing while the issue was still hotly debated, Justin Winsor raised strong objections to canonization: "He had nothing of the generous and noble spirit of a conjoint lover of man and of God, as the higher spirits of all times have developed it. There was no all-loving Deity in his conception." Even an admirer like Taviani concedes that Columbus was no saint.*

In 1892 and 1893, Columbus the man and the symbol was treated to a year-long commemoration throughout the United States. To the beat of brass bands and a chorus of self-congratulation, Americans hailed the man who had crossed uncharted seas as they had now leaped a wide and wild continent. Antonin Dvořák composed his symphony *From the New World* as an evocation of the sweep and promise of the beckoning American landscape. President Benjamin Harrison proclaimed: "Columbus stood in his age as the pioneer of progress and enlightenment." In New York, the ethnic hero was commemorated with a statue atop a column of Italian marble placed at the corner of Central Park that was renamed Columbus Circle; the money for it was raised by Italian immigrants, who had joined the Irish in search of an identity with the larger American community. There was a nighttime parade and fireworks from the Brooklyn Bridge re-creating Niagara Falls. In Baltimore, Herbert B. Adams, a professor at Johns Hopkins University, delivered a lecture extolling the spirit of Columbus and its continuing relevance:

*A current movement to confer sainthood on Queen Isabella is not likely to be any more successful. Petitioners to the Vatican cite her commanding role in bringing Christianity to the Americas. But Jews and Muslims in particular are outraged, seeing Isabella as a symbol of intolerance for her part in the Inquisition and the expulsion of Moors and Jews from Spain.

> In the fields of science and religion, in art and letters, in civic and social reform, in the improvement of great peoples and in the elevation of mankind, there are still new worlds for discovery and conquest. The heavens above and the earth beneath and even the depths of the great sea are full of fresh materials for observation and research. The beauty of this rolling cosmos is that the infinitely small is as wonderful as the infinitely great. From the red planet Mars and the new moon of Jupiter to a microscopic germ of life or black death, the range of all scientific inquiry is equally noble and rewarding. Let us then, comrades all, press forward. As Aeneas said to his companions, "It is not too late to seek another world."

The grandest of all the celebrations, the World's Columbian Exposition in Chicago, was billed as "the jubilee of mankind." It was so grand and ambitious, in fact, that the opening had to be delayed until 1893. President Grover Cleveland threw the switch on that new invention, electricity, to set in motion the many machines and architectural marvels by which the United States advertised itself as an emerging giant among the nations. Columbus was now the symbol of the American success. The invocation was a prayer of thanksgiving for "that most momentous of all voyages by which Columbus lifted the veil that hid the New World from the old and opened the gateway of the future of mankind." Clearly, the exposition was more than a commemoration of the past; it was also the exclamation of a future that self-confident Americans were eager to shape and enjoy.

A few historians, seeking the man behind the myth, struck chords in refreshing counterpoint to the adulatory hymns to Columbus. Harrisse's diligent examination of all known Columbus materials left scholars no excuse for continuing to treat the man as a demigod. One American writer, Aaron Goodrich, went so far as to publish in 1874 an intemperate denunciation of Columbus, describing the history of him as nothing "but a gilded lie." Still, Harrisse himself rendered a largely favorable judgment. "My admiration is the result of reflection, and not blind hero-worship," he writes in *Columbus and the Bank of St. George.* "Columbus removed out of the range of mere speculation the idea that beyond the Atlantic Ocean lands existed and could be reached by sea, made of the notion a fixed fact, and linked forever the two worlds. That event, which is unquestionably the greatest of modern time, secures to Columbus a place in the pantheon dedicated to the worthies whose courageous deeds mankind will always admire."

Justin Winsor, more than any other respected historian of the day, cast a cold light on the dark side of Columbus's character. He grants the man's courage and the discovery's surpassing significance. But he does not mince words regarding the behavior and moral responsibility of Columbus, who, in his view, forfeited any claim to sympathy when he robbed the lookout who had cried *"Tierra!"* of proper credit and thus took for himself the lifetime pension promised to the first person to see land. In his 1891 biography, Winsor delivers a harsh judgment:

> No man craves more than Columbus to be judged with all the palliations demanded of a difference of his own age and ours. No child of any age ever did less to improve his contemporaries, and few ever did more to prepare the way for such improvements. The age created him and the age left him. There is no more conspicuous example in history of a man showing the path and losing it.
>
> . . . He mourned bitterly that his own efforts were ill requited. He had no pity for the misery of others, except they be his dependents and co-sharers of his purposes. He found a policy worth commemorating in slitting the noses and tearing off the ears of naked heathen. He vindicates his excess by impressing upon the world that a man setting out to conquer the Indies must not be judged by the amenities of life which belong to a quiet rule in established countries. Yet, with a chance to establish a humane life among peoples ready to be moulded to good purposes, he sought from the very first to organize among them the inherited evils of "established countries." He talked a great deal about making converts of the poor souls, while the very first sight which he had of them prompted him to consign them to the slave-mart, just as if the first step to Christianize was the step which unmans.
>
> . . . It was indeed the misery of Columbus to miss the opportunity of being wiser than his fellows, the occasion always sought by a commanding spirit, and it was offered to him almost as to no other.
>
> . . . Hardly another character in the world's record has made so little of its opportunities. His discovery was a blunder; his blunder was a new world; the New World is his monument! Its discoverer might have been its father; he proved to be its de-

spoiler. He might have given its young days such a benignity as the world likes to associate with a maker; he left it a legacy of devastation and crime. He might have been an unselfish promoter of geographical science; he proved a rabid seeker for gold and a viceroyalty. He might have won converts to the fold of Christ by the kindness of his spirit; he gained the execrations of the good angels. He might, like Las Casas, have rebuked the fiendishness of his contemporaries; he set them an example of perverted belief.

Winsor's withering assault on the heroic Columbus of legend was the exception in the late nineteenth century, and not taken kindly by those who held to the prevailing image. Another American historian, John Fiske, felt that his colleague was overreacting "against the absurdities of Roselly de Lorgues and others who have tried to make a saint of Columbus." Winsor's Columbus was surely unthinkable. "How could Las Casas," Fiske asks, "ever have respected the feeble, mean-spirited driveller whose portrait Mr. Winsor asks us to accept as the Discoverer of America?" Speaking at Columbus Day ceremonies in 1892, Chauncey Depew, president of the New York Central Railroad, tore into scholars like Winsor. "If there is anything which I detest more than another," he declared, "it is that spirit of critical historical inquiry which doubts everything; that modern spirit which destroys all the illusions and all the heroes which have been the inspiration of patriotism through all the centuries."

Most people living in America four centuries after the voyages of discovery had created the Columbus they wanted to believe in and were quite satisfied with their creation. But scholars were already finding grounds for a major reassessment of Columbus's reputation in history.

Early in the twentieth century, a few researchers like Henry Vignaud approached new materials from the archives with an increasingly critical eye and exposed contradictions, lacunae, and suspected fictions in the familiar story passed down from Hernando Columbus, Oviedo, Las Casas, and other contemporary accounts. Parts of the story unraveled. No one could be so sure anymore when and how Columbus arrived at his idea, what his real objective was, or what manner of man he was—an inspired but rational genius, a lucky adventurer clouded by mysticism, a man of the Renaissance or from the Middle Ages. But doubt and skepticism about the real Columbus seldom found expression in popular discourse. In textbooks, statuary, and Columbus Day rhetoric, the estimate of the man changed little from that of Edward Channing in 1905, who concluded in his *History of the United States:* "No man has done more to change the course of human history than Christopher Columbus."

Drawing on the accumulating documents and his own seafaring expertise, Samuel Eliot Morison in 1942 rescued Columbus from mythology and portrayed the man as what he had been first and foremost: an inspired mariner of the fifteenth century. Morison's biography, *Admiral of the Ocean Sea,* is written with verve and authority. His Columbus is no saint, but he could sail a ship and possessed the will and courage to go where no one had presumably gone before. His Columbus deserves the fame he has been accorded. His Columbus was a satisfying exemplar of the humble individual who through heroic exertions could change history. But Morison chose to stress the one aspect of Columbus—his skill as a mariner, demonstrated in four daring voyages—that has been beyond serious dispute.

The world was changing, though, and so was Columbus's reputation in history. World war and relentless strife, tyranny and greed, widespread poverty amid plenty, and economic expansion that ravages nature without necessarily satisfying basic human needs—modern life was making disbelievers of many who once worshipped at the altar of progress. If they now doubted progress, they also came to question Columbus, who had been the icon of progress. The idol had been the measure of the worshippers, but now there were atheists all around. In the years since World War II, nearly all of the colonies of the major empires won their independence and, like the United States in its early days, began to view world history from their own anticolonial perspective. And in their view, the Age of Discovery initiated by Columbus was not the bright dawning of a glorious epoch in history, but an invasion, a conquest, and the end of their own peculiar histories. To them Columbus was no hero, no symbol of progress, but the avatar of oppression.

With critics chipping away at the pedestal on which Columbus has stood for so long in history, the hero is tottering and at risk of falling in a crumbling heap. The Columbus who symbolized new beginnings and progress seems anachronistic, diminished and cast aside by the iconoclasm, pessimism, and cynicism in vogue. The Columbus of

1992 is the post-colonial and demythologized Columbus. He has been stripped of the symbolic cloak of optimism and exposed as a human being whose flaws were many and of reverberating consequence. The imagery imposed on him is now more apt to be that of pessimism concerning the human condition. Another Columbus for another age. Such, it seems, is the fate of great figures in history.

"A funny thing happened on the way to the quincentennial observation of America's 'discovery,' " historian Garry Wills writes in *The New York Review of Books* in 1990. "Columbus got mugged. This time the Indians were waiting for him. He comes now with an apologetic air—but not, for some, sufficiently apologetic. . . . He comes to be dishonored."

The rhetoric of Columbus scholarship has changed, more concerned as it is with exploring and assessing the man and his motives and filled with reproof instead of adulation. The Columbus whom Winsor had limned a century ago to widespread disapproval is now in fashion.

Francis Jennings, a historian at the Newberry Library in Chicago, reflects the increasingly critical approach in a book, published in 1975, examining the European incursion in America more from the standpoint of the native Americans. The title is revealing: *The Invasion of America: Indians, Colonialism, and the Cant of Conquest.* Another influential book is *The Columbian Exchange,* in which Alfred W. Crosby, a historian at the University of Texas at Austin, examines the biological consequences of the discovery—the exchange of plants and animals between continents, the spread of devastating disease, the eventual globalization of biology. Historians are increasingly addressing consequences as well as actions. In deference to Indian sensitivities, and the obvious fact that, strictly speaking, America had been discovered thousands of years before, scholars eschew the words "discovery" and "discoverer" in their discourse. They speak of the "encounter" or the "contact." Typically, a research group at the University of Florida is named the Institute for Early Contact Period Studies.

In public forums, the atmosphere is even more emotionally charged. Columbus is tarred as the precursor of exploitation and conquest. Kirkpatrick Sale, in *The Conquest of Paradise,* argues that Columbus was a grasping fortune-hunter whose legacy was the destruction of the native population and the rape of the land that continues to this day. Descendants of the native Americans and the African slaves brought to the New World, as well as those who sympathize with their causes, are understandably reluctant to celebrate Columbus and the 500th anniversary of his landfall. In Madrid, a group known as the Association of Indian Cultures has threatened to sabotage celebratory ceremonies in Spain and throughout Latin America. Basque separatists in 1986 murdered Admiral Cristóbal Colón, a descendant of the explorer. In politically troubled Haiti, demonstrators descended from African slaves tossed a statue of Columbus into the bay. In the United States, leaders of Indian organizations condemned Columbus as a pirate or worse; Russell Means of the American Indian Movement said that Columbus "makes Hitler look like a juvenile delinquent." Vernon Bellecourt, another leader of the movement, called for "militant demonstrations" against celebrants in 1992 "to blow out the candles on their birthday cake."

A sense of guilt has spread among others. The governing board of the National Council of Churches, a predominantly Protestant organization, resolved that, in consideration of "genocide, slavery, 'ecocide' and exploitation" that followed Columbus, the quincentenary should be a time of penitence rather than jubilation. The National Conference of Catholic Bishops, though acknowledging the "harsh and painful" treatment of indigenous Americans, cautioned that "the effort to portray the history of the encounter as a totally negative experience in which only violence and exploitation of the native peoples were present is not an accurate interpretation of the past."

In 1986, after four years of impassioned debate, the United Nations abandoned its attempt to plan a quincentennial celebration. Spain had made the proposal, and the United States, Canada, and a number of Latin American countries had supported it. But opposition came from many quarters. The Scandinavians argued that it ignored the exploits of Leif Eriksson. Ireland touted St. Brendan as the discoverer. Most African and some Asian states opposed any celebration that, in effect, glorified the colonial past. And some American states, where African and Indian blood runs thick, expressed strong reservations about honoring Columbus.

Once again, Columbus has become a symbol, this time of exploitation and imperialism. Garry Wills observes that the "issues that ramify out from the revolt against European imperialism are everywhere evident around us—in the feminist and minority questioning of 'dead white males' as the arbiters of our culture. The battles over a standard or core curriculum are simply this same war fought on slightly different grounds. So is the political struggle over one official language for the United States." In reviewing *The Conquest of Paradise,* Wills points out that the author "is on to something when he makes Columbus the deadest whitest male now offered for our detestation. If any historical figure can appropriately be loaded up with all the heresies of our time—Eurocentrism, phallocentrism, imperialism, elitism, and all-bad-things-generally-ism—Columbus is the man."

It was time that the encounter was viewed not only from the European standpoint, but from that of the indigenous Americans. It was time that the sanitized storybook version of Europeans bringing civilization and Christianity to America was replaced with a more clear-eyed recognition of the evils and atrocities committed in wresting a land from its original inhabitants. It was time that Columbus was judged by the evidence of his actions and words, not by the legend that had been embedded in our imaginations. But are we burdening him with more guilt than any one man should have to shoulder? Surely we have not finally established Columbus's place in history. It would be interesting to know how he will be characterized in 2092. For it seems that Columbus's destiny is to serve as a barometer of our self-confidence and complacency, our hopes and aspirations, our faith in progress and the capacity of humans to create a more just society.

Herbert Butterfield complained of the tendency of many historians to look in the past for "roots" and "anticipations" of their own time, and to single out and praise only those personalities who turned out to have been successful in fighting for causes and values esteemed in the historian's contemporary society. He called this the Whig interpretation of history—"the theory that we study the past for the sake of the present." Some historians can be said to be guilty of this in both gilding the image of Columbus and, in more recent times, tarnishing it almost beyond recognition. They should, instead, strive to reconstruct the person who really was, insofar as the record allows, and the times as they really were—and leave to others, who are never in short supply, the task of measuring the person for the hero's cloak.

Here is a summary of what can be said. Columbus was, as far as we can tell, a man from Genoa who grew up in a family of wool-weavers and then went to sea. He found his way to Portugal, where exploration of the sea was a dynamic of the age and the search for a new route to the Indies was an economic and religious imperative. There he became obsessed with an idea of sailing across the sea to reach the

Indies. He was ambitious for fame and wealth and, quite likely, to serve as God's messenger to the world and restore the Holy Sepulcher to Christendom. Some of his ancestors may have been Jewish, but he was a devout Christian who sailed for the crown of Spain. Through single-minded persistence and the charisma to make friends in high places, he prevailed on Ferdinand and Isabella to back his bold scheme. He was not the only European to believe the world was round, but he seems to have been the first to stake his life on it.

He was a consummate mariner, everyone seemed to agree. As Cuneo, who sailed with him, said: "By a simple look at the night sky, he would know what route to follow or what weather to expect; he took the helm and once the storm was over, he would hoist the sails, while the others were asleep." And he found a new world. Though he probably never realized it, and certainly never admitted it, he made a discovery that would change the world. If there had not been an America to find, he would probably have sailed to his death and certainly to oblivion. He could never have made the Indies, which lay far beyond where his miscalculations had placed them. He was wrong, but lucky. No explorer succeeds without some luck. But his skill and fortune deserted him on land. He was an inept administrator of the colony he established at La Isabela, ruling by the gibbet, antagonizing his own men to insurrection, and goading the Tainos into bloody rebellion. At the first opportunity, he captured Tainos and shipped them to Spain as slaves, a practice not without precedent in Europe or even among the people of pre-Columbian America.

His geographic interpretations were muddled by preconceptions and a blind reliance on venerated church teachings. His was not an open mind. He sought confirmation of received wisdom rather than new knowledge. Enthralled by the proximity of what he believed was the earthly paradise, he failed to appreciate that he had reached the South American continent. Yet he persevered, often wracked with the pain of arthritis and fevers, completing four epic voyages that showed the way to countless others. As he approached death, his mind was consumed with self-pity, mysticism, and a desperate desire to seize Jerusalem in preparation for Judgment Day.

Here is how Columbus himself, in his Letter to Santángel in February 1493, judged the meaning of his life and achievement:

> . . . the eternal God, Our Lord, Who gives to all those who walk in His way victory over things which appear impossible, and this

was notably one. For although men have talked or have written of these lands, all was conjecture, without getting a look at it, but amounted only to this, that those who heard for the most part listened and judged it more a fable than that there was anything in it, however small.

So, since our Redeemer has given this victory . . . for this all Christendom ought to feel joyful and make great celebrations and give solemn thanks to the Holy Trinity with many solemn prayers for the great exaltation which it will have, in the turning of so many peoples to our holy faith, and afterwards for material benefits.

But how are we to judge the historical Columbus, the man and not the legend? Was he a great man?

No, if greatness is measured by one's stature among contemporaries. Justin Winsor said a century ago: "The really great man is superior to his age, and anticipates its future." We will never know whether the course of history might have been any different if Columbus had been a kinder, more generous man, like Las Casas. But, then, Las Casas himself went to the Caribbean, like so many others, with every intention of exploiting it for personal gain. Or if he had been more like Captain James Cook—stern, unyielding, a peerless mariner, but also a commanding spirit, intellectually curious and hospitable to the sciences, devoted completely to the mission of exploration and discovery. But Cook lived in a different time, about three centuries later. To argue that Columbus was acting in the accepted manner of his time is to concede that he was not superior to his age. To contend (with ample supporting evidence) that, even if Columbus had set a better example, others who followed would eventually have corrupted his efforts, is to beg the question. Moreover, the only example Columbus set was one of pettiness, self-aggrandizement, and a lack of magnanimity. He could not find in himself the generosity to share any credit for his accomplishments. Whatever his original objective, his lust for gold drove him from island to island and, it seems, to the verge of paranoia. And the only future he could anticipate was wealth for himself and his heirs and the chimera of the imminent end of the world.

Yes, if greatness derives from the audacity of his undertaking, its surprising revelation, and the magnitude of its impact on subsequent history. Columbus did cross the uncharted Atlantic Ocean, no mean feat. He did find new lands and people, and he returned to tell of it so that others could follow, opening the way to intercontinental travel and expansion. True, if he had never sailed, other mariners would eventually have raised the American coast, as the Portuguese did in reaching Brazil by accident in 1500. But it was Columbus who had the idea, ill-conceived though it was in many respects, and pursued the idea with uncommon persistence, undeterred by the doubters and scoffers. As it was put in the apocryphal story, Columbus showed the world how to stand an egg on its end.

Whether he was a great man or merely an agent of a great accomplishment, the issue is his standing in history. And that, Butterfield notwithstanding, depends on posterity's changing evaluation—Whitman's "ever-shifting guesses"—of him and the consequence of Europe's discovery of America. His reputation is inextricably linked to America. Ultimately, Columbus's place in history can only be judged in relation to the place accorded America in history over the last five centuries.

17

America's Place in the World

Europeans took a long time appreciating their discovery of the New World. At first, Columbus and succeeding explorers looked upon the islands and mainland as an inconvenience, the barrier standing in their way to Asia that must be breached or circumnavigated. That was what Magellan was up to, and also the British navigators probing the northern inlets for a passage to India. The conquerors and then the settlers who did push into the interior were forced to come to terms with the land, if only to assure their survival. Their reports back home excited curiosity and further exploration—but could not overcome the bewilderment of Europe in the face of the discovery.

All in all, Europeans were unprepared by experience, learning, or philosophy for what stood revealed to them. The Portuguese Pedro Nunes, writing in 1537, expressed what must have been their feelings of being overwhelmed by the astonishing newness of everything: "New islands, new lands, new seas, new peoples; and, what is more, a new sky and new stars." J. H. Elliott notes that Europeans had known something, however vaguely, about Africa and Asia, but absolutely nothing of America. "It is a striking fact," wrote Etienne Pasquier, a Parisian lawyer, in the 1560s, "that our classical authors had no knowledge of all this America, which we call New Lands."

As a result, Elliott postulates in *The Old World and the New, 1492–1650,* the response of Europeans in making the mental adjustments required to incorporate America within their field of vision was slow and uncertain. Like Columbus, they sought initially to assimilate the discoveries in light of what they already knew or thought, which was perfectly natural. They averted their eyes to the utter unfamiliarity of the land and people, and so could not see what there was to discover. It was a paradoxical attitude for Renaissance Europe. On the one hand, the Europe of "the discovery of the world and of man," in the summing up of the Renaissance by Jules Michelet, was reaching out to distant horizons in the emerging spirit of exploration. On the other hand, its comprehension of what explorers had come upon was constrained, Elliott says, by that other aspect of the Renaissance: the veneration of antiquity. The Renaissance in Italy had been stimulated by the rediscovery of the writings of classical Greece and Rome. It is not surprising, therefore, that the early European response to America was influenced, above all, by their understanding of the classical world as celebrated in a Christian world emerging from the Middle Ages.

"For there was always something narcissistic in Europe's approach both to antiquity and to America," Elliott writes in a later essay amending his thesis. "In observing America it was, in the first instance, observing itself—and observing itself in one of two mirrors, each of which distorted as it revealed. It could see in America its own ideal past—a world still uncontaminated by greed and vice, where men lived in felicity and prelapsarian innocence. Or, as occurred increasingly with the advance of the sixteenth century, it could see in America its actual past—a time when Europe's rude inhabitants were as yet untouched by civil manners or by Christianity."

As early as Peter Martyr, Europeans colored their interpretations of explorers' reports with images of the Noble Savage, to use a later expression for the same perception, and of the Golden Age. Columbus's first reports praised the generosity and guilelessness of the naked islanders. Vespucci's popular accounts described people living without possessions or laws, kings or lords, churches or idolators. "What more can I say?" Vespucci asked, and then went on in a typical allusion to the classical world. "They live according to nature, rather as Epicureans so far as they can, than Stoics." The inhabitants of the New World, Martyr wrote, "seem to live in that golden world of which old writers speak so much, wherein men lived simply and innocently without enforcement of laws, without quarrelling, judges and libels, content only to satisfy nature, without further vexation for knowledge of things to come." Is this not a humanistic version of the Biblical paradise Columbus thought he was on the verge of finding? Neither was, in fact, close to the truth. The innocence of these indigenous Americans was more imagined than real; to one degree or another, they knew warfare, brutality, slavery, human sacrifice, and cannibalism, among unattractive human practices. Columbus did not "introduce" slavery to the New World; the practice existed there before his arrival, though his shipments of Tainos to Spain presaged a transoceanic traffic in slaves unprecedented in history.

The idealized image of people living in nature persisted, nonetheless, and inspired the occasional questioning of Europe's own values and also a more favorable appreciation of the plurality of cultures. In his essay "Of the Cannibales," Michel de Montaigne in 1582 wrote of the Brazilian Indians as a prototype of "natural man" living outside civilized society, who should not be judged by conventional European standards. "It seems to me that what we actually see in these nations surpasses . . . all the pictures in which poets have idealized the golden age," Montaigne writes. "Those people are wild in the sense which we call wild the fruits that Nature has produced by herself and her ordinary progress; whereas in truth it is those we have altered artificially and diverted from the common order, that we should rather call wild. In the first we still see, in full life and vigour, the genuine and most natural and useful virtues and properties, which we have bastardized in the latter, and only adapted to please our corrupt taste." Because these people lacked Europe's obsession with property and political power, Montaigne says, so were "the very words denoting falsehood, treachery, dissimulation, avarice, detraction, pardon, unheard of."

Europe's emerging vision of America, Elliott contends, reflected a "sense of self-dissatisfaction" and a longing for a better state of things, either in a return to the lost Christian paradise or to the Golden Age of the ancients, or "to some elusive combination of both these imagined worlds." No wonder that Sir Thomas More, in 1516, located his imaginary Utopia on an island near those recently discovered by Vespucci.

The first artistic expressions of America were no more enlightening of reality than the written records. In *The New Golden Land: European Images of America from the Discoveries to the Present Time,* Hugh Honour notes that an edition of Columbus's Letter to Santángel printed in Basel in 1493 was illustrated by woodcuts previously issued with accounts of Mediterranean voyages: a ship supposedly arriving at a Caribbean island is a forty-oared galley resembling Roman vessels. A Florentine edition of the same letter included as a frontispiece a scene that "might equally well have served to embellish a Renaissance version of the Troy legend." De Bry's images of indigenous Americans were nudes in the heroic Greek mold. An Albrecht Dürer drawing depicts accurately an Indian's headdress, but the man himself, Honour says, "looks more like a snub-nosed German youth dressed up for a Nuremberg pageant than a genuine Tupinamba."

It was almost a century before artists, in representing the New World, broke away from Eurocentric preconceptions and classical or medieval styles. Sir Francis Drake was one of the first explorers to be accompanied by artists. They left an impressive collection of watercolors of plants, animals, and people in the West Indies and Panama of the late sixteenth century. The drawings were found recently in a manuscript entitled *Histoire Naturelle des Indes,* usually referred to as the Drake manuscript. The anonymous artists drew the Indians with seeming admiration as strong and skillful people. They delighted in scenes of Indian domestic life. One of the most affecting series of watercolors tells a tale of courtship and marriage. A young man is shown bearing all he owns—canoe, arrows, and fishnets—to the father of the woman he wishes to marry. He is ordered off on a hunt and told not to return until he can bring enough food to feed the young woman's whole family. Then, on their marriage day, the bridegroom holds a rabbit in one hand as a symbol of his hunting prowess, and the bride grinds maize in a basin. But for the most part in these and other early drawings, European artists concentrated on such practical matters as Indians sowing grain, weaving hammocks, hunting with bow and arrow, or collecting gold in streams. African slaves—the newfound land had already lost whatever innocence might have been claimed for it—were depicted diving for pearls and smelting silver. Of all the Indian scenes, only one in this collection shows warlike behavior or an allusion to cannibalism. Artists in the New World at this time generally put the best face on conditions, because, in their patrons' eyes, realism was not to be taken so far as to discourage investors and colonists.

America was being measured by its economic potential. Verlyn Klinkenborg, curator of a recent exhibition of drawings from the Drake manuscript, notes that plants are represented mainly as resources for man's use, and man dominates all the landscapes. "In that sense," he says, "*Histoire Naturelle* is an early exercise in economic geography, charting use and profit in the New World."

By this time, much of America as it was when encountered by Europeans was disappearing in reality and in myth. Disease was wiping out the indigenous populations, who were being replaced by slaves from Africa. As Europeans pushed inland, establishing their own communities, native cultures collapsed. The opportunity to discover pre-Columbian America and Americans was passing. The Noble Savage living in the Golden Age was only a myth of European creation, and now it was too late, if it had ever been possible, to learn who the American people really were and, accepting them for what they were, to find a way to live and let live. The Las Casases and Montaignes were outnumbered. Europeans had begun to invent America, as Edmundo O'Gorman argues, in their own image and for their own purposes. They had set upon a course of creating Neo-Europes, in Alfred Crosby's phrase. America's place in history is almost invariably judged not by what was or what might have been, but by what the Europeans invented when they planted their Neo-Europes on the two continents they came to possess as a result of Columbus's voyages.

In contrast to the sanguinary language of patriots in colonial and post-Revolutionary North America, European intellectuals of the eighteenth century engaged in a searching reappraisal of America.

To support his concept of human social development, Jean-Jacques Rousseau revived the romanticized Noble Savage, contending that "most of the savage nations" of America lived in "the state least subject to revolution, the best state of man." Their state, he believed, "is the veritable youth of the world; and that all subsequent advances have been so many steps, in appearance towards the perfection of the individual, in reality towards the decrepitude of the species." European portraiture generally celebrated the popular Rousseau image. But Voltaire took an opposite position, seeing the Indians as solitary hunters "forced, naked and unarmed, to defend themselves and their prey from other ferocious animals."

The French naturalist Georges-Louis Leclerc de Buffon conferred scientific respectability upon the impression growing among European intellectuals that America was somehow inferior, either immature or degenerate, in relation to the Old World. This was, Buffon writes, the "greatest fact, the most general, the least known to all naturalists before me." As evidence of the inferiority of nature in America, he offered denigrating comparisons between the "ridiculous" tapir and the elephant, the llama and the camel, and the "cowardly" puma and the noble lion. Moreover, Old World animals introduced there fared poorly, declining in health and size, with the sole exception of the pig. It was Buffon's thesis that America suffered an arrested development because of a humid climate, a legacy of what he said was its relatively late emergence from the waters of the Biblical flood.

Buffon's ideas enjoyed a certain vogue in the eighteenth century and encouraged more extreme elaborations on the theme of "America's weakness." Expressions of European superiority were perhaps a reaction to the threatening assertiveness of the British colonies of North America. In *Philosophical Researches on the American,* published in Berlin in 1768, Cornelius de Pauw, a Dutch author, declared: "It is without doubt a terrible spectacle to see one half of the globe so disfavoured by nature that everything there is degenerate or monstrous." Not only were the animals inferior to those in the Old World, in his view, but so were the indigenous Americans; likewise, Europeans who settled there soon degenerated. To De Pauw, who never traveled to the New World, it was regrettable that Europeans had ever had anything to do with the place. He described the discovery of America as the most calamitous event in human history.

If nothing else, De Pauw's provocative exposition revealed Europe's new preoccupation with the meaning of America. There was no gainsaying the importance of the discovery in history. In *Wealth of Nations,* Adam Smith in 1776 echoed Gomara's assessment: "The discovery of America, and that of a passage to the East Indies by the Cape of Good Hope, are the two greatest and most important events recorded in the history of mankind." In 1770, Abbé Guillaume-Thomas Raynal had put it only slightly differently: "No event has been so interesting to mankind in general, and to the inhabitants of Europe in particular, as the discovery of the new world, and the passage to India by the Cape of Good Hope." So saying, he undertook a philosophical history of the European colonial experience in the East and West Indies in which he amplified De Pauw's interpretations and expressed other doubts about how beneficial the discovery had been for Europe. As Elliott points out, Raynal later challenged others to consider the following questions: Has the discovery of America been useful or harmful to mankind? If useful, how can its usefulness be magnified? If harmful, how can the harm be ameliorated? He offered a prize for the essay that would best answer those questions.

Of the respondents whose essays have survived, the optimists and pessimists were evenly divided, but the judges at Lyon decided that no entry was worthy of the prize. Raynal's own essay enumerated what he considered positive effects: improvements in ships, navigation, geography, astronomy, medicine, natural history, and other branches of knowledge, as well as wealth and power to the nations that found and colonized the lands. But at what price in lives and values had these gains been bought?

Although "Europe is indebted to the New World for a few conveniences, and a few luxuries," Raynal observes, they were "so cruelly obtained, so unequally distributed, and so obstinately disputed" that they may not justify the costs. The Europeans who yielded to America's temptations became "a new species of anomalous savages" who thought nothing of acquiring "riches in exchange for their virtue and their health." In conclusion, the abbé asks, in effect, if we had it to do over again, would we still want to discover the way to America and India? "Let me suppose that I address myself to the most cruel of the Europeans in the following terms," he says. "There exist regions which will furnish you with rich metals, agreeable clothing, and delicious food. But read this history, and behold at what price the discovery is promised to you. Do you wish or not that it should be made? Is it to be imagined that there exists a being infernal enough to answer this question in the affirmative? Let it be remembered that there will not be a single instant in futurity when my question will not have the same force."

The American experience was forcing some Europeans back home to take an even more critical look at themselves. The anti-imperialist Samuel Johnson was impelled to write in 1759: "Much knowledge has been acquired, and much cruelty been committed; the belief of religion has been very little propagated, and its laws have been outrageously and enormously violated. The Europeans have scarcely visited any coast but to gratify avarice, and extend corruption; to arrogate dominion without right, and practise cruelty without incentive."

So far, Columbus had not occupied a central place in these critical reappraisals. He had generally escaped being blamed for the perceived negative consequences. In the 1770s, Johnson did not exactly reproach Columbus himself, but, as Garry Wills notes, Johnson was one of the first to make a connection between the conquest of America and its original conqueror. Columbus, Johnson writes, had to travel "from court to court, scorned and repulsed as a wild projector, an idle promiser of kingdoms in the clouds: nor has any part of the world yet had reason to rejoice that he found at last reception and employment." This was certainly not the Columbus then being mythologized in America itself.

Despite some pangs of guilt and expressions of moral outrage, nothing stayed the momentum of European expansion in America. Immigration continued to grow, mainly among the British, French, and Germans to North America and the Spanish and Portuguese to the south. Most of them had never heard of the "weakness of America" or read the intellectuals who either idealized or despised the Indians or deplored Europe's bloodstained seizure of the lands from their original inhabitants. Millions more people from all over Europe came to take their chances on America in the nineteenth century, particularly after the introduction of the steamship, and on through World War I. Crosby calls it "the greatest wave of humanity ever to cross the oceans and probably the greatest that ever will cross oceans." Their migrations reshaped America and history.

The America these millions of people flocked to promised a fresh start. The image of America had become that of a haven from Old World tyranny and restricted opportunity and a promised land where people could make something of themselves and prepare for a better life for their children. This was the image of Columbia. Not only American chauvinists believed in this image; the idea of steady progress was now woven into the fabric of Western thought, and those denied its benefits in Europe sought them across the ocean. Their dreams had been fired by reports of plenitude that had become even more alluring since J. Hector St. John de Crèvecoeur, in *Letters from an American Farmer,* wrote in 1783: "We have a bellyful of victuals every day, our cows run about, and come home full of milk, our hogs get fat of themselves in the woods: oh, this is a good country."

With the immigrations and widespread settlement, particularly in North America, America seemed to confirm the validity of progress as an inexorable force of history. It afforded people room and resources for growth, and as they prospered, so did the United States as a nation and an experiment in democracy. Its influence extended beyond what was perceived as political progress. In so many practical, everyday ways, the new and old worlds were being united in a global economy and biology. Europeans had been seeking gold and spices, but they brought back not only gold but tobacco, maize, and potatoes.

The new wealth and improved nutrition had an incalculable impact on the growth of a more prosperous, confident Europe and on the Industrial Revolution. In turn, the Europeans transplanted in America their wheat, turnips, oats, and ryegrasses and introduced cattle, pigs, goats, sheep, chickens, and horses. The swift success of European agriculture in temperate America has had tremendous consequences. It underlay the economic growth of the United States, Canada, Uruguay, and Argentina—Crosby's Neo-Europes. And the rest of the world has come to depend on this transplanted agriculture for much of its food. As Crosby points out, the share of world grain exports of the Neo-Europes of America, as well as Australia and New Zealand, is greater than the Middle East's share of petroleum exports.

Columbus's reputation in history was never higher than it was when the achievements and promise of America seemed so bright and were extravagantly proclaimed both at home and abroad. But a more sobering approach to thinking about the European discoveries, exemplified in the use of the term "encounter," has brought about a sea-change in the interpretation of history flowing from 1492. Columbus's reputation has suffered. So has America's self-image.

As recently as 1974, Samuel Eliot Morison concluded *The European Discovery of America: The Southern Voyages* with a paean in the manner of the old-school history: "To the people of the New World, pagans expecting short and brutish lives, void of hope for any future, had come the Christian vision of a merciful God and a glorious heaven." It is hard to imagine those words' being written today. Fashions in historical interpretation have changed once again.

More recently, in 1986, D. W. Meinig, a geographer at Syracuse University, called attention to the change by noting the dual meaning of the word "encounter." In the benign sense, it means "to meet unexpectedly." But in its root sense, it means "to meet in conflict," and the current revisionist views of Columbus and European imperialism have stressed this root meaning. In *The Shaping of America,* Meinig says: "It is important for Americans to understand more clearly than they do that their nation has been created by massive aggression against a long succession of peoples. That is an ineluctable part of the 'frontier,' the 'westward movement,' the 'growth' of the republic and similar themes so long celebrated in American history. Just as in the cases of China, Rome, Russia, and other macrosocieties and empires, such expansion resulted in the destruction or displacement, capture, and deep deformation of all societies in its path."

Meinig's is a mild expression of the new recognition that the traditional history had not always reflected the costs and sufferings accompanying the European discovery and settlement of America. Others have expanded the theme to support vitriolic attacks on Western culture and politics. They reject the chauvinists' Columbus.

In 1988, at a conference of scholars held at the University of Florida, Alfred Crosby sought to explain the sources of revisionist thinking in terms of a new *Zeitgeist.* No new data on the encounter have come to light. Instead, he says, the "primary factor behind our reassessment of the encounter is a general reassessment of the role of rapid change, even catastrophe, in human history, and even the history of the earth and of the universe."

An earlier faith in progress was founded on a Western belief that change came gradually, and almost invariably was for the better. The principle underlay and was a justification for capitalism and the Industrial Revolution. Even Marxism, in its original form, presupposed a ladder of change leading to improvement in a classless society. In science, the uniformitarian geology of Charles Lyell and the evolutionary theory of Charles Darwin were widely accepted because, in part, they seemed to confirm the idea of progress; the present world and its inhabitants were the products not of global disasters and multiple creations, but of slow and steady change.

By contrast, Crosby observes, the twentieth century has experienced the two worst wars in history, genocide, the invention of more ominous means of destruction, revolutions and the collapse of empires, rampant population growth and the threat of ecological disaster. Catastrophism, not steady progress, is the modern paradigm. It has been made respectable in science through the new understanding of how restless continents bring disaster through earthquakes, volcanoes, and climate change; of the periodic waves of mass extinctions of life (the dinosaurs perhaps were victims of a global catastrophe, not their own incompetence); even of the birth of the universe in one explosive moment—the Big Bang.

"The rapidity and magnitude of change in our century has prepared us to ask different questions about the encounter than the older schools of scientists and scholars asked," Crosby believes. Asking these questions, he says, is a step toward finding answers responsible for "our catastrophic rethinking of the encounter."

Where does this lead? For some it provokes a bitter recital of brutality and slavery, oppression and exploitation, and it subjects Columbus to some rough debunking as a man and a symbol. If Raynal held his essay contest today, the pessimistic assessments might outnumber the optimistic ones. But the new paradigm can also give rise to thinking that actually magnifies the significance of the reunion between two worlds.

"The encounter marks one of the major discontinuities in the course of life on this planet," Crosby asserts. "Its significance towers far above the origins of this or that kind of government or even the fate of this or that group of humans." Its importance he compares to the great geologic changes in the past: the separation of the continents and the mass extinctions that altered the direction of evolution. Did not Columbus, as a practical matter, bring about a reversal in the millions of years of continental drift? Horses, which had died out in the New World, were reintroduced by the Spaniards. The Europeans accelerated the rate of extinctions of species in the Americas, but also transplanted new species to stunning effect. In Crosby's view, Columbus and later explorers, and lately the aviators, have drawn "the continents together to produce what is not geographically, but certainly is politically, socially, economically, botanically, zoologically and bacteriologically a supercontinent."

William McNeill has also written of the encounter's sweeping effect on the entire planet. "Before Columbus's time," he says, "the globe was divided by barren ocean spaces into a large number of separate human, plant, and animal communities, each an island unto itself with only sporadic and accidental connections with anything outside. But European navigation was such that what Columbus started in 1492 was carried forward by others unrelentingly, until the entire globe became a single interacting whole. The unification of the globe inaugurated by Columbus, therefore, damaged and sometimes destroyed many local forms of life—human as well as nonhuman. No one planned it that way. No one intended it to happen. But the different levels of ecological and cultural development in the separate world islands of preceding ages made such an upshot inevitable once communication and contact across the ocean barriers began."

The triumph of European life forms and of human immigrants coming from the Old World to the New is the familiar stuff of national histories throughout the Americas. In less obvious but equally transforming ways, McNeill says, the encounter changed Europe as well, through new ideas, new resources, and new models of political and social life. The change in Europe was less immediate and catastrophic than in America, but ultimately it proved nothing short of revolutionary. It led, McNeill believes, to the Enlightenment of the eighteenth century and thus to the philosophical, political, and scientific foundations of modern Western civilization.

As McNeill writes:

> The variety of religions and ways of life that clearly existed and continued to exist in Asia and Africa as well as in America suggested to some that perhaps the Christian faith and the customs familiar in Europe were not uniquely and universally true, but were only one set of ideas and practices among others, none of which could claim to be really valid because they were not based on reason or any other genuinely universal foundation. But the light of reason, such thinkers hoped, might yet prevail, and we are accustomed to agree with them by calling their assault on Europe's established ideas and institutions "the Enlightenment." Other developments within Europe fed into the Enlightenment, of course, but knowledge about the New World, and realization of how awkwardly it fitted into the biblical record, gave powerful impetus to the propagation of Enlightenment ideas. Thus, instead of reinforcing commitment to and confidence in their cultural heritage, as the first European encounter had done, by the eighteenth century an influential group of European thinkers began to question their inherited ideas, especially religious ideas; and they set out instead to construct a new set of enlightened beliefs and of institutions to match. Without the New World, the European Enlightenment would scarcely have occurred.

Attributing so much to one historical development might make a historian like Butterfield uneasy. In cautioning against the presentism of much historical interpretation, he recalled "the schoolboy who, writing on the results of Columbus's discovery of America, enumerated amongst other things the execution of Charles I, the war of the Spanish Succession and the French Revolution." No one will ever know what the world and subsequent events would have been like if the discovery had not been made, or if it had occurred much later. But the impact of the European discovery of America, for good or ill, can hardly be underestimated. Nor can one credibly minimize America's place in history. And it all began with Christopher Columbus, who acted on a consuming idea.

The encounter, its many critics insist, should not be celebrated. They are correct, if to celebrate perpetuates a view of the events that ignores the terrible toll. But neither should the encounter be measured only in terms of Columbus's failings or its consequences to the native Americans and their land. This must be acknowledged and memorialized in the hope that nothing like it is ever repeated in any form. Even so, there can be no denying that the reverberating significance of the events over the last five centuries—the good and the deplorable—stemmed from the act of Columbus and the European response to his discovery. Call what happened the "encounter" or the "contact," as fashion dictates, but the historical truth is that Europeans made known something that had been unknown—which is the definition of discovery. Columbus and those who followed discovered lands that were new to them, and they acted upon their discovery. The means and ends can be lamented or celebrated, as they have been, but it was the European response to discovery, bringing two worlds together, that changed history.

Columbus simply showed the way and, regrettably, set a poor moral example. It must be remembered who he was—not who we wish he had been. He was a European Christian of the fifteenth century sailing for the crown of Spain. There can be no expiation, only understanding. His single-mindedness and boldness, and the magnitude of his achievement, give him heroic standing in history. In so many other respects, he failed to rise above his milieu and set a more worthy example, and so ended up a tragic figure. But he does not deserve to bear alone the blame for the consequences of his audacious act. Such a defamed image would be as unwarranted and unhistorical as the deified Columbus of a century ago.

As the wise Butterfield cautions: "It may be true to assert that there are many things in history and in the present day which would never have happened in the way they have happened if Martin Luther had not defied a Pope; there are equally many things which would not have taken place as they have done if Columbus had not discovered America; but it is as fallacious to ascribe paternity to Luther in the one case as it is to make Columbus responsible for modern America; we can only say that both men added a conditioning circumstance to a whole network of other conditioning circumstances."

Addressing the question once posed by Raynal, whether the discovery of America was the greatest feat of the Christian West or one of history's monumental crimes, Mario Vargas Llosa, the Peruvian novelist, finds little to admire in the early Spanish conquerors but suggests the dangers inherent in transferring to them an inordinate share of the blame for modern America. He asks: "Why have the postcolonial republics of the Americas—republics that might have been expected to have deeper and broader notions of liberty, equality, and fraternity—failed so miserably to improve the lives of their Indian citizens?" Then, speaking primarily of Latin America, he adds: "Immense opportunities brought by the civilization that discovered and conquered America have been beneficial only to a minority, sometimes a very small one; whereas the great majority managed to have only a negative share of the conquest. . . . One of our worst defects, our best fictions, is to believe that our miseries have been imposed on us from abroad, that others, for example, the conquistadores, have always been responsible for our problems. . . . Did they really do it? We did it; we are the conquistadores."

In Columbus we see the embodiment and instrumentality of the duality of human nature and recognize the inextricable tie between the two, the Promethean seeker chained to the rock with the squalid spoiler. This is not the Columbus as seen by his son Hernando. Or the Columbus of Roselly de Lorgues or early-American boosterism.

An inspired Columbus responded to the urge to reach out and discover, applying intelligence, zeal, and fortitude to expand knowledge and human potential, as had the first Americans in their own way when they trekked across Beringia. His urge, like theirs, was acted on without comprehension of all the ramifications, most of which were, as often is the case, unknowable. Confronted with the discovery and possessed of the new knowledge, however, Columbus and others lapsed into indifference to anything but their own immediate appetites and their own values. With few exceptions, they regarded the people they encountered, their long-separated brothers, as benighted people to be subdued, subjugated, and converted to Christianity. The Europeans had the power to subdue and the duty, as they saw it, to save these people from the damnation that awaited those outside the Christian faith, and so they did both without considering the wishes of the native Americans. But even if they had acted more charitably toward these strangers, their very act of discovery, a manifestation of some of the more esteemed human qualities, would alone have spelled disaster for the discovered through disease and displacement.

Encounters of this kind, between the seeker and the spoiler in us all, are enacted every day. Christa Wolf, the German writer, opens *Accident: A Day's News,* a rumination on life under the ominous cloud from the Chernobyl nuclear disaster, with an epigraph from Konrad Lorenz, the ethologist. Lorenz had written: "The long-sought missing link between animals and the really humane being is ourselves."

People have choices, but they do not always choose well. Following the course of Columbus from island to island, through four voyages, we know what will happen not because of our familiarity with the history in books but because, recognizing ourselves in him, we sense the inexorability of events and consequences. One wishes Columbus had acquitted himself more nobly, in the full knowledge that, even if he had, others who came after would have almost surely squandered the opportunity presented them to make a truly fresh start in human history: a new world in more than the geographic sense. But wishes, yesterday's self-congratulation, or today's self-flagellation are not history. Columbus's failings, as well as his ambitions and courage, are beyond historical doubt—and are all so human.

Bibliographical Notes

Specific documents, books, and articles consulted in writing this book are cited by chapters. The following are among the many invaluable sources of general knowledge and interpretations of Columbus and his times:

Writings of Columbus

Dunn, Oliver, and Kelley, James E. Jr. (translators). *The Diario of Christopher Columbus's First Voyage to America, 1492–1493.* Norman, Okla., 1989. The abstract of the Columbus journal by Bartolomé de las Casas, with notes and a concordance. The most recent translation into English, and considered by scholars the most authoritative, this is used as the source for quotations in the book concerning the first voyage.

Fuson, Robert H. (translator). *The Log of Christopher Columbus.* Camden, Me., 1987. Another recent version of the Las Casas abstract of the Columbus journal. A somewhat freer, more fluent translation, with an excellent summary of how the document survived through time. On this interesting subject, see also Fuson, "The Diario de Colón: A Legacy of Poor Transcription, Translation, and Interpretation," in *Terrae Incognitae,* 15, 1983.

Jane, Cecil (editor). *Select Documents Illustrating the Four Voyages of Columbus.* 2 volumes. London, 1932–33. A revised and annotated edition by L. A. Vigneras, published in New York, 1960.

Lyon, Eugene. "The Diario of Christopher Columbus: October 10–October 27, 1492." In *A Columbus Casebook,* supplement to *National Geographic,* 170, Nov. 1986.

Major, R. H. *Select Letters of Christopher Columbus, with Other Original Documents, Relating to His First Four Voyages to the New World.* London, 1847. Corinth Books edition, 1961.

Markham, Clements. *The Journal of Christopher Columbus and Documents Relating to the Voyages of John Cabot and Gaspar Corte Real.* London, 1893.

Morison, Samuel Eliot. *Christopher Columbus, Mariner*. Boston, 1955. Includes a translation of the Letter to Santángel.

——— (editor). *Journals and Other Documents of the Life and Voyages of Christopher Columbus.* New York, 1963. Includes translations of the Capitulations of Santa Fé, the Toscanelli letter, and the Letter to Santángel.

Navarrete, Martín Fernández de. *Viajes de Cristóbal Colón.* Madrid, 1934. Reprint of 1825 edition.

Stevens, Benjamin F. (editor). *Christopher Columbus: His Own Book of Privileges, 1502.* With translation and introduction by Henry Harrisse. London, 1893.

West, Delno C., and Kling, August. *The Libro de las Profecías of Christopher Columbus.* Gainesville, Fla., 1991. English translation of the *Book of Prophecies,* with an excellent interpretative essay.

Other Documents and Contemporary Accounts

Bernáldez, Andrés. *Select Documents Illustrating the Four Voyages of Columbus.* London, 1930. English translation of *Historia de los reyes católicos don Fernando y doña Isabel.*

Keen, Benjamin (editor and translator). *The Life of the Admiral Christopher Columbus by His Son Ferdinand.* New Brunswick, N.J., 1959. The standard version of Ferdinand Columbus's influential biography. Cited hereafter as *Ferdinand's Life of the Admiral.*

Las Casas, Bartolomé de. *Historia de las Indias.* Edited by Agustín Millares Carlo, with introduction by Lewis Hanke. 3 volumes. Mexico, 1951. No complete English translation is available. But ample excerpts are included in Henry Raup Wagner and Helen Rand Parish, *Documents and Narrative Concerning the Discovery and Conquest of Latin America.* Albuquerque, N.M., 1967.

Lollis, Cesare de (editor). *Raccolta de documenti e studi pubblicati della Real Commissione Colombiana pel quarto centenario della scoperta dell'America.* 14 volumes. Rome, 1892–96.

Markham, Clements (editor). *The Letters of Amerigo Vespucci.* London, 1874.

Martyr d'Anghiera, Peter. *De Orbe Novo.* First three decades published in 1516, and the complete eight decades in 1530. For the first English translation of the three decades pertaining to the time of Columbus, see Richard Eden, *The Decades of the Newe Worlde or West India,* London, 1555. Also, Edward Arber, *First Three English Books on America,* Birmingham, Eng., 1885. For a modern English translation of the entire Martyr collection, Francis A. MacNutt, *De Orbe Novo,* 2 volumes, New York and London, 1912. The MacNutt translation is the primary source of quotations in this book.

Olsen, J. E., and Bourne, E. G. (editors). *Original Narratives of Early American History: The Northmen, Columbus and Cabot.* New York, 1906. Reprinted 1967.

Oviedo y Valdés, Gonzalo Fernández de. *Historia general y natural de las Indias.* 4 volumes. Madrid, 1851–55. English translation of excerpts by Sterling A. Stoudemire, Chapel Hill, 1959. For an interpretation of Oviedo's writings and extensive quotations in English, see Antonella Gerbi, *Nature in the New World,* translated by Jeremy Moyle, Pittsburgh, 1985.

Tyler, S. Lyman (editor and translator). *Two Worlds: The Indian Encounters with the Europeans, 1492–1509.* Salt Lake City, 1988. Well-organized excerpts mainly from Las Casas and also from Ferdinand Columbus and Oviedo.

Varela, Consuelo. *Cristóbal Colón: Textos y documentos completos.* Madrid, 1982.

Biographies, Histories, and Interpretations

Aston, Margaret. *The Fifteenth Century: The Prospect of Europe.* New York, 1979.

Beazley, C. R. *Prince Henry the Navigator.* London, 1895.

Chiapelli, Fredi (editor). *First Images of America: The Impact of the New World on the Old.* 2 volumes. Berkeley, 1976. Excellent collection of essays on the European response to the discoveries.

Crosby, Alfred W. *The Columbian Exchange: Biological and Cultural Consequences of 1492.* Westport, Conn., 1972.

———. *Ecological Imperialism: The Biological Expansion of Europe, 900–1900.* Cambridge, 1986.

De Vorsey, Louis Jr., and Parker, John (editors). *In the Wake of Columbus: Islands and Controversy.* Detroit, 1985.

Dobyns, Henry. *Their Number Become Thinned.* Knoxville, 1983.

Elliott, J. H. *The Old World and the New, 1492–1650.* Cambridge, 1970. A concise, perceptive essay on the European response to the New World.

Fiske, John. *The Discovery of America.* 2 volumes. Boston, 1902.

Gerace, Donald T. (editor). *Columbus and His World: Proceedings of First San Salvador Conference.* Bahamian Field Station (Fort Lauderdale, Fla.), 1987.

Goldstein, Thomas. "Geography in Fifteenth-Century Florence." In John Parker (editor), *Merchants and Scholars,* Minneapolis, 1965.

Granzotto, Gianni. *Christopher Columbus.* Translated by Stephen Sartarelli. New York, 1985. A recent, impressionistic biography.

Hale, J. R. *Renaissance Exploration.* New York, 1968.

Hanke, Lewis. *All Mankind Is One.* DeKalb, Ill., 1974.

———. *Aristotle and the American Indians.* London, 1959. Reprinted in paperback, 1970. This, and the previously cited book, discuss the famous confrontation between Las Casas and Sepúlveda.

———. *Bartolomé de las Casas: Bookman, Scholar and Propagandist.* Philadelphia, 1952.

Harrisse, Henry. *Christophe Colomb.* Paris, 1884.

———. *The Discovery of America.* London and Paris, 1892.

———. *Notes on Columbus.* New York, 1866 (privately published).

Irving, Washington. *A History of the Life and Voyages of Christopher Columbus.* 3 volumes. New York, 1828.

Landström, Björn. *Columbus.* New York, 1966.

Madariaga, Salvador de. *Christopher Columbus.* London, 1949. Originally published 1939. An engaging biography, but of particular interest because of its argument about the Jewish origins of Columbus.

Mariéjol, Jean Hippolyte. *The Spain of Ferdinand and Isabella.* Translated and edited by Benjamin Keen. New Brunswick, N.J., 1961.

Martínez-Hidalgo, José María. *Columbus' Ships.* Barre, Vt., 1966.

Molinari, Diego Luis. *La Empresa Colombiana.* Buenos Aires, 1938. Morison considers this the best biography of Columbus in Spanish.

Morison, Samuel Eliot. *Admiral of the Ocean Sea: A Life of Christopher Columbus.* 2 volumes. Boston, 1942. A single-volume edition was published at the same time, but lacks the substantial bibliographical notes of the former. A more accessible edition was published in 1983, with a foreword by David B. Quinn. Cited hereafter as *AOS.*

———. *The European Discovery of America: The Northern Voyages.* New York, 1971.

———. *The European Discovery of America: The Southern Voyages.* New York, 1974.

———, and Obregón, Mauricio. *The Caribbean as Columbus Saw It.* Boston, 1964.

Newton, Arthur P. (editor). *The Great Age of Discovery.* Freeport, N.Y., 1969. Lectures at the University of London first published in 1932.

Nunn, George E. *The Geographical Conceptions of Columbus.* New York, 1924.

O'Gorman, Edmundo. *The Invention of America.* Bloomington, Ind., 1961.

Olschki, Leonardo. "What Columbus Saw on Landing in the West Indies." In *Proceedings of the American Philosophical Society,* 84, 1941.

Parry, J. H. *The Age of Reconnaissance.* Cleveland, 1963.

———. *The Discovery of the Sea.* Berkeley, 1981.

Payne, Stanley G. *A History of Spain and Portugal.* 2 volumes. Madison, Wisc., 1973.

Pohl, Frederick J. *Amerigo Vespucci, Pilot Major.* New York, 1944.

Quinn, David B. *North America from Earliest Discovery to First Settlements.* New York, 1977.

Sale, Kirkpatrick. *The Conquest of Paradise: Christopher Columbus and the Columbian Legacy.* New York, 1990. A polemical work, but well researched and with some keen insights and a good treatment of the changing Columbus reputation through history.

Sauer, Carl O. *The Early Spanish Main.* Berkeley, 1966.

Taviani, Paolo Emilio. *Christopher Columbus: The Grand Design.* London, 1985.

Thacher, John Boyd. *Christopher Columbus: His Life, His Work, His Remains.* 3 volumes. New York, 1903–4.

Todorov, Tzvetan. *The Conquest of America.* Translated by Richard Howard. New York, 1985.

Vignaud, Henry. *Toscanelli and Columbus.* New York, 1902.

Winsor, Justin. *Christopher Columbus, and How He Received and Imparted the Spirit of Discovery.* Cambridge, Mass., 1891. A comprehensive one-volume work, incorporating materials that surfaced in the nineteenth century and providing a more critical look at Columbus than was customary in those days. All quotations attributed to Winsor are from this volume.

———. *Narrative and Critical History of America.* 8 volumes. Boston, 1884–89.

Young, Filson. *Christopher Columbus and the New World of His Discovery.* New York, 1912.

The following are sources, including those cited above and many others, consulted in writing specific chapters:

Preface

Lewis, Bernard. *History: Remembered, Recovered, Invented.* New York, 1987. For the quote from Ranke and discussion of problems in trying to write history as it really is.

Morison, S. E. *AOS.* The 1983 edition has the foreword by Quinn.

———. "Faith of a Historian." In *American Historical Review,* 50, Jan. 1951. Adapted from his speech as president of the American Historical Association.

Stoner, Winifred Sackville. "The History of the United States." The 1919 poem about Columbus sailing the ocean blue.

1. An Exclamation of Discovery

Boland, Charles M. *They All Discovered America.* Garden City, N.Y., 1961.

Boxer, C. R. *The Portuguese Seaborne Empire, 1415–1825.* New York, 1969.

The Columbus Papers. Translation of the Letter to Santángel used for all quotations.

Crosby, Alfred W. *Ecological Imperialism.*

Jones, Gwyn. *The Norse Atlantic Saga.* Oxford, 1986.

Magnusson, Magnus, and Palsson, Hermann (editors and translators). *The Vinland Sagas.* Baltimore, 1965.

Morison, S. E. *AOS.*

———. *The European Discovery of America: The Northern Voyages.*

Parry, J. H. *The Discovery of the Sea.*

Quinn, D. B. *North America from Earliest Discovery to First Settlements.*

Washburn, Wilcomb E. "The Meaning of 'Discovery' in the Fifteenth and Sixteenth Centuries." In *American Historical Review,* 68, Oct. 1962.

2. His Shining Hour

Aston, Margaret. *The Fifteenth Century.*

Braudel, Fernand. *The Structures of Everyday Life.* Vol. 1 of *Civilization and Capitalism, 15th–18th Century.* New York, 1981.

Chiapelli, Fredi (editor). *First Images of America.* Vol. 1.

...aissance Europe: The Individual and Society, 1480–1520,* New

...jamin. *Ferdinand's Life of the Admiral.*

Krause, Michael. *The Writing of American History.* Norman, Okla., 1953. Influ ence of the invention of printing on the history of the discovery. Review of the early historians of Columbus.

Mariéjol, Jean Hippolyte. *The Spain of Ferdinand and Isabella.*

McMurtrie, Douglas C. *The Book: The Story of Printing and Bookmaking.* New York, 1943.

Morison, S. E. *AOS.*

Newton, Arthur P. (editor). *The Great Age of Discovery.*

Payne, Stanley G. *A History of Spain and Portugal.* Vol. 1.

Rumeu de Armas, Antonio. *La Rábida y el descubrimiento de América: Colón, Marchena, y Fray Juan Pérez.* Madrid, 1968. For discussion of Pinzón's request to come to Barcelona and Medina Celi's letter to Mendoza. Attention to this publication was brought by Foster Provost in *1492: A Columbus Newsletter,* 11, Spring 1990, a useful periodical of the John Carter Brown Library at Brown University.

Sauer, Carl O. *The Early Spanish Main.*

Steinberg, S. H. *Five Hundred Years of Printing.* London, 1961.

Thacher, John Boyd. *Christopher Columbus.* Vols. 1 and 3.

3. Witnesses to History

Bernáldez, Andrés. *Select Documents Illustrating the Four Voyages of Columbus.*

Fuson, Robert H. *The Log of Christopher Columbus.* Summary of how the Las Casas abstract passed through history to us.

Gerbi, Antonello. *Nature in the New World.*

Hanke, Lewis. *Bartolomé de las Casas: Bookman, Scholar and Propagandist.*

Harrisse, Henry. *The Discovery of America.* Also, *Notes on Columbus.*

Irving, Washington. *A History of the Life and Voyages of Christopher Columbus.*

Keen, Benjamin. *Ferdinand's Life of the Admiral.*

Larner, John. "The Certainty of Columbus: Some Recent Studies." In *History,* 73, Feb. 1988.

[Las] Casas, Bartolomé de. *Historia de las Indias.* The Hanke and Wagner-Parish [int]erpretations and excerpts were most useful.

[Ma]rtyr, Peter. *De Orbe Novo.* The Arber and MacNutt editions were consulted.

Morison, S. E., *AOS.*

Navarrete, Martín Fernández de. *Viajes de Cristóbal Colón.*

Thacher, J. B. *Christopher Columbus.* Vol. 1.

Wagner, Henry R. "Peter Martyr and His Works." In *Proceedings of the American Antiquarian Society,* 56, 1947.

Williams, Stanley T. *The Life of Washington Irving.* 2 volumes. New York, 1935. Vol. 1, ch. 8, pertains to his years in Madrid, during which Irving wrote the biography.

Winsor, Justin. *Christopher Columbus.* Ch. 1.

4. The Many Faces of Columbus

Elliott, J. H. *Imperial Spain 1469–1716.* New York, 1963. For information on Jews in fifteenth-century Spain and the Inquisition.

Harrisse, Henry. *Christopher Columbus and the Bank of St. George.* New York, 1888. Documents pertaining to his origins.

Kayserling, Meyer. *Christopher Columbus and the Participation of the Jews in the Spanish and Portuguese Discoveries.* Hermon, N.Y., 1968. Reprint of 1893 book.

Keen, Benjamin. *Ferdinand's Life of the Admiral.*

Lasansky, Leonardo. Hamline University, St. Paul. Personal communication with the author.

Madariaga, Salvador de. *Christopher Columbus.*

The Manifest. Newsletter of the James Ford Bell Library, University of Minnesota. Sept. 1983. Columbus portraits.

Menéndez Pidal, Ramón. *La lengua de Cristóbal Colón.* Madrid, 1942. Cited and quoted by Taviani.

Milani, Virgil I. "The Written Language of Christopher Columbus." In *Forum Italicum.* Buffalo, 1973.

Taviani, Paolo Emilio. *Christopher Columbus.* Most detailed discussion of documents supporting his Genoese origins.

Thacher, John Boyd. *Christopher Columbus.* Vol. 3. Extensive description styles of Columbus portraiture.

Wassermann, Jacob. *Columbus.* Translated by Eric Sutton. Boston, 1930.

Wesenthal, Simon, *Sails of Hope.* Translated by Richard and Clara Winston. New York, 1973.

5. *Genesis of the Idea*

Aston, Margaret. *The Fifteenth Century.* Quotes from a diary by a participant on a trip with Leo Rozmital of Bohemia to Cape Finisterre, in 1466.

Beazley, C. R. *Prince Henry the Navigator.*

Boxer, C. R. *The Portuguese Seaborne Empire.*

Crone, Gerald. *The Discovery of America.* New York, 1969. Ch. 5.

Goldstein, Thomas. "Geography in Fifteenth Century Florence." In John Parker (editor), *Merchants and Scholars.*

Hale, J. R. *Renaissance Exploration.*

Keen, Benjamin. *Ferdinand's Life of the Admiral.*

Kimble, George H. T. *Geography in the Middle Ages.* London, 1938.

Larner, John. "The Certainty of Columbus." Discusses thesis of Juan Manzano's *Colón y su secreto: El predescubrimiento,* Madrid, 1976. Also comments on Vignaud's arguments about the Toscanelli correspondence.

Morison, S. E. *AOS.*

Nunn, George E. *The Geographical Conceptions of Columbus.*

Parry, J. H. *The Discovery of the Sea.*

Penrose, Boies. *Travel and Discovery in the Renaissance, 1420–1620.* Cambridge, Mass., 1955.

Prestage, Edgar. *The Portuguese Pioneers.* London, 1933.

Quinn, D. B. *North America from Earliest Discovery to First Settlements.* Ch. 3 summarizes knowledge of the ocean and early explorations prior to Columbus.

Taylor, E. G. R. "Idée Fixe: The Mind of Columbus." In *Hispanic American Historical Review,* 11, 1931.

Taviani, Paolo Emilio. *Christopher Columbus.* Ch. 18–32 are on Columbus in Portugal and the sources of his idea, with an extensive appendix elaborating on the evidence.

,naud, Henry. *Toscanelli and Columbus.*

Vilford, John Noble. *The Mapmakers.* New York, 1981. Ch. 2 for Ptolemy, 3 for medieval cartography, and 4 for developments leading up to 1492.

6. *The Road to Palos*

Carpentier, Alejo. *The Harp and the Shadow.* Translated by Thomas Christensen and Carol Christensen. New York, 1990. First published in 1978.

Harrisse, Henry. *Notes on Columbus.*

Keen, Benjamin. *Ferdinand's Life of the Admiral.*

Irving, Washington. *A History of the Life and Voyages of Christopher Columbus.*

Morison, S. E. *AOS.*

Olsen, J. E., and Bourne, E. G. (editors). *Original Narratives of Early American History.* Text of the contract between Columbus and Ferdinand and Isabella.

Parry, J. H. *The Discovery of the Sea.*

Rumeu de Armas, Antonio. *La Rábida y el descubrimiento de América.*

Sauer, Carl O. *The Early Spanish Main.* Ch. 2 for arguments that the Columbus objective was other than reaching the Indies.

Taviani, Paolo Emilio. *Christopher Columbus.* Especially for discussion of Columbus's planned destination.

Thacher, John Boyd. *Christopher Columbus.*

Varela, Consuelo. "Florentine Friendship and Kinship with Christopher Columbus." In Donald T. Gerace (editor), *Columbus and His World.*

Vignaud, Henry. *Toscanelli and Columbus.* Also see Vignaud, *The Columbian Tradition.* New York, 1920.

Winsor, Justin. *Christopher Columbus.*

7. *Masterpieces for Discovery*

Cipolla, Carlo M. *Guns, Sails and Empires: Technological Innovation and the Early Phases of European Expansion 1400–1700.* New York, 1965.

Keith, Donald, Carrell, Toni, and Lakey, Denise C. "The Search for Columbus' Caravel Gallega and the Site of Santa María de Belén. In *Journal of Field Archeology,* 17, 1990.

———, et al. "The Molasses Reef Wreck, Turks and Caicos Islands, B. A Preliminary Report." In *International Journal of Nautical Archeology* *Underwater Exploration,* 31, 1984.

Lyon, Eugene. "Niña." In *National Geographic,* 170, Nov. 1986. Also, personal communication with the author.

Martínez-Hidalgo, José María. *Columbus' Ships.*

Morison, S. E. *AOS.*

Oertling, Thomas J. "A Suction Pump from an Early 16th-Century Shipwreck." In *Technology & Culture,* 30, July 1987.

Parry, J. H. *The Age of Reconnaissance.*

Phillips, Carla Rahn. "Sizes and Configurations of Spanish Ships in the Age of Discovery." In Donald T. Gerace (editor), *Columbus and His World.*

Smith, Roger C. *Vanguard of Empire: Fifteenth- and Sixteenth-Century Ships of Exploration and Discovery.* Ph.D. dissertation, Texas A & M, 1985. Also, research papers presented by Smith and others at a symposium, "The Potential Contributions of Nautical Archeology to Understanding Voyages of Exploration and Discovery in the New World," held at Annual Conference on Underwater Archeology, Boston, Jan. 9–13, 1985.

Taviani, Paolo Emilio. *Christopher Columbus.*

Wilford, John Noble. "Columbus' Ships: A Quest for Facts in Time for 1992." In *New York Times,* June 4, 1985.

———. "Translated Documents Capture Ambience and Aroma of the Niña." In *New York Times,* Oct. 14, 1986.

8. The Columbian Argonauts

Gould, Alice Bache. *Nueva lista documentada de los tripulantes de Colón en 1492.* Edited by José de la Peña y Camara. Madrid, 1984. A posthumous publication of her invaluable research.

Granzotto, Gianni. *Christopher Columbus.*

Lamb, Ursula. "Pioneers of Discovery History in the Spanish Archives." Unpublished manuscript, 1990. Also, personal communication with the author.

Morison, S. E. *AOS.*

Parry, J. H. *The Discovery of the Sea.*

…ips, Carla Rahn. *Life at Sea in the Sixteenth Century: The Landlubber's Lament of Eugenio de Salazar.* Minneapolis, 1987. No. 24 in series of James Ford Bell Lectures at the University of Minnesota.

Pleitos de Colón. Testimony in lawsuit brought by heirs of Martín Alonso Pinzón. See Morison (editor), *Journals and Other Documents.*

Sherman, Stuart P. (editor). *The Poetical Works of Joaquin Miller.* New York, 1923.

Taviani, Paolo Emilio. *Christopher Columbus.*

Winsor, Justin. *Christopher Columbus.*

9. Landfall—But Where?

Becher, A. B. *The Landfall of Columbus.* London, 1856.

De Vorsey, Louis Jr., and Parker, John (editors). *In the Wake of Columbus.* Thorough and scholarly discussion of the controversy, introduced with a historical essay by Parker. Also, personal communications with most of the contributors.

Fuson, Robert H. *The Log of Christopher Columbus.* Appendix B, for arguments favoring a Samana Cay landfall.

Gerace, Donald T. (editor). *Columbus and His World.* Several contributors discuss their landfall theories.

Judge, Joseph. "Where Columbus Found the New World." In *National Geographic,* 170, Nov. 1986. Also, personal correspondence with the author. The society published a supplement to this issue, *A Columbus Casebook,* which includes more elaborate evidence used to establish Samana Cay as its candidate for the landfall site.

Keegan, William F. "The Columbian Chronicles." In *Sciences,* 29, Jan.–Feb. 1989. One of the most succinct reviews of evidence for Columbus's route after leaving Guanahani.

Marsden, Luis. "The First Landfall of Columbus." In *National Geographic,* 170, Nov. 1986.

Marvel, Josiah, and Power, Robert H. "In Quest of Where America Began: The Case for Grand Turk." In *American History Illustrated,* 25, Feb. 1991.

Morison, S. E. *AOS.*

Parry, J. H. *The Discovery of the Sea.*

Richardson, Philip L., and Goldsmith, Roger A. "The Columbus Landfall: Voyage Track Corrected for Winds and Currents." In *Oceanus,* 30, Fall 1987.

10. The Encounter

Axtell, James. *After Columbus: Essays in the Ethnohistory of Colonial North America.* New York, 1988. Also, personal communication with the author.

Bryan, Alan L. (editor). *New Evidence for the Pleistocene Peopling of the Americas.* Orono, Me., 1986.

Crosby, Alfred W. *Ecological Imperialism.*

Dillehay, Thomas D. "A Late Iron Age Settlement in Southern Chile." In *Scientific American,* 251, Oct. 1984.

Fagan, Brian M. *The Great Journey: The Peopling of Ancient America.* London, 1987.

Guidon, Niedé, and Delibrias, G. "Carbon 14 Dates Point to Man in the Americas 32,000 Years Ago." In *Nature,* 32, June 19, 1986.

Jennings, Francis. *The Invasion of America: Indians, Colonialism, and the Cant of Conquest.* New York, 1976.

Keegan, William F. "Creating the Guanahatabey (Ciboney): The Modern Genesis of an Extinct Culture." In *Antiquity,* 63, June 1989. Also, personal communication with the author.

McNeill, William H. "How Columbus Remade the World." In *Humanities,* 6, Dec. 1985. Publication of the National Endowment of the Humanities.

Meltzer, David J. "Why Don't We Know When the First People Came to North America?" In *American Antiquity,* 53, 3, 1989.

Olschki, Leonardo. "What Columbus Saw on Landing in the West Indies."

Parry, J. H. *The Age of Reconnaissance.*

Purdy, Barbara A. "American Indians After A.D. 1492: A Case Study of Forced Culture Change." In *American Anthropologist,* 90, Sept. 1988.

Rose, Richard. "Lucayan Lifeways at the Time of Columbus." In Donald T. Gerace (editor), *Columbus and His World.*

———. "The Pigeon Creek Site, San Salvador, Bahamas." In *Florida Anthropologist,* 32, Dec. 1982.

Rouse, Irving. *Migrations in Prehistory.* New Haven, 1986.

Sauer, Carl O. *The Early Spanish Main.*

Todorov, Tzvetan. *The Conquest of America.*

Tyler, S. Lyman. *Two Worlds: The Indian Encounters with the Europeans.* For translations of several accounts of the encounter, including Las Casas.

Wilford, John Noble. "Findings Plunge Archeology of the Americas into Turmoil." In *New York Times,* May 30, 1989.

———. "New Finds Challenge Ideas of Earliest Americans." In *New York Times,* July 22, 1986.

Wilson, Samuel W. "Peopling the Antilles." In *Archeology,* 43, Sept.–Oct. 1990.

11. The Foreshadowing

Cruxent, José Mariá. "The Origin of La Isabela: First Spanish Colony in the New World." In David Hurst Thomas (editor), *Columbian Consequences.* Vol. 2. Washington, 1989.

Deagan, Kathleen. "Columbus's Lost Colony: La Navidad." In *National Geographic,* 172, Nov. 1987. Also, personal communication with the author.

———. Report on the 1989 Sub-Surface Test Program at La Isabela. Submitted to Director of National Parks, Dominican Republic. June 15, 1989.

Fleming, John V. "Columbus and the Cannibals." Unpublished lecture, Committee for Medieval Studies, Princeton University. Analysis of how Columbus communicated with the Indians.

Fuson, Robert H. *The Log of Christopher Columbus.* Appendix E on La Navidad.

Gannon, Michael V. "The New Alliance of History and Archaeology in the Eastern Spanish Borderlands." In *William and Mary Quarterly*, 39, April 1991.

Keen, Benjamin. *Ferdinand's Life of the Admiral.*

Major, R. H. *Select Letters of Christopher Columbus.*

Morison, S. E. *AOS.*

———. "The Route of Columbus Along the North Coast of Haiti and the Site of La Navidad." In *Transactions of the American Philosophical Society,* 31, 1940.

Schwartz, Stuart B. *The Iberian Mediterranean and Atlantic Traditions in the Formation of Columbus as a Colonizer.* Minneapolis, 1986.

Todorov, Tzvetan. *The Conquest of America.*

Tyler, S. Lyman (editor). *Two Worlds: The Indian Encounters with the Europeans.* Several chapters include extensive excerpts of contemporary accounts of conflict on Hispaniola, especially translations of Las Casas.

Wilford, John Noble. "Dominican Bluff Yields Columbus's First Colony." In *New York Times,* Nov. 27, 1990.

Wilson, Samuel W. "Columbus, My Enemy." In *Natural History,* Dec. 1990.

———. *Hispaniola: Caribbean Chiefdoms in the Age of Columbus.* Tuscaloosa, Ala., 1990.

12. A Question of Humanity

Arens, William. *The Man-Eating Myth.* Oxford, 1979.

Baker, Brenda J., and Armelagos, George J. "The Origin and Antiquity of Syphilis." In *Current Anthropology,* 29, Dec. 1988.

Benditt, John. "The Syphilized World." In *Scientific American,* 260, March 1989.

Crosby, Alfred W. *The Columbian Exchange.*

Dickey, J. M. (compiler). *Christopher Columbus and His Monument: Columbia.* Chicago, 1892. A collection of encomiums, with only a footnote on the issue of slavery.

Dobyns, Henry F. *Their Number Become Thinned.* For updating of his view, "Reassessing New World Populations at the Time of Contact," lecture at symposium, "Rethinking the Encounter," University of Florida, Gainesville, April 1988.

Fiske, John. *The Discovery of America.* Vol. 2.

Fuson, Robert H. *The Log of Christopher Columbus.* Ch. 2 for comments on Columbus and slavery.

Hanke, Lewis. *All Mankind Is One.*

———. *Aristotle and the American Indians.*

Keen, Benjamin. *Ferdinand's Life of the Admiral.*

Kirsner, Robert. "North American Views of Spain." In *Five Hundred,* 1, May–June 1989. Publication of the Columbus Quincentenary Jubilee Commission, Washington. Comments on the Black Legend.

Kolata, Gina. "Are the Horrors of Cannibalism Fact—or Fiction?" In *Smithsonian,* 17, March 1987.

Koning, Hans. "Don't Celebrate 1492—Mourn It." In *New York Times,* Aug. 14, 1990.

MacNutt, Francis A. (editor). *De Orbe Novo,* by Peter Martyr d'Anghiera.

McNeill, William H. *Plagues and Peoples.* Garden City, N.Y., 1976.

Morison, S. E. (editor). *Journals and Other Documents of the Life and Voyages of Christopher Columbus.* For quotations from Cuneo and Coma.

Phillips, William D. Jr. *Slavery from Roman Times to the Early Transatlantic Trade.* Minneapolis, 1985.

Ramenofsky, Ann F. *Vectors of Death: The Archeology of European Contact.* Albuquerque, 1987.

Rawley, James A. *The Transatlantic Slave Trade.* New York, 1981.

Riley, Thomas J. "Existence of Cannibalism." Letter to the editor in *Science,* 233, Aug. 29, 1986.

Roberts, Leslie. "Disease and Death in the New World." In *Science,* 246, Dec. 8, 1989.

Sale, Kirkpatrick. *The Conquest of Paradise.*

Swagerty, W. R. "World Demography and Epidemiology." Lecture at University of Florida symposium, "Rethinking the Encounter," Gainesville, April 1988.

Todorov, Tzvetan. *The Conquest of America.*

Tyler, S. Lyman (editor). *Two Worlds: The Indian Encounters with the Europeans.* For Las Casas and the conflicts on Hispaniola.

13. A Name for the New World

Arciniegas, Germán. *Amerigo and the New World: The Life and Times of Amerigo Vespucci.* Translated by Harriet De Onís. New York, 1955.

Boorstin, Daniel J. *The Discoverers.* New York, 1983. Ch. 33 for Vespucci.

———. "From Patrons to Publics." In *Earth '88: Changing Geographic Perspective.* Washington, 1988.

Gerbi, Antonello. *Nature in the New World.* Ch. 6 and 7 on Vespucci's descriptions of nature and the people.

Harrisse, Henry. *Notes on Columbus.*

MacNutt, Francis A. (editor). *De Orbe Novo,* by Peter Martyr d'Anghiera.

Magnaghi, Alberto. *Amerigo Vespucci.* 2 volumes. Rome, 1924. Revised edition, 1926.

Major, R. H. *Select Letters of Christopher Columbus.*

Markham, Clements (editor). *The Letters of Amerigo Vespucci.*

Morison, S. E. *The European Discovery of America: The Southern Voyages.* Cites the quotation from Emerson, "English Traits," 1855.

O'Gorman, Edmundo. *The Invention of America.*

Parry, J. H. *The Discovery of the Sea.*

Pohl, Frederick J. *Amerigo Vespucci, Pilot Major.*

Skelton, R. A. *Explorers' Maps.* London, 1958.

Todorov, Tzvetan. *The Conquest of America.*

Waldseemüller, Martin. *The Cosmographiae Introduction of Martin Waldseemüller in Facsimilie.* With introduction by Joseph Fischer and Franz von Wieser. New York, 1907.

Washburn, Wilcomb E. "The Meaning of 'Discovery' in the Fifteenth and Sixteenth Centuries."

West, Delno C., and Kling, August. *The Libro de las Profecías of Christopher Columbus.*

Winsor, Justin. *Narrative and Critical History of America.* Vol. 2.

14. God's Messenger

Fleming, John V. Personal communication with the author.

Jennings, Francis. *The Invasion of America.*

Larner, John. "The Certainty of Columbus."

Morison, S. E. (editor). *Journals and Other Documents of the Life and Voyages of Christopher Columbus.*

Phelan, John Leddy. *The Millennial Kingdom of the Franciscans in the New World.* Berkeley, 1956. Revised edition, 1970.

Reeves, Marjorie. *The Influence of Prophecy in the Later Middle Ages.* Oxford, 1969.

Taylor, E. G. R. "Idée Fixe: The Mind of Columbus."

Todorov, Tzvetan. *The Conquest of America.*

Wassermann, Jacob. *Columbus.*

Watts, Pauline Moffitt. "Prophecy and Discovery: On the Spiritual Origins of Christopher Columbus's 'Enterprise of the Indies.'" In *American Historical Review,* 90, Feb. 1985.

West, Delno C. *Joachim of Fiore in Christian Thought: Essays on the Influence of the Calabrian Prophet.* New York, 1975.

———. "Wallowing in a Theological Stupor or a Steadfast and Consuming Faith: Scholarly Encounters with Columbus." In Donald T. Gerace (editor), *Columbus and His World.*

———, and Kling, August. *The Libro de las Profecías of Christopher Columbus.*

15. In Death No Peace

Benton, Frederick L. *The Last Resting Place of Christopher Columbus.* Santo Domingo, 1953.

Ericson, Jonathon. Personal communication with the author.

Granzotto, Gianni. *Christopher Columbus.* Suggests that the Columbus remains may never have left Valladolid, and so are still buried under what is now a pool room.

Jane, Cecil. *Select Documents Illustrating the Four Voyages of Columbus.*

Keen, Benjamin. *Ferdinand's Life of the Admiral.*

Matthews, Jay. "In Quest of the True Columbus." In Los Angeles *Times,* Oct. 13, 1986. On plans for scientific examination of the disputed bones.

Morison, S. E. (editor). *Journals and Other Documents of the Life and Voyages of Christopher Columbus.*

Sale, Kirkpatrick. *The Conquest of Paradise.*

Thacher, John Boyd. *Christopher Columbus.* Vols. 2 and 3 for Columbus's ideas of what he had discovered. Vol. 3 for account of his remains.

Weissman, Gerald. *They All Laughed at Christopher Columbus: Tales of Medicine and the Art of Discovery.* New York, 1987. The title essay develops the theory that Columbus suffered from Reiter's syndrome.

Winsor, Justin. *Christopher Columbus.*

16. His Place in History

Adams, Herbert B., and Wood, Henry. *Columbus and His Discovery of America.* Baltimore, 1892.

Barlow, Joel. *The Vision of Columbus.* Hartford, 1787.

Belknap, Jeremy. *A Discourse Intended to Commemorate the Discovery of America by Christopher Columbus.* Boston, 1792.

Boorstin, Daniel J. *Hidden History: Exploring Our Secret Past.* New York, 1987. The essay "A Flood of Pseudo-Events" considers the role of heroes in history.

Butterfield, Herbert. *The Whig Interpretation of History.* New York, 1965. First published 1932. A classic essay on the distortions of history that occur when historians impose a rigid point of view on the study of the past.

Channing, Edward. *History of the United States.* New York, 1905.

Dickey, J. M. (compiler). *Christopher Columbus and His Monument: Columbia.* Collection of various poems, orations, and other writings about the heroic Columbus.

Elson, John. "Good Guy or Dirty Word?" *Time,* Nov. 26, 1990.

Fiske, John. *The Discovery of America.* Vol. 2.

Goodrich, Aaron. *A History of the Character and Achievements of the So-called Christopher Columbus.* New York, 1874.

Harrisse, Henry. *Columbus and the Bank of St. George.*

Irving, Washington. *A History of the Life and Voyages of Christopher Columbus.*

Memorial Volume: Dedicatory and Opening Ceremonies of the World's Columbian Exposition. Chicago, 1893.

Morison, S. E. *AOS.*

Sale, Kirkpatrick. *The Conquest of Paradise.*

Schwartz, Stuart B. *The Iberian Mediterranean and Atlantic Traditions in the Formation of Columbus as a Colonizer.*

Sewall, Samuel. *Some Few Lines Towards a Description of the New Heaven as It Makes to Those Who Stand Upon the New Earth.* Boston, 1727.

Taviani, Paolo Emilio. "Columbus the Man: A Modern Psychology on a Medieval Basis." In Donald T. Gerace (editor), *Columbus and His World.*

West, Delno C., and Kling, August. "Columbus and Columbia: A Brief Survey of the Early Creation of the Columbus Symbol in American History." In *Studies in Popular Culture,* 12, 1989.

Whitman, Walt. "Prayer of Columbus." In *Two Rivulets,* Camden, N.J., 1876.

Wills, Garry. "Goodbye, Columbus." In *New York Review of Books,* Nov. 22, 1990.

Winsor, Justin. *Christopher Columbus.*

17. America's Place in the World

Butterfield, Herbert. *The Whig Interpretation of History.*

Chiapelli, Fredi (editor). *First Images of America.*

Crosby, Alfred W. *Ecological Imperialism.* An elaboration of Crosby's ideas, including discussion of the new *Zeitgeist,* is from his lecture at the University of Florida symposium, "Rethinking the Encounter," 1988.

Elliott, J. H. *The Old World and the New, 1492–1650.* The best single volume on the early reaction to the discovery, including Raynal's essay contest and what Elliott calls the "uncertain impact."

———. "Renaissance Europe and America: A Blunted Impact?" In Fredi Chiapelli (editor), *First Images of America,* vol. 1. A reassessment of his thesis.

Gerbi, Antonello. *Nature in the New World.*

Honour, Hugh. *The New Golden Land: European Images of America from the Discoveries to the Present Time.* New York, 1975. Excellent review of first impressions of the New World in art and literature.

Klinkenborg, Verlyn. "The West Indies as Freshly Seen in the 16th Century." In *Smithsonian,* 18, Jan. 1988.

McNeill, William H. "How Columbus Remade the World."

Meinig, D. W. *The Shaping of America: A Geographical Perspective on 500 Years of History.* New Haven, 1986.

Morison, S. E. *The European Discovery of America: The Southern Voyages.*

O'Gorman, Edmundo. *The Invention of America.*

Pagden, Anthony. *The Fall of Natural Man.* Cambridge, 1982.

Penrose, Boies. *Travel and Discovery in the Renaissance, 1420–1620.*

Raynal, Guillaume. *A Philosophical and Political History of the Settlements and Trade of the Europeans in the East and West Indies.* Translated by J. Justamond. 4 volumes. Dublin, 1776.

Sturtevant, William C. "First Visual Images of America." In Chiapelli, Fredi (editor), *First Images of America.*

Wilford, John Noble. "First Brush with a Brave New World." In *New York Times,* Feb. 7, 1988. For description and interpretation of the exhibition "Sir Francis Drake and the Age of Discovery" at the Pierpont Morgan Library, New York. The exhibition was based on the Drake manuscript.

Wills, Garry. "Goodbye, Columbus." In *New York Review of Books.* Cites Samuel Johnson on imperialism. The quotations are from Samuel Johnson, *The Political Writings.* Edited by Donald J. Greene. New Haven, 1977.

Wolf, Christa. *Accident: A Day's News.* New York, 1989. Quotation from Konrad Lorenz, *On Aggression,* translated by Marjorie Latzke, New York, 1966.

Acknowledgments

I hope it is clear that I have attempted to write a somewhat different book about Columbus, one that tells not so much the story of Columbus as the story of the history of Columbus and how it has changed with the passing generations. The timing was, of course, dictated by the approach of 1992. The inspiration, as noted in the preface, was my discovery of how little we know about those three ships of familiar name. Roger C. Smith, then of Texas A & M and now a nautical archeologist for the State of Florida, called this to my attention. Then I found myself in the thick of the landfall controversy—and I was sure the Columbus history encompassed my special interests in exploration, cartography, archeology, and history.

At a critical moment, Daniel J. Boorstin treated me to lunch and encouragement, and over the last five years my editor, Ashbel Green, listened with sympathy and steered my thinking as I struggled to develop the concept for this book and bring it to pass. An author needs encouragement and guidance.

A journalist who plunges into the thickets of historical scholarship must depend on the help of experts wise to the territory. I was fortunate to have the counsel of Michael V. Gannon, director of the Institute for Early Contact Period Studies at the University of Florida. He was generous with his time, advice, and friendship. Through him I was included as a participant in the conference of Columbus scholars held at San Salvador Island in 1986, and was able to visit several archeological dig sites related to Columbus. Kathleen A. Deagan of the Florida Museum of Natural History was my expert and patient guide to Columbus archeology. And she was a serene hostess amid the primitive conditions of the La Isabela site. I am equally grateful to Delno C. West of Northern Arizona University, who shared his pre-publication manuscript on the *Book of Prophecies* and brought to my attention other valuable pieces of research.

Many others who were helpful through interviews and shared works-in-progress included James Axtell, José M. Cruxent, Jonathon E. Ericson, John V. Fleming, Robert H. Fuson, Charles A. Hoffman, William H. Hodges, Joseph Judge, William F. Keegan, Donald Keith, James E. Kelley, Jr., Ursula Lamb, Leonardo Lasansky, Eugene Lyon, Josiah Marvel, Jerald T. Milanich,

Arne B. Molander, Helen Nader, Mauricio Obregón, John Parker, Carla Rahn Phillips, Foster Provost, Richard Rose, W. R. Swagerty, John Russell-Wood, Paolo Emilio Taviani, and Consuelo Varela. Taviani and Christian Zacher were with me on an illuminating flight low over the Bahamian islands involved in the landfall dispute. Those who were kind enough to read and comment on parts of the book were: Kathleen Deagan, Ursula Lamb, John Russell-Wood, and Del West.

No one can write about Columbus without being intimidated and, eventually overcoming that, being inspired by Samuel Eliot Morison's *Admiral of the Ocean Sea.* This was the Polaris of my research. If I have criticized some of Morison's attitudes and conclusions, my respect for his scholarship and literary style is in no way diminished. Nor should the reader be discouraged from shipping out with Columbus through Morison. I also enjoyed making the acquaintance of Ferdinand Columbus, Peter Martyr, Fernández de Oviedo, and, above all, the estimable Bartolomé de las Casas.

My thanks go to the editors of *The New York Times* for indulging another of my literary enthusiasms and agreeing to have me report on some of the Columbian controversies covered in this book. Also, I am grateful to the University of Tennessee for the honor of being the first occupant of its Chair of Excellence in Science Journalism, in 1989–90. This required me to reflect on my vocation and try to explain how I go about it, while at the same time it gave me an opportunity to immerse myself in some of the research for this book.

Finally, but actually foremost, to my wife, Nancy, goes my deepest gratitude. She should be pleased that another book is done, and should know that it could not have been done without her.

Index

PERMISSIONS ACKNOWLEDGMENTS

Grateful acknowledgment is made to the following for permission to reprint previously published material:

Doubleday: Excerpts from *Prince Henry and the Discovery of the Sea* by John H. Parry. Copyright © 1974 by John H. Parry. Reprinted by permission of Doubleday, a division of Bantam Doubleday Dell Publishing Group, Inc.

Donald T. Gerace: Excerpts from *Columbus and His World: Proceedings of First San Salvador Conference* (1987), Donald T. Gerace, Editor. Reprinted by permission.

HarperCollins Publishers and *Editions du Seuil:* Excerpts from *The Conquest of America: The Question of the Other* by Tzvetan Todorov, translated by Richard Howard. English translation copyright © 1984 by Harper & Row Publishers, Inc. Originally published in French as *Conquête de l'Amérique* by Tzvetan Todorov. Copyright © 1982 by Editions du Seuil. Reprinted by permission of HarperCollins Publishers and Editions du Seuil, Paris.

Little, Brown and Company: Excerpts from *Admiral of the Ocean Sea: A Life of Christopher Columbus* by Samuel Eliot Morison. Copyright 1942, copyright renewed 1970 by Samuel Eliot Morison. Excerpts from *Christopher Columbus, Mariner* by Samuel Eliot Morison. Copyright 1942, 1955 by Samuel Eliot Morison. Reprinted by permission of Little, Brown and Company.

National Endowment for the Humanities: Excerpts from "How Columbus Remade the World" by William H. McNeill (Humanities 6, Dec. 1985). Reprinted by permission of the National Endowment for the Humanities.

The New York Review of Books: Excerpt from "Goodbye, Columbus" by Garry Wills (Nov. 22, 1990). Copyright © 1990 by Nyrev, Inc. Reprinted by permission of The New York Review of Books.

Penguin Books Ltd.: Excerpt from *The Lusiads* by Luis Vaz de Camoëns, translated by William C. Atkinson (Penguin Classics, 1952). Copyright 1952 by William C. Atkinson. Reprinted by permission of Penguin Books Ltd., London.

Rutgers University Press: Excerpts from *The Life of the Admiral Christopher Columbus by His Son Ferdinand* translated and annotated by Benjamin Keen. Copyright © 1959 by Benjamin Keen. Reprinted by permission of Rutgers University Press.

TAB Books: Excerpt from book #60660, *The Log of Christopher Columbus* by Robert H. Fuson. Copyright © 1987 by Robert H. Fuson. Published by International Marine/TAB Books, a division of McGraw-Hill, Blue Ridge Summit, PA 17294 (1-800-233-1128 or 1-717-794-2191). Reprinted by permission.

University of New Mexico Press: Excerpts from *Historia de las Indias* by Bartolomé de Las Casas, translated by Henry Raup Wagner and Helen Rand Parish in *Documents and Narrative Concerning the Discovery and Conquest of Latin America*. Copyright © 1967 by University of New Mexico Press. Reprinted by permission of University of New Mexico Press.

University of Oklahoma Press: Excerpts from *The Diario of Christopher Columbus's First Voyage to America, 1492–1493*, translated by Oliver Dunn and James E. Kelley, Jr. Copyright © 1989 by Oliver Dunn and James E. Kelley, Jr. Reprinted by permission of University of Oklahoma Press.

University of Pittsburgh Press: Excerpts from *Nature in the New World: From Christopher Columbus to Gonzalo Fernandez de Oviedo* by Antonello Gerbi, translated by Jeremy Moyle. Translation copyright © 1985 by Jeremy Moyle. Reprinted by permission of the University of Pittsburgh Press.

University of Utah Press: Excerpts from *Historia de las Indias* by Bartolomé de Las Casas, translated by S. Lyman Tyler in *Two Worlds: The Indian Encounter with the European, 1492–1509* (Salt Lake City: University of Utah Press, 1988). Reprinted by permission of the University of Utah Press.

University Presses of Florida: Excerpts from *The Libro de las Profecias of Christopher Columbus*, translated with commentary by Delno C. West and August Kling (Gainesville: University of Florida Press, 1991). Reprinted by permission of University Presses of Florida.

ILLUSTRATION CREDITS

page 25 Art Resource
page 26 The Bettmann Archive
page 55 The Bettmann Archive
page 57 Courtesy of the James Ford Bell Library, University of Minnesota
page 104 The New York Times
page 225 Courtesy of Professor John V. Fleming, Princeton University